The History of Scientific Thought

Volume 1

THE

From Anaximander to Proclus

ORIGINS OF

600 B.C. to 300 A.D.

SCIENTIFIC

by Giorgio de Santillana

THOUGHT

The University of Chicago Press

Q
125
.D34 7
1961

THE UNIVERSITY OF CHICAGO PRESS, CHICAGO 37
The University of Toronto Press, Toronto 5, Canada
© 1961 by Giorgio de Santillana. Published 1961
Printed in the United States of America

CONTENTS

Of High and Far-off Times

THE BIBLE is not a very scientific book. Yet we notice that it opens with a theory about the beginning of the world. Cosmogonies, whenever they occur, are an attempt to give an answer to important questions. The Hebrews may be forgiven for not being primarily interested in what things are made of, so long as they stay the way they are. What preoccupied them was a more serious question, namely: Why is it that the condition of man is miserable; and is it due to an initial "unfair deal" on Someone's part? The answer of Genesis is: man has forfeited his initial condition by becoming conscious of his separateness (this is the Tree of Knowledge) and is thrust out of the unconscious communion of living things. He alone is responsible for having gained selfhood, with what it entails, and—as Plato would say—God is innocent. Another statement of Genesis is that the force which made the world remains equal to itself through time, although we and all things perish, "for the Lord thy God endureth forever." That power might very well have been imagined otherwise, as in other religions: e.g., a creator who gives up his identity in bringing the world into being and fades away leaving only a set of behaviors; or a ruler doomed to eventual failure which will plunge the world into chaos again, as predicted in Norse mythology.

These and such are fairly serious answers to serious questions. In fact, no more interesting answers on these points have been obtained of late. Thus, if first things come first, it should be conceded that the author of Genesis had grabbed the right sow by the ear.

The story of the Fall, as it occurs in various versions in early thought, reveals a considerable amount of obscure puzzlement and ambiguous wisdom among those forgotten thinkers. There is a persistent idea (the root of later Gnostic philosophies) that nature, as we know it, is cruel and wrong and need not have been so. When the world was made, "the lion and the lamb lay down together." By "taking knowledge," we have broken the unconscious harmony: animals now behave like beasts, and we realize it. Hence we have fraught ourselves with dire prohibitions, sex taboos and the like; but, however much we enforce those and try to go straight, we keep being hopelessly wrong. Primitives consider it a sinister and grievous act to kill their quarry, yet they have to do it, but then surround themselves with rites of atonement meant to placate their victims. Our predicament, properly speaking, remains inextricable. The desire for total redemption, for being washed in the blood of the Lamb, lies deep in the soul.

On another level, it is all of life itself which presents an inextricable ambiguity. There is an Indian tale to explain the difference between organic and inorganic. The stone and the pumpkin had a quarrel about their respective merits. The stone at last jumped on the pumpkin and smashed it, hoping to prove its point. But right then the offshoots of the pumpkin burst forth in blossom. The price of life is death and vice versa. If we face it as a problem, it leads nowhere. As a myth, it carries its own acceptance.

This kind of explaining is surely not science; it implies no theory or definition; but it is a kind of knowledge: mythical knowledge, which means explaining something by telling a tale about it which should show it in the light of an essential truth. The story of Genesis is such a myth. The plight of Man looks "telltale" (an old word which keeps close to the old meaning). The tale will now be unfolded. The listener is brought to an "understanding." Then follows the tale of redemption still enacted among us with the ritual which gives it the power to save. From there on, however, explaining has no further role. Revealed religions tend to leave events to the unaccountable will of a supreme personality, and it is only the end of that line when Islam refers to the laws of nature as "Allah's habits."

But besides the gradual maturing of such strictly religious conceptions, which are as it were the warp of our civilization, there is another line of thought we have to trace back as far as possible because it forms the weft with which we are concerned here.

We know next to nothing of thought, either religious or scientific, among people in the Stone Age. But we are certainly indebted to those ingenious technologists for the basic principles in handling matter and energy: coaxing fire into the hearth, discovering leverage for the spear thrower, using tension and twist to send the arrow hurtling through the air, snap the trap shut, fasten the axhead to the handle. As first things come hardest, let us not think of such achievements as natural. Even less obvious are the achievements of the Neolithic revolution and the Bronze Age: the sowing of wheat, the smelting, the weaving, the pottery, and all the crafts. Nor is it easy to comprehend how men came upon such ideas as raising four-cornered step pyramids as pedestals for the habitation of their gods. None but high cultures can be credited with such performances. The humanists and philologists in charge of history may consider them rude and simple, the obvious beginnings in a still earth-bound society. To them we might oppose what Galileo had to say, who understood somewhat more of these matters: "I think that antiquity had very good reason to enumerate the first inventors of the noble arts among the gods, seeing that the common intellects have so little curiosity. . . . The application to great invention moved by small hints, and the thinking that under a primary and childish appearance admirable arts may be hidden is not the part of a trivial but a superhuman spirit."

Nothing, then, very "primitive" in all this. Scholars once took for granted the identity of our past with contemporary "savages" who perversely abstain from food production and hence have entered the files sub "Old Stone Age." The "primitive" of nineteenth-century scholars was safely "prelogical," a child prattling artless tales to himself, to which we listen with amused condescension. The ladder of Progress went up from there. But great discoveries were also made in those decades. Sir James Frazer in his *Golden Bough* revealed the early world-wide spread of beliefs, magic operations, and fertility rites which apparently preceded known civilization, and showed them as the deep universal substructure of our historic cultures, still alive and pervasive up to our own times. Classical scholars shivered when they saw their one and only Greece thus lost in the barbaric backdrop; anthropologists rejoiced.

A timeless uniform past, where nothing much happened except seasonal rites, where civilizations are an occasional —and unexplained—growth, such is the picture which caused historical thought to be forgotten, especially in this country, and replaced by social anthropology with claims to objective science. And then came Freud. What greater temptation, where there are only fertility cults and sex taboos and primitive hordes in sight, than to interpret the feelings of the past in terms of that familiar and horrendous mystery, our own unconscious? Everything became smothered in the weeds of amateur psychoanalysis.

If we have been rescued from this melancholy predicament, we owe it to the ethnologists and prehistoric archaeologists, who labored on to produce evidence instead of psychological generalities. We are indebted to Leo Frobenius and the German Historical School for the theory of "culture circles" which again brought historical perspective into the flat picture. We owe it to modern research in prehistory, and in particular to von Heine-Geldern and Baumann, if the conventional notion of progress has been stood on its head—and if justice will be done eventually to the achievements of W. H. R. Rivers and the British School of Diffusionists. The point is this: that what we observe as "primitive" conditions are, with very few exceptions (like Bushmen and some of the Australian aboriginal tribes) only what is left of the rise and fall of past higher cultures; what appeared to be a universal steady state of superstitions from which thought grows is only the common denominator to which decaying civilizations run in the end. We uncover in our search what is not virgin soil but areas once cultivated and still full of ancient seeds. The image is no longer that of a static state but of restless design, transmission, and change over the millennia since the New Stone Age. It could hardly be otherwise, if we want to account for the variety which has given us China and Babylon, Greece, Mexico, Egypt, and India.

Once the possibility had been revived of a universal history of culture, the road was opened to promising rediscoveries and new adventures: we are able not only to put to good use the labors of great nineteenth-century scholars like Boeckh, Ideler, Brugsch, and such of their eighteenth-century forerunners as Charles Dupuis, but to recognize that only when fitted into this rediscovered "old-fashioned" historical frame, could the amount of new data presented to us by Thureau-Dangin, Kugler, Boll, and Seler be interpreted and evaluated in a reasonable way. Thus, the work of L. de Saussure and Laufer, of Eisler and Gundel, after due critical revision, yields now returns beyond expectation. It is to be hoped that work in progress by Werner, Stecchini and von Dechend will bring further light in this far-reaching enterprise.

How could such new things be found in already well-known ancient texts? Science, at all times, involves a technical language which can hardly be understood if it is not even recognized. Nobody can interpret farther than he understands, nor can anyone translate technical terms from an utterly foreign language if he is not first acquainted with the corresponding technical terms in his own. This should strike one as rather elementary. The vast amount of ancient Near Eastern and related "mythological" texts are at best obscure and ambiguous, often strangely incongruous. The most refined philological methods in the hands of expert philologists will yield only childish stuff out of them, if childish stuff is expected. Technical indications which would make clear sense to scientists go unnoticed or mistranslated. How, e.g., could anyone recognize planetary periods who has never known them, and has cut the line of millennial tradition which valued astronomy as the Royal Art? * It should be kept in mind

---

* To take a simple example: in an otherwise excellent and authoritative work on Egypt we find that the Sun, Amun Ra, stands in tradition as Egypt's first king, which shows Egypt's culture to have been sun-centered as all proper agrarian cultures are. But elsewhere the author has to admit that a still earlier god-king was Ptah, Lord of Memphis, the original capital of the "United Kingdom" (Upper and Lower Egypt). He leaves us—and himself—to conclude that Ptah was another version of the Sun. Still, there is a demotic ostracon not to be ignored which actually states the star of Ra to be Kronos, i.e., Saturn. We are led to suppose that the Sun had been superimposed on the original role of Saturn; the more so as astronomical cuneiform tablets call Saturn by the name of the Sun, Shamash, and as there is sufficient reason to take the Greek Sun for Kronos wherever he is spoken of as "Helios the

that every translation is a mere function of the translator's expectation. If his own way of thinking is under the influence of the psychoanalytical pattern, whether consciously or not, it will cause him to accept any amount of terrifying nonsense as "sacred" lore, and to translate it accordingly. It is, in fact, a wonder how pleased most readers seem to be when fed lunatic utterances, without ever wondering how the devil the pyramids happened to get built in spite of the strange frame of mind their constructors were cursed with.

It is the observation of celestial motions which challenged men to search for the impersonal *invariants* behind events. This is after all what science means. Astronomy was already present in Sumer, whose recorded history begins about 3000 B.C. We have the Sumerian names of constellations and planets, surviving in Babylonian cuneiform tablets, but we have reason to think that they were inherited from unknown predecessors. As concerns the Egyptian names of constellations, it is evident from the most ancient star lists that they were, already then, no longer grasped in their original significance.* So we conclude that what looked to us like a point of departure is only a phase in a line of thought which stretches back into the dim regions of predynastic origins everywhere. But the extraordinary wealth of rites, tales, and traditions found

---

Titan." Irrelevant, say the well-specialized philologists: it is only the matter of a late ostracon, and good method teaches us to discount anything late. Well and good, but they might have taken into account that Ptah, from the beginning, bears the title of "Lord of the Thirty-Year Cycle." It would be enough to show that, whether it be early or late, the ostracon is to the point. A check would have shown them that it is explicitly confirmed by Hyginus, *Astronomica* 42, and Diodorus 2. 30.3. This in turn might have led them to discover many further remarkable connections which had been systematically ignored; e.g., in China (surely another agrarian state) Saturn was the Imperial Star.

* When writing appeared for the first time in history as Mesopotamian cuneiform (Uruk IV, about end of 4th millennium B.C.) the system of measures which is at the basis of all metric systems of the ancient world and of China had been already established and formalized. It was linked with cosmic measurements. This system continued into our days. The pre-Sumerian pound is exactly the English pound avoirdupois within less than one grain, i.e., within ¹⁄₁₀₀ of a gram. Instrumental precision in angular measurement seems to have reached 3'.

more or less uniformly around the world, in certain distinct parts of Africa, in China, Polynesia, and Mexico, points to a time of great migrations and also to a center of diffusion somewhere in the Middle East (we might call it, with Henry Field, the Proto-Mediterranean) in the far-back millenaries where archaeological excavation yields only uncertain clues. We are, in fact, beginning to understand that the vast protohistoric material of myths and legends of gods and heroes founding cities, bringing culture, undertaking great voyages, going on a "Hunt for the Sun," can be deciphered as the technical language of the yet unknown archaic astronomers who are also responsible for the naming of the constellations. Surely, it implies a conscious intention, not mere idle fancy, to read those figures out of the confusion of stars. Someone before history must have blocked them out for reasons known to himself, and with such an authority that they were repeated without question, substantially the same from Mexico to Africa and Polynesia—and have remained with us to this day. And this is datable back to sometime between 4000 and 6000 B.C. as part of the Neolithic revolution.

In the light of this theory, many seemingly absurd stories begin to make sense. Sunday-school pupils must have long been puzzled about how Samson slew a thousand Philistines with the jawbone of an ass. But that "jaw" is in heaven. It was the name given by the Babylonians to the Hyades, which were placed in Taurus as the "Jaw of the Bull." * In their creation epic, which antedates Samson, Marduk uses it as a boomeranglike weapon. It is known to the Dyaks of Borneo. In South America, where bulls were unknown, it reappears as the "jaw of the tapir" and it is connected with the great god Hunracán, the hurricane, who certainly knows how to slay his thousands. In our sky, the name of the celestial Samson is Orion, the mighty hunter, alias Nimrod. He remains such even in China as "War Lord Tsan," the huntmaster of the autumn hunt, but the Hyades are changed there into a net for catching birds. In Cambodia, Orion himself became a trap

---

* Hyades is the Greek name, which means simply "watery." But it is said also: "God clave an hollow place that was in the jaw and there came water thereout, and when Samson had drunk his spirit came again, and he revived."

for tigers; in Borneo, tigers not being available, pigs have to substitute; and in Polynesia, bereft of every kind of big game, we find Orion in the shape of a huge snare for birds. It is the snare that Maui, the creator-hero, used to catch the sun-bird; but having captured it, he proceeded to beat it up, and with what? The jawbone of Muri Ranga Vhenua, his own respected grandmother.

There would be much, much more to say of blinded Orion/Samson with the wounded heel (like Krishna, like Wotan as "Wild Hunter," not least, like Talos, the bronze automat that Hephaestus wrought)—turning the mill wheel of the stars like Helge the Dane or the Hamlet of the ancient North (the original powerful personage that was later transformed into the gentle prince), pulling down the pillars of heaven over his enemies like Whakatau the Maori hero, doing many other Samson-like things like the Amlethos-Kyros of Persian lore; but let this suffice, that in the original astronomical scheme we find the reason for the changes that are rung upon the one constellation: Orion is not himself the hunter, he is the hunting dress and the proper outfit for the planet which appropriates his garments for a time as a "paranatellon" and thus makes him live and see; left to himself, the poor thing is blind.

We can see then how so many myths, fantastic and. arbitrary in semblance, of which the Greek tale of the Argonauts is a late offspring, may provide a terminology of image motifs, a kind of code which is beginning to be broken. It was meant to allow those who knew: (a) to determine unequivocally the position of given planets in respect to the earth, to the firmament, and to one another; (b) to present what knowledge there was of the fabric of the world in the form of tales about "how the world began." The code was exceedingly difficult, for the heroes, i.e., the wandering stars, moved through the constellations in a way that men knew then how to describe only by giving them a bewildering variety of names, attributes, and disguises according to position. It was only the much later Babylonian astrological tablets which allowed us to make the first steps toward the unraveling of the tangle; because they were still couched in the language of those myths, while the *astronomical* texts of the same time (around 500 B.C. and later) are already taken down in an exact notation. Here we come across the first known parting of the ways between science and pseudo science. While astrology kept (and keeps) pumping the same old and ever muddier water through the old tortuous channels without paying heed to new facts (the astrological spring equinox "stands" still today in Aries, as in 2000 B.C.), astronomy discovered a more direct and shorter way of approach: the new technical language.

But economy is not an unmixed blessing; it flattened out the picture. Mathematical techniques may sometimes detract from thought. This is not said to underrate the great computational feats of the Babylonians, of which more hereafter. But they did not cut themselves free from the old-fashioned language alone: the passage from mythical to mathematical language corresponds to a basic shift in relevance. Protohistoric, archaic astronomy concentrated on conjunction periods of planets. They served to determine the various types of "great years" of cosmic recurrence, all referred to some given time zero. And here also begin the calendaric fittings of the cycles of the sun and moon inside the greater cycles. The placement of a planet did not imply simply its position in the zodiac and with respect to the sun; to fix that, it would have been sufficient to make a hero, say, ride a lion, while pinning down the time of his lion ride within the solar year through one seasonal motif or the other, e.g., the blowing of conch trumpets by Capricorn which meant the hibernal solstice. But the placement had to be unequivocally determined with reference to a complex system of time proportions, establishing the places, and the "age" of the other planets. Which meant that one had to weave around the heroes such plots as family tragedies, which allowed covering relatively long spaces of time under the guise of many "generations"; which meant, furthermore, that a technical term had to be used for each type of conjunction, as the Chinese did: "When Jupiter met Venus it was a 'combat,' but when Mars did so it was a 'fusion.' Another metallurgical term, 'quenching,' applied to conjunctions of Mars with Mercury, while irrigation engineering gave 'blocked channels,' as Needham informs us. The terms come from the usual blending of astrology with alchemy.

Suppose we try to cover, by means of telling adventures,

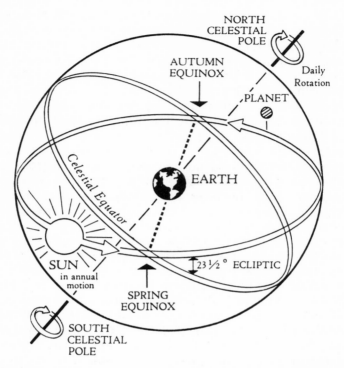

Fig. 1. Equator and Ecliptic on the Celestial Sphere. The spectator on earth sees the heavens rotating in twenty-four hours around the North-South Pole axis. The sun, moon and planets have their own proper motions along the band of the ecliptic, inclined 23½° on the equator. The fixed stars placed along the ecliptic are called the Zodiac and divided into twelve constellations. The two circles, equator and ecliptic, meet at the equinoctial points. They are widest apart from each other at the solstices. The inclination of the ecliptic causes the path of the sun to swing up and down according to the seasons: it is highest at the summer solstice, lowest in the winter one. Therefore, to someone on earth, the sun will appear to describe in the sky through the year a spiral up and down between the two solstitial latitudes (Tropics); and so, of course, will the moon and planets. To visualize the separate circles of equator and ecliptic in the sky was already a feat of considerable abstraction.

the heavenly "situation" in the 56th year, for instance, of the shortest "great year," determined by the conjunction of Jupiter and Saturn at almost the same place in the zodiac, which covers 60 years (exactly 59.5779). We shall have to consider the significance of this year with respect to every involved "personage": Saturn is coming close to the end of his 2nd sidereal revolution, Jupiter has already completed 4½ of them, while Venus has gone through 35 synodic revolutions—the term indicates the period between two successive conjunctions with the sun—equal to 91 sidereal revolutions, and Mars is starting on his 26th synodic (30th sidereal) voyage around the world; nor has the puzzle-player to forget which zodiacal station everybody is dwelling in for the time being. The more items, meant to narrow down as best as possible the ambiguity, the better. The variety of names given to each planet and the multiplicity of mythical motifs to accompany them were made necessary by the almost incalculable complexity of relations to be expressed. All this had to be set down without coordinates, probably without the aid of writing, in one synoptic vision, and memorized as legends. The colossal intellectual effort, the abstraction, that this entailed are worthy of the greatest modern theorists. We must assume every age has minds of the order of Archimedes, Kepler, or Newton. In the lost millenaries, as well as yesterday, those minds had to create within the context of their time.

The creation had its usefulness, too. The sailing directions for Polynesian navigators in the Pacific were embodied in a carefully organized sequence of tales spun around known heroes, and kept a trade secret, which seems a pity; this method worked under the supposition that the navigator knew the star groups going through the zenith of every isle belonging to his "program" of regularly undertaken voyages—as he did in fact know. Some popular hero, having set out on a journey to a particular place, came, as Grimble reports from the Gilbert Islands,

across an old woman sitting at the door of her house (Pleiades), on whom he played some familiar trick, which caused her to run away westwards (i.e., decline towards her setting). Next, he met a man coming in a canoe from the east (this is to say, he then steered by the star Aldebaran in the constellation of Taurus, which is V-shaped, like the section of a canoe). With him he held converse until the old woman, who had run away from him, fell into the sea (the Pleiades set); she made such a dreadful noise that the hero of the tale ran away to eastward and took refuge with two old lepers (Gemini). And so on, until the tale has unfolded the whole series of stars by which an outrigger is guided to some particular land.

The thought behind these constructions of the high and far-off times is equally lofty, even if its forms are strange. The theory about "how the world began" seems to involve the breaking asunder of a harmony, a kind of cosmogonic "original sin" whereby the circle of the ecliptic (with the zodiac) was tilted up at an angle with respect to the equator. The stories go something like this all over the world: the Powers fell out—whether it was the fight of the Asuras and Devas in Indian tradition, or the struggle between Kung Kung and Chuan Hsü for the Empire of the Middle —or the challenge offered by the Titans to the gods of Greece. The well-known tales of Tantalos the Titan and Lykaon serving the gods with the flesh of their own sons carry with them a curse: the gods "upset the table" in horror, the sun shrinks away, tragedy follows. The war of the Titans against Olympus in Greece has strange analogies in all mythologies. Thus, the fall of Satan, the fall of the Aztec gods thrown down from the heights of heaven because they had plucked the forbidden flowers; all of them were set into "lower motion" in new paths where they keep trying to reconquer the heights by building towers and world axes which lean to one side. In every case there is a breaking or tilting or skewing of mountains or pillars or levels whereby "the path of the sun receded" or "heaven leaned over to the northwest" and "the sun and the moon were shifted." Always there is an implicit image of the "rending" of a unity into cycles of unceasing change, and it is tied up with the separation of two poles in heaven, the alternation of seasonal death and rebirth, the search for a paradise lost. "Before the coming of the Enemy it was always midday," as the Persian *Bundahishn* words it. That original fall was seen as the cause of the fateful polarity in things, eternity and perishability, power and downfall, light and dark, male and female. As a consequence we have the theme of great world cycles, in which celestial configurations come back into place and the world is supposed to start anew.

The dust of centuries had settled upon the remains of this great world-wide archaic construction when the Greeks came upon the scene. Yet something of it survived in traditional rites, in myths and fairy tales no longer understood. Taken verbally, it matured the bloody cults intended to procure fertility, based on the belief in a dark universal force of an ambivalent nature, the source of good and evil at the same time, bringing forth and destroying. Its original themes could flash out again, preserved almost intact, in the later thought of the Pythagoreans and of Plato.

But they are tantalizing fragments of a lost whole. They make one think of those "mist landscapes" of which Chinese painters are masters, which show here a rock, here a gable, there the tip of a tree, and leave the rest to imagination. Even when the code shall have yielded, when the techniques shall be known, we cannot hope to gauge the thought of those remote ancestors of ours, lost as it is in its symbols.

> Their words are no more heard aright
> Through lapse of many ages. . . .

What is the meaning, for instance, of the number 432,-000, that universal multiple, which occurs in so many contexts of myth and cycle and is also the number of syllables of the *Rig-Veda?* Who was the original Rip van Winkle, compelled to watch the dreadful game that the great ones played with rolling globes in heaven—a game where a thousand years were as one day, so that he awoke to find the haft of his ax moldered into dust? Why did the Mexican god Tezcatlipoca drill fire in heaven in the cyclical year 2-*acatl,* that is "2-reed," called after the same "reed" in which Prometheus stole the fire from on high, while the Sumerian word for reed is *gi,* "to burn," and Gibil the God of Fire? What is the real riddle of the Sphinx? Why did the Flood recede when Capricorn blew upon the conch of the winter solstice? Why was the kingly power still described in Old Norse as "the License from the Great Bear"? What is the idea behind the seven-league boots of the

Ogre or the tale of Snow White? Why is it always the Third Son, the simple one, who wins the Princess with the aid of the Animals? For certain allusions are clear. There are thousands of clues to the gigantic puzzle which is waiting to be reassembled.

We have called this a Prologue because its subject does not fall as yet within the frame of the established history of science. Very few among the specialists who have done such brilliant work on early mathematics are willing to venture out into areas where numerical data becomes insecure, and where they feel evidence to yield clues as frail as "the calcimine imprint of a fern in chalk." But we believe the reader should not be denied a sight of new horizons. Kepler seems to have understood the role of science in culture better than many moderns, when he wrote: "The ways in which men came into the knowledge of things celestial appears to me almost as marvelous as the nature of those things itself."

So much concerning heaven, and man's fate. But what about nature itself? When does science, in *our* sense, begin? Even Babylonian mathematics, with its prodigious sophistication and its equivalent of Fourier series, does not deal with nature at all, or with ideas either. We have to skip vast ages of time and reach that brief and magic period, from 600 to 300 B.C., when Greece comes to flower.

1

On the Nature of Things

THE HELLENES with their Olympian gods were Indo-European invaders who had established themselves rather late upon the scene, about 1500 B.C. In Homeric times they had been, like their Persian cousins, a "horsey" lot; then they had turned to seafaring and commerce. Like Ulysses of old, they were adventurous, resourceful and wide-awake. A worldly and sensible civilization, they knew how to colonize and legislate for themselves and their subjects. They founded the first modern type of commonwealths with their pattern of political life. It seems due to this independence, to this sense of law and proportion, that they expressed their philosophical views not in the language of priest castes, but in the language of the legislator.

The first men who insisted upon "speaking in terms of nature," as Aristotle says, are certain wise men of Ionia who were legislators and merchant princes in their own seafaring republics precariously perched on the rim of Asia Minor in very much the same way as the early North American settlements were perched on the rim of our continent. They were the Jeffersons and Franklins of their time (the seventh and sixth centuries B.C.).

ANAXIMANDER

They were not trying to give a scientific system, since no one yet had told them what "science" ought to be. They were stating that there is an order of things, that this order is of justice and reciprocity very much like that of men, and that men should understand that order the better to fit into it. The initial sentence, and the only one preserved, of what we can consider the first Greek book on science, that of Anaximander of Miletus (about 590 B.C.), runs thus:

That from which all things are born is also the cause of their coming to an end, as is meet, for they pay reparations and atonement to each other for their mutual injustice in the order of time.

This is all that we have of it, but it is meaningful enough. What had been with Sappho lyrical awareness and despair, what had been the poetic lament of Mimnermus about "the generations of men being dispersed like autumn leaves," is transformed here into impassive understanding. Anaximander, like Aeschylus in the next century with his tragedies, like many prophets and seers also before his time, is perceiving an order which is at the same time natural and moral. What blossoms forth must die eventually; what grows to strength must yield in the end and return to nothingness in order to make way for new beings and new forces; what tries to monopolize power must fall; if the balance between opposing forces moves one way it will have to swing back the other way, because that order is impartially just. We note that it is still, as in all archaic doctrine, the cyclical all-comprising Order of Time.

A fundamental theme of Greek thought has been set. The vision will be reached again by Sophocles's King Oedipus, once fallen from power, self-blinded and a wandering beggar: "Notwithstanding the extremity of my sufferings, I am led in my old age and in the greatness of my soul to judge that all is well."

The rest is silence. But it is from themes such as this that the philosopher starts out on his way. What made the Ionian way "physical" is that the cause of things is no longer imagined in a dramatic or mythical way, but as some kind of primordial—and stable—substance.

IONIAN THOUGHT

A first attempt in this direction had been made by an elder contemporary of Anaximander, also a Milesian, called Thales. He had said that water is the substrate and all things are derived from it. His name, because of this, usually stands at the beginning in our histories of philosophy. But we simply do not know enough about Thales to decide exactly what he meant by it. Aristotle, who is our authority, seems uncertain himself and wonders whether the idea may not have been transposed from the mythical cosmogonies which reigned at the time, such as are echoed for us in Genesis: ". . . and darkness was upon the face of the deep, and the spirit of God moved upon the face of the waters." But these of Genesis are such waters as never were on sea or land; they are still the archaic "waters" in heaven. It is like making things arise from the bosom of Night; it is mythical "begetting." Aristotle is careful to insist that this cannot be quite what Thales meant, for these Milesians, as we saw, "intended to speak in terms of nature." But how far did Thales go, and how did he organize his thought? That is where he and we are left guessing. Did he choose water because of the essential part it plays in the origin and nourishing of life? Because of its changes which cause it to go from sediment to ex-halations of mist and vapor, which then was considered all one with air and hence also one with life's breath? Did he take life to germinate spontaneously from it? He saw the earth as a disk, floating on water. But he did not go on to tell us what that water rests on in its turn. He also held that "all things are full of gods," which would be enough to dissolve any attempt at a real system into spontaneous behavior, very much on the old mythical pattern. On the other hand, he is said to have reached that conclusion from the properties of the magnet and of rubbed *elektron,* i.e., amber, which would make him an uncommonly ob-servant character. Here again, although he stands in his-tory as the initiator of the "Milesian School," he looks like a transitional figure.

But a transition from what? It would be very wrong to imagine only medicine men behind him, or sad mythog-raphers like Hesiod. Ionia is moving out of those four centuries of darkness which have been called the "Greek Middle Ages" with an already strong civilization, and a worldly one at that. The Ionians have just achieved what is their equivalent to the discovery of America, that is, they have sailed out of Gibraltar into the Atlantic as far as Britain. They have founded colonies and trading sta-tions from Trebizond to Lisbon. The seamen of Teos and Samos have beaten the Phoenicians at their own game. It all happened within the preceding century or two. Iron in the form of steel has come in; "black iron," wrote Hesiod,

"discovered for the misfortune of men." It is still manufactured with much secrecy and hocus-pocus, mainly by
the people of Urartu in the Asian interior, around Lake
Van. Those remarkable innovations, coined money and
the alphabet (if not writing itself, which is much more
ancient) are in common use, and fifty-oared ships of a
new type have taken to the high seas able to sail by dead
reckoning. Writers are trying their hand at the earliest
chronicles (that of Hecataeus of Miletus dates back to
before 550 B.C.); Ionian voyagers come back from ancient
countries like Egypt, where the Pharaoh has set up official
guides to take them sight-seeing. They admire but are not
overwhelmed. The crocodiles that were shown them they
crisply call by the name of "lizards." The huge monoliths
are to them "obeliskoi," that is, "pinlets," a name the
Cockneys were to reinvent in our time, as they dubbed
one of them "Cleopatra's Needle." They do not think they
have to feel inferior to anybody. As Herodotus will write
sadly in the following century, "So long as they remained
free of painful foreign oppression, they had taken to living
in continental luxury beyond their needs. They went
around the forum clad in purple vestments, prompt to
boast of their condition, vain of their well-oiled and
scented coiffure." It is still early in the history of Greek
citizen states, but it is already the Indian summer of Ionia.

Of such a proud republic, then, were merchant princes
like Thales and Anaximander citizens. What we discern in
their background are not priests and prophets, but legislators, engineers, and explorers. There is Solon, who taught
justice to the Athenians; and Eupalinus the architect, who
pierced the mountain of Samos almost a mile for an aqueduct; there are Mandrokles the bridge-maker, Rhoikos,
Chersiphron, Theodoros, on whose name tradition accu-
mulates the invention of such various devices as the water-
level, the lathe, and the key; all of them (except for Solon)
Ionians, and quite certainly participant of Babylonian
techniques which had come to them through the highlands
of Asia Minor and, once, through ancient international
ports like Ugarit.

Thales himself is credited with building bridges, divert-
ing the course of rivers, compiling almanacs, and it is only
from Babylonian data, clearly, that he could have derived

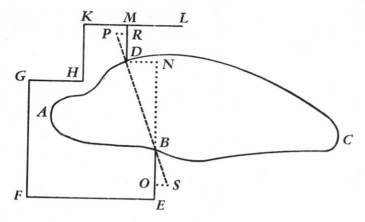

Fig. 2. Eupalinus's method for digging an aqueduct through a mountain in Samos, 1 kilometer in length, 7 feet high and wide, with vertical
vents. The working men approaching from both ends were able to meet
at the center with an error of only 30 feet horizontally and 10 feet
vertically. When King Hezekiah of Judea had a similar aqueduct dug
in Jerusalem at about the same time, his workers had such primitive
methods of sighting that they produced a zigzag tunnel, twice as long
as necessary.

Eupalinus laid out on the ground around the mountain a series of
lines perpendicular to one another, which connected the two ends B
and D. This allowed him to complete the figure and to derive the
ratios of the two sides DN and NB, and hence, by way of similar tri-
angles outside, the direction for boring.

his prediction of the solar eclipse in 585 B.C., which is the
first date in Western astronomy. He seems to have been
interested in the study of climates and seasons, which to
him were all one with astronomy, for at that time there
still was no idea at all of what we call "outer space." There
was only the air, which lost itself in the empty shimmering
above, called the "fiery aether" (the word *aither* means
"burning"), circumscribed by the heavenly vault. Celestial
phenomena were called *meteora,* which means, literally,
"above the air," but yet somehow in the upper atmosphere
of fire, whence came the lightning. Thales apparently did
not go beyond that. What little we know of him shows him
rather as a statesman of curious and widely ranging interests. Political projects must have involved him more seriously than science, as when he urged the Ionian cities to
federate in order to resist the Persian danger. What was
achieved, as usual, was too little and too late, but for the

farseeing minds of the time it must have been the Grand
Design, a matter of profound concern and much diplo-
macy.

"NATURE"

Anaximander, too, was a statesman and a legislator.
He founded a colony at Apollonia on the Black Sea; he

Anaximander's Map in a Modern Reconstruction. The earth is still
disk-shaped. The land is girdled by the "River Ocean" of unknown
width. The center is, more or less conventionally, the sanctuary of
Delphi, said to be "the navel of the earth." This map marked also the
beginning of geopolitics. Some time later Miletus sent an embassy to
the Spartans asking them to help them out of their danger by heading a
coalition and marching straight on Susa, the capital of the Persian
empire. They had with them the bronze table, says Herodotus, "on which
the earth was depicted with all its seas and rivers," and demonstrated it
freely in support of their plans. The stolid Spartans were much impressed, and asked for three days to consider. At the end of this time
King Cleomenes summoned the ambassadors and told them the plan
looked good on bronze. Susa seemed within reach; how far was it
actually? "Three months' march from the sea," said the ambassadors.
The king ordered them to leave the town before sunset.

also drew what seems to be the first map of the known world and had it engraved on a bronze table. But, with him, we find ourselves facing not only the "wise man" but a mind capable of high abstraction. If we have only one authentic sentence from his work, we are told enough—although in a miserably fragmentary and inadequate way—about his ideas to show that he was a daring and systematic thinker. The title of his book (it was said) was *On the Physis*—a word which became later the Latin *natura rerum,* and thus, our "nature"; but we should be mindful of what it could mean originally. *Physis,* "the physis of things," from which comes our own "physics," is an old word, already found in Homer, used in a sense very similar to our colloquial "the nature of the animal." More amply, it is "what makes beings the way they are." It is etymologically related to our verb "pushing"; its verb *phynai,* like the Latin *nasci, natura,* means "to grow," hence we might translate it "what things grow from." Thales' suggestion, as we have seen, was that they come out of water, and he had let it go at that. For Anaximander, so we are told, this was too commonsensical an answer. Water is itself one of the things we have to account for; it does not even account for everything else. Take that most comprehensive and awesome of phenomena, the revolution of the sky—could water account for that? Anaximander had raised a problem for which not even the beginning of an answer was given in ancient lore. It had always been taken for granted. With his thought now beyond the study of "meteors" and constellations, concentrating on the sky itself, he searched for some mechanism, and hit upon one of the great motifs of scientific cosmology: that of the fluid vortex. The eddies or whirlpools which appear in the flow of a stream must have become his guiding image. He conceived, therefore, of a vast flow, shoreless and endless, in which this our world is but a passing eddy. And, since there is no reason to suppose that in such a flow there should be only one, he announced that there must be many. Anaximander, reports Cicero, "is of the opinion that gods are born at vast intervals throughout east and west, and that they are the innumerable worlds." But, he adds with a frown, how can we think of a god other than sempiternal? Obviously, five centuries before Cicero, this requirement was not felt to be compelling. A world is a god to Anaximander, and there are innumerable such: they are born and pass away forever. The source of godhead, as well as of physical reality, is the great Flow itself, instinct with the seeds of all life, eternal, without beginning and end. Not having a name for it, since it comes before any distinction, Anaximander simply called it *Apeiron,* "the Unbounded." He also says that it is "the divine" and the *archē* of things, a word which would mean several things at once in our own language: "rulership," "principle," and also "beginning."

The equation has thus been set up in its amplest form, from which is to be developed the thought of Greece. In the first term we have the principle, nature and her changes, "that from which things come"; in the other ("as is meet"), the order which rules all things and becomes justice to men.

Things come into being and pass away. If Anaximander had been a moralist like Ecclesiastes or Aeschylus, he would have left it at that. Being that new personage, a physicist, he had to work out the first term: how do they? He let his physical imagination take over. In that world-eddy, he thought, what is mixed in the uniform boundless must come to separate out; and the familiar image that came to his mind must have been the winnower's sieve, rotating and shaken, where the heavy grain remains in the middle and the chaff wanders toward the rim. For he said that contraries "separated out," earth going to the center and fire to the outside, water and air remaining in between. And he must have thought of the concentrated fire envelope as becoming a kind of reverberating oven, for he said that it caused the water to boil up and to push back the fire in great billows of steam, until a stable balance was established which became our world. But some of the fire was rolled up and trapped in the surging billows, forming a kind of rotating inner tube (to use a rubber-age simile) of steam. There are vents in those tubes "like the nozzle of a pair of bellows," where the fire shows through, and those circular vents we call the sun and the moon. They are about the size of the earth. The size he assigned to the tubes was 27 and 18 earthly diameters respectively, which makes already a huge, non-familiar-sized world. A highly

mechanized one at that. Why so big? A plausible suggestion is that Anaximander wanted to account for the equality
of the days and nights, and had to place the sun far
enough away to have its rays practically parallel all over
the earth. The figures of 18 and 27 are chosen as multiples
of the number three. But it all remained somewhat "mete-
orological" in the old manner, for we are told that he
connected the varying inclinations of the sun with the
changes in seasonal winds. If the sun was still caught in
the clouds, one could certainly conceive of it as drifting
with the seasons. And of course the whole system might
dissolve sometime as an eddy in the stream, leaving
scarcely a ripple behind.

The rule he had set compelled Anaximander to ask himself further how living things had arisen, and he conceived
of a true evolutionary theory. Most of the world must have
been, at some time, covered by water, as he showed from
the evidence of fossil shells on dry land (an idea which
was not to be taken up again until Leonardo da Vinci)
and life must have come from the waters. Creatures arose
from the moist element as it was evaporated by the sun.
They must have had a "bark" to protect themselves from
evaporation, and could not live long in the beginning.
Men must have been fishlike creatures too, but as their
young require a long period of suckling before they can be
on their own, they must have been, or have depended on,
some kind of sea mammal at the outset. This is not very
explicit, but it is as much as we can make out owing to the
wretched incompetence of scribes and collectors of scattered "opinions" from third-hand texts who lived ten centuries later, and who are our main source of information.

Even as we have it, all this is a startling departure from
the spirit of Genesis in all its versions (Babylonian, Jew-
ish, or Greek) as it was strongly present at the time and
even in much more recent times. Such departures can be
violently disturbing to public opinion. But the Ionians
were singularly free of the atavistic taboos still so strong in
Greece. They worshiped their city gods dutifully, but they
were quite willing to discuss comparative religion.

That inquisitiveness and free logical reasoning were
traits of the educated man of the time we can see from
Herodotus of Halicarnassus, who wrote about 450 B.C.

Another wandering Ionian, whose restless life, after so-
journs in Samos and in Athens, was concluded in the
Sicilian colony of Thurii, Herodotus was the first to under-
take to write a *historiā* or "inquiry" about the known
world of his time. His main aim is to recount the Persian
wars, just concluded, but as the Greeks were newcomers
(their memory, he says, reaches back only a few centuries) to a context in which their victory had made them
a dominant factor, he feels the need to explain, in the first
part of his book, the growth of Near- and Mid-Eastern
power over a vaster span of time, omitting nothing he
knows about populations, climate, geography, etc. His
travels were, for his time, prodigious. They took him from
Babylon, Egypt, and Italy to the Black Sea and to the
Scythian hinterlands, over an arc of 1,800 miles. The following discussion of the floods of the Nile will show his
critical mind at work. The conclusion he draws is, of
course, wrong. It is on the Anaximandrean pattern, based
as it is on the "drift" of the sun. He actually examines the
possibility of a melting of the snows in Central Africa and
discards it. But then in his time nothing at all was known
or understood of the equatorial regions. And nothing went
on being known of the sources of the Nile until our times
(Speke, 1862). David Livingstone, who spent his years of
exploration searching for them, came to believe in Herodotus's story of two fountains of bottomless depth in the
heart of Africa. His last journey to the North was a half-
mystical attempt to rediscover those fountains, and on it
he perished. The passage we quote is thus also part of
modern history.

In the lack of any text from the Ionian scientists, of
whom we have only a few scattered sentences, we may
take this discussion * as the one which must have been
closest to their style. Anaximander was no doubt more
concise and solemn in his writing, but we might say: this
is probably the way in which he spoke.

About why the Nile behaves precisely as it does I could get
no information from the priests or anyone else. What I par-

---

* Herodotus, *The Histories,* translated and edited by Aubrey de
Selincourt. London: Penguin Books, Ltd., 1954.

ticularly wished to know was why the water begins to rise at the summer solstice, continues to do so for a hundred days, and then falls again at the end of that period, so that it remains low throughout the winter until the summer solstice comes round again in the following year. Nobody in Egypt could give me any explanation of this, in spite of my constant attempts to find out what was the peculiar property which made the Nile behave in the opposite way to other rivers, and why—another point on which I hoped for information—it was the only river to cause no breezes.

Certain Greeks, hoping to advertise how clever they are, have tried to account for the flooding of the Nile in three different ways. Two of the explanations are not worth dwelling upon, beyond a bare mention of what they are: one is that the Etesian [trade] winds cause the water to rise by checking the flow of the current towards the sea. In fact, however, these winds on many occasions have failed to blow, yet the Nile has risen as usual; moreover, if the Etesian winds were responsible for the rise, the other rivers which happen to run against them would certainly be affected in the same way as the Nile—and to a greater extent, in that they are smaller and have a less powerful current. There are many such rivers in Syria and Libya, but none of them are affected in the same way as the Nile. The second explanation is less rational, being somewhat, if I may so put it, of a legendary character: it is that the Nile exhibits its remarkable characteristics because it flows from the Ocean, the stream of which encircles the world. The third theory is much the more plausible, but at the same time furthest from the truth: according to this, the water of the Nile comes from melting snow—but as it flows from Libya through Ethiopia into Egypt, that is, from a very hot into a cooler climate, how could it possibly originate in snow? Obviously, this view is as worthless as the other two. Anyone who can use his wits about such matters will find plenty of arguments to prove how unlikely it is that snow is the cause of the flooding of the river: the strongest is provided by the winds, which blow hot from those regions; secondly, rain and frost are unknown there—and after snow rain is bound to fall within five days. So that if there were snow in that part of the world, there would necessarily be rain too; thirdly, the natives are black because of the hot climate. Again, kites and swallows remain throughout the year, and cranes migrate thither in winter to escape the cold weather of Scythia. But if there were any snow, however little, in the region through which the Nile flows and in which it rises, none of these things could possibly be; for they are contrary to reason. As to the writer who mentions the Ocean in this connection, his account is a mere fairy-tale depending upon an unknown quantity and cannot therefore be disproved by argument. I know myself of no river called Ocean, and can only suppose that Homer or some earlier poet invented the name and introduced it into poetry. If after criticizing these theories, I must express an opinion myself about a matter so obscure as the reason why the Nile floods in summer, I would say (to put the whole thing in the fewest words) that during winter the sun is driven out of his course by storms towards the upper parts of Libya. It stands to reason that the country nearest to, and most directly under, the sun should be most short of water, and that the streams which feed the rivers in that neighbourhood should most readily dry up.

But let me explain in somewhat greater detail my view of what happens when the sun passes across the upper regions of Libya. The atmosphere there is always clear, and there are no cold winds to temper the heat; and the result of this is that the sun, as it passes over, has the same effect as it normally has elsewhere in summer on its passage through the mid-heaven: namely, it draws the water towards itself and then thrusts it into those parts of the country still further inland, where it comes under the influence of the winds which scatter and disperse it in vapour—so naturally the winds (the south and southwest) which blow from this region are the most rainy. . . . These, then, are my reasons for thinking that the sun is the cause of this phenomenon, as also, I believe, of the dryness of the atmosphere in Egypt; the sun parching whatever lies in its path—so that in the upper parts of Libya it is always summer. Suppose for a moment the relative positions of north and south were changed—suppose, that is, the north wind and the south wind each, so to speak, usurped that part of the heavens which now belongs to the other: if such a thing occurred, the sun, when driven from its normal course by the northerly gales of winter, would pass over the north of Europe instead of—as now—over the south of Libya, and I have no doubt that during its passage across Europe its effect upon the Danube would be precisely the same as its present effect upon the Nile. I mentioned the fact that no breeze blows from the Nile: I would suggest, in explanation of this, that the usual thing is for winds to originate in a cold region, not in a hot one.

Well, these things have been as they are since the beginning of time, and there is no changing them; so I will pass to another subject. Concerning the sources of the Nile, nobody I have spoken with, Egyptian, Libyan, or Greek, professed to have any knowledge, except the scribe who kept the register of the treasures of Athene in the Egyptian city of Sais. But even this person's account, though he pretended to exact knowledge, seemed to me hardly serious. He told me that south of Syene [Aswan] there were two mountains of conical shape called Crophi and Mophi; and that the springs of the Nile, which were of fathomless depth, flowed out from between them. The fact that the springs were bottomless he said had been proved by the Egyptian king Psammetichus, who had a rope made many thousands of fathoms long which he let down into the water without finding the bottom. I think myself that if there is any truth in this story of the scribe's, it indicates the presence of powerful whirlpools and eddies in the water, caused by its impact upon the mountains, and it was these eddies which prevented the sounding-line from reaching the bottom.

2

Reason and the Vortex

WE MUST SEE what is the manner of thinking which allows exceptional men to go their own way undeterred. When he asked himself how the earth "stood," Anaximander found in his own bringing-up only the vague explanation that it rested "upon the foundations of the deep," which is common sense and reassuring enough. It soothes some dark apprehensions with a familiar image, and one which leads to no thought, only to embellishments, as in the Hindu tradition which figures the earth as supported by twelve elephants, who in their turn stand on the back of the great tortoise which floats on the waters of the deep. Anaximander preserved from that background the idea of a disk-shaped earth surrounded by the "Ocean River." But once his attention had become fixed on the obviously all-around turning of the heavens, he had to think of a vast whirl as the real situation. Then the earth was just "in the middle." Asked how it was supported, he replied that there was no reason why it should go this way or that, since all directions around the center are the same, and the outside swirling "forced" it to be where it was. This singular way of thinking has become a pillar of scientific thought, and it is known as the *principle of sufficient reason*. Anaximander went on using it with revolutionary conclusions springing up at every step. Since the situation of the earth is symmetrical with respect to the rest, there is no reason for an absolute *up* and *down*—that dominant feeling built into us by the fear of falling since earliest babyhood. The primal substance has to be "boundless" because we cannot see where it should stop. And inside that boundless, as we have seen, there is no sufficient reason for imagining our own world as a special singularity, since the forces that brought it about extend without limit; so there ought to be an unlimited number of worlds in what is beginning to look like infinite space. (Two types of symmetry come up here. In uniform space, the symmetry is random distribution; in the circular pattern of the whirl, it is radial. In the throw of the dice, it would be six-fold, which was to be later the starting point of the theory of probabilities.) This is of course exactly the way modern speculation proceeds: *Until a definite reason to the contrary can be assigned, we have to suppose a symmetrical distribution of things or possibilities.* It is an aspect of the principle of sufficient reason. It can be called, in this form, the *principle of symmetry,* or of *indifference,* or of *equally distributed ignorance.* In itself, it is simple enough. It states that causes which are undistinguishable intrinsically, when considered by themselves, cannot produce distinguishable effects. Archimedes uses it in a way which would look platitudinous to the outsider, to define the equilibrium in a balance. Experience has shown that the principle is one of the hardest to grasp for the unscientific mind.

Let us try to make our point clear. Surely, there is *a* principle of sufficient reason which is accepted by all, and we use it all the time. It is the same as to say that things are expected to make sense. Whenever we are faced with something, be it in experience or in experiment, for which we can imagine no sufficient reason, discomfort results. Even the story of Eve and the apple is there to provide sufficient reason for our human condition. In the Age of Belief it was taught by venerable Fathers that God made animals for our culinary or other convenience; that seemed to provide sufficient reason for their existence. Aristotle, as we shall see, thinks the universe is so constructed that all its points are distinguishable with as little symmetry as possible, and that the business of philosophy is to assign proper formal cause or sufficient reason for all the differences. He believes only in positive or specific sufficient reason. So do all philosophers. But it can be cause, judgment, or motive, general or particular, moral, esthetic, or otherwise; and thereby hang all kinds of philosophies. Leibniz tried to unify them all by a rigorous formulation of the principle: Nothing can be true, nothing can happen in reality, unless there is a sufficient reason for its being exactly so and not otherwise. Now, conversely, it becomes clear that if a theory cannot deduce for a given feature a sufficient reason why it should be thus and so and not otherwise, that feature has no place in the theory. This is the *negative* aspect of the principle, as it was applied by Anaximander: "If we can assign no specific boundary, we had better assume there is none." This way of thinking is what makes for the power and openness of the scientific imagination with respect to other forms: it takes calculated risks by creating its own symmetries; it can play with possibilities; it can deduce what is from what is not without losing its coherence. Today, still, it may seem strange to many that Anaximander's thought, starting from a wrong idea, such as the rotation of the sky, and leading to a wrong conclusion, such as the central position of the earth, should be considered justified and important because of the reasoning which joins the two. This simply goes to show how much miscomprehension there may be today concerning the true nature of science.

One thing at least should be intuitively clear, that this way of theorizing continuously undermines the instinctive assumption of a specific pattern ordained by a Providence for a limited purpose—any purpose that man can imagine being always limited. It is a remarkable testimonial to the maturity of the free republics of Ionia that Anaximander was not formally stoned to death in the public square, but that instead a statue was set up in his honor.

So the thing took place without bloodshed after all. Trouble was to come later, when people began to understand what had happened. But even that trouble (and we include in it the death of Socrates) amounts to little in the great slaughter of history, if we consider that this was one of the most momentous breaks in the career of humanity, comparable only to the discovery of fire. For it is not a paradox to say that Anaximander's system is as much an innovation on the way of thinking that came before as the whole of science has been since, from Anaximander to Einstein.

If we look today at the photograph of a great spiral nebula such as that of Andromeda, we cannot avoid feeling as if Anaximander's universe had appeared in the field of our telescope; and recent cosmological speculations on matter and antimatter "separating out" of some primeval entity and then annihilating each other when they chance to meet, releasing the kinetic energy needed to move the galaxies, are one more impressive rehearsal of the ancient motif.

Yet, let us not be fenced in by familiar similarities. These physical images arose from a background of thought very far from ours. The very word *cause* at that time has a strictly juridical connotation; it means "responsibility." In Latin, always conservative, usage preserves *causa* as the legal procedure itself, aimed at establishing responsibility. The universe which is taking shape in Anaximander's mind (and it is difficult for us to place ourselves in the position of a man trying to project a "universe") is still a vast community of forces which bring forth other forces which in turn fall into place; instead of the moderating will of a Zeus, it has its own inner necessity as a ruler, for it is itself "the divine." Contrast and balance, equalization, acceptance, justice are the intelligible mainsprings of it all. This it is that makes it a *kosmos,* which in the early language of politics refers to the well-ordered community; a concept perhaps less defined than visualized, as we still can see it portrayed in Lorenzetti's fresco *Il Buon Governo.* The famous lines of Solon's elegy on immanent justice ("Most hard is it to apprehend the unapparent measure of judgment, which alone holds the limits of all things") show how the idea had been taking shape in contemporary Greece. Traditionally, Solon comes just before Anaximander. But the chronology we have is not sufficiently secure to bear this out, and it may well be that Solon's voyage to Ionia played an important part in the formation of his own thought.

Here is a world of immanent function, manifesting its own severe will to order to which man must adjust, but in adjusting he will find himself "at home" in it—an expression which runs through the whole of Greek thought. It is quite possible that even the formation of our vortex is conceived of somehow as the foundation of an active unit, in which the contrary forces are at the same time released and controlled. It is clear, conversely, that in Anaximander's underlying scheme of a human community those drives are singled out which make of man the equivalent of a simple force—greed, aggrandizement, what used to be called *pleonexia.* Twenty-two centuries later Thomas

Hobbes will start from those same elements in his attempt to mechanize the workings of society.

SYSTEM ANALYSIS

Is there a superconsciousness in this universe, corresponding to what we of the later tradition would call God? The answer should be: Not any more than in Hesiod, Anaximander's direct predecessor. Hesiod's *Theogony* is the story of the successive generations of the gods, arising from heaven and earth; they, too, pay reparations to one another in their downfall, until Zeus is established, who reigns on more or less constitutional lines. The universe is a coexistence of forces which can be dethroned when they go wrong. They are timebound, if not necessarily mortal. Anaximander starts from there. His Unbounded is certainly meant to develop the Hesiodic idea of Chaos, the "yawning gap." What he does is to remove the animistic and personalized elements of the primitive version and to replace them with constant behaviors. Thus, even the other image of the community which predominates in his mind becomes one of an order. The actions attributed to the gods are explicitly transformed into physical mechanisms. Thus, the lightning is taken away from Zeus and becomes fire "bursting" from a cloud. In much of his account Anaximander has to preserve the language and images of his predecessors in order to make himself understood. When he speaks of the clouds as a "bark," he has probably in mind Pherecydes' myth of the world-tree draped in a starry mantle, a very ancient *physis;* when he speaks of the Unbounded as a "germ" from which the world grew, he has another similar myth in mind. Even when he speaks of contraries "separating" out from the original stuff, he illustrates it (if we are to believe Alexander of Aphrodisias) with the Hesiodic image of that "in between" from which Light and Night separate out—and we may recognize here a barely fitting piece left over from the great days of archaic astronomy. But we see that he is using all these images and is not controlled by them. He builds up a scheme whereby what comes first is that if things belong to one order as they change into one another, they must be of the same One Substance. It is this substance, then, which has to be germ and womb and system all in one, matrix, begetter, and controller in an unending process. That is what he calls "the divine." The gods are left aside. "The Unbounded," he says, "comprehends the whole and steers all things." This word "steering," *kybernān,* natural to a seafaring civilization, has remained through the Latin *gubernare* in our language: our mechanics speak of the "governor" of a steam engine, whence in our times arose the science of cybernetics. The term for governing, retranslated into Greek by Wiener, turns out to be Anaximander's very own. But it implies now what he meant and could not express—automatic control.

Anaximander, like Solon, thought half-consciously in terms of the city because it was the only self-regulating system that he knew. But as he identified its immortal element with the intermortal relationships which live in us, and must live in the universe, his imagination went one step further "into the unseen," as the Greeks used to say. He saw it as automatic control. Wisdom, *sophia,* is etymologically being *saphēs* about these things, that is, "sharp," using sharp discernment. Anaximander had to devise some kind of coherent mechanism, and he did. Aristophanes was to say bitterly: "They have dethroned Zeus, and Vortex is King." The divine mechanism did not have to be true in detail, but it expressed on this new level what had to be there—the impersonal equivalent of a consciousness, which makes its stipulations alive not only in nature but in men's minds, and superior to all and each.

This is where real poetic capacity is brought to bear, where the powerful originality of invention breaks through. One has only to think of the other, more biological, images adopted by our medieval thinkers twenty centuries later in the name of good sense to theorize about the good society, with the community as a body, the people as the limbs, the ruler as the head, and so forth, and the interminable inconclusive discoursing and exhorting which go with it, to realize what a uniquely lucky throw of the intellectual dice it was to have these men imagine their first model in the language of wind and steam, whirlpool and winnowing sieve, borrowed from their technology—imagine it, and then be fascinated by it; for the model acquires a "sharpness" of structure which leads the mind from one acute question to another toward the discovery of new philosophical horizons.

What we called the "cosmic community" is not interpreted in terms of social reason; it takes on the character of another reason, another justice, which is necessity. There is no mention of law anywhere, for "law" means a command, and the Unbounded exercises no more command than Mother Earth had done in previous theogonies. It brings forth and takes back. The conflict between contraries may be a communal one; it is nonetheless blind. The green log in the fire sizzles and sputters indignantly in vain; the flames have it. But if the rains fall, then fire is overcome, it is in "the nature of things." Thus do the elements come to equalize out dynamically in the balance of the cosmos. The inherent rule is only the result of the necessary behavior of parts, just as we would think today in thermodynamics. "The divine" comes out as unfree as Spinoza's deity; it is the bearer of "the force of things." Surely, the mind may still have been struggling with ancestral notions like "the dark counsels of necessity," and Time may have appeared as a sovereign disposing and ordering power. We may discern poetic ambiguity in Anaximander's words, charged with all the themes of the past. But the light of reason has dispelled Chthonian darkness. If what emerges is not physical thought, one may ask what is. The anthropomorphic mold has been broken; it is no longer nature viewed as an image of society, but much rather the reverse, in the great equation which embraces both aspects. *Physis,* whose justice has become identified with abstract reason, has become autonomous, even more, automatic.

What has been founded here is a way of thought which has since been called *scientific rationalism.* It may be stated thus: *Whatever can be deduced necessarily from premises that we consider true will be found sometime, somewhere, somehow, to exist.* This is the mainspring of discovery; it is what guides us in research and in the construction of theories. Without it, science would be the accumulation of empirical facts that certain outsiders imagine it to be. The principle works also negatively, as we have seen in *sufficient reason,* where it requires indeed a full measure of faith and audacity. Since no reason can be assigned for our world-vortex to be unique in the universe, Anaximander decided that there must be innumerable such worlds. This point of view was strikingly expressed in the next century by Metrodorus: a single world in the immensity of space, he said, would be as unnatural as a single ear of wheat in a limitless plain.

ANAXIMENES

Anaximenes, another Milesian—"an associate of Anaximander," say our sources, and add nothing beyond that—picked up the mechanistic aspect and made it more consistent. In his thought, there is no longer the separation of opposites out of the primal matter, nor that balance of contrasts which makes for harmony; there is the single process of change from dense to rare and inversely. The philosophical idea of balance having been dropped, Anaximenes no longer feels the need of a substrate underlying all elements equally, but can go back to choosing one of them, and this time it is air. "Everything, according to him, is made by condensation and rarefaction, but motion is from eternity," says a commentator. It is the process of packing or "felting" (this is the word actually used) which makes the dense out of the rare. Rarefied air becomes vapor and fiery exhalation; "felted," it becomes water and ice and stone. "It becomes visible in heat and cold, in moisture and in movement. It is in perpetual motion, since without motion it would not change." Here is a fascinating theoretical departure. It might have looked uncouth on the face of it to go back to one of the "beggarly elements," but it allows us to explain the difference in behaviors. Air is compressible; water is not, because it is "felted." We can hope to find reasons for the multiple aspects of matter. The theory looks as though it were going to succeed; it fails, yet it has marked an advance in setting up a new problem. Instead of undefined opposites which can be understood only qualitatively, as different essences, so to speak, we have a first scheme of matter and motion, both apparently unbounded in time and space.

"From air," says Anaximenes, "the things that are and have been and will be, and things divine and the gods, took their rise, while other things came from its offspring."

This comes to us not as a quotation, but it is surely a close paraphrase of his own way of speaking. Of him, as of his master, we have only one directly quoted sentence: "As our soul, being air, holds us together, so do breath and air surround the whole universe."

Something has been gained over Anaximander's system in further mechanization; something has been lost in philosophical scope, but we see that at the core the thought remains the same. Air as primordial substance, like Anaximander's indefinite seed, has to play an ambivalent role, both matter and *psyche,* the "breath of life." Traditional religious thought traced everything that happened back to the gods. If the principle and cause were one, the Unbounded, it must be the original unitary form of the divine energy, which then took the shape of individual worlds and gods, but it goes on "surrounding the whole and ruling all things." This definition of the Divine is open, general, and abstract enough to resist the challenge of later and more sophisticated analysis. It was to remain the model for the Greek philosophical conception of godhead, and it is striking to see it advanced again and even in the original Greek word, *periekhon,* "the Surrounding," by a master of contemporary existentialism, K. Jaspers. It is for him, again, the cosmic counterpart of what we can deal with in our sphere of human purpose and understanding: the infinite and unknowable, which actually surrounds and comprehends it, concealing in itself the source of all being and value.

"The ancients had a solemn way of speaking about these things," remarks Aristotle (for him they are "the ancients," although they come only two centuries before him). They well might have. They had laid the firm foundations for a natural philosophy which was also a theology and a theodicy and a physical science at the same time. The link between the various aspects of the one undertaking was never again to be broken, at least in our own civilization for as long as it lasts.

3

The Logos in the Lightning

THERE WAS one last change to be rung upon the elements (Mother Earth having remained the dark preserve of the mythologists) and it was the work of a great mind, later by perhaps two generations, who seems to have had little patience for the mechanisms of his predecessors: Heraclitus (Herakleitos) of Ephesos. Says Diogenes Laertius, a late compiler on whom, unfortunately, we have to depend for so much of our information on this period: "His detailed doctrines are as follows: that Fire is the Element, and that all things are 'an exchange of Fire,' coming into being by rarefaction and condensation. But he expounds nothing clearly." This complaint is worthy of the hack whom Flaubert called "the greatest jackass of antiquity," for even that "rarefaction and condensation," which make no sense here, he has added by way of trying to puzzle out the meaning of the word "exchange." We have by luck a number of oracular sayings of Heraclitus himself, which in their paradoxical brevity did not stand paraphrasing and had thus to be quoted directly by successive authors. These sentences are meant to startle by way of unexpected contrasts ("We never step twice into the same river, we are and are not" *), and there is a self-conscious artistry and reticence in them which fit Heraclitus's character as a disdainful aristocratic temper and a conservative irritated by the commonness of the common man. "The god whose oracle is in Delphi neither speaks out nor conceals: he indicates." The cryptic style is meant to stress the central ideal, which to intuitive minds shines forth "indicated" with undeviating sureness. Here is what was prob-

* This and subsequent quotations from Heraclitus in this chapter are from *Early Greek Philosophy,* translated and edited by John Burnet. London: Basil Blackwell.

ably the opening statement of his book. It sounds like a flourish of trumpets:

This Word [*Logos*] is from everlasting, yet men understand it as little after the first hearing of it as before. For though all things come to pass according to this Word, men seem wanting in experience when they examine the words and deeds I set forth, distinguishing each thing in its nature and showing how it truly is. But other men know not what they do when awake, even as they forget what they do in sleep.

The idea is this: the substrate, the underlying reality, is not some one unchanging primordial matter; it is nothing but the pure flow of change, represented by Fire, that which devours and brings forth. A perfect image of the conception is the flame itself, which subsists in apparent stillness on its wick, but whose shape is nothing but the restless flow of fuel being exchanged into something else.

This order, the same for all things, no god or man has made, but it always was, is, and shall ever be, an ever-living fire, kindling and going out according to fixed measure.—All things are exchanged for fire, and fire for all things, as goods are exchanged for gold, and gold for goods.

The "measure" of change replaces, or rather determines, what to us are the distinctions of reality. Air, earth, and water are transmutations of fire, but in that qualitative elemental continuum their "measure" is a geometric mean proportionality. Fire : Air :: Air : Water :: Water : Earth.
There is, then, nothing fixed and stable except the measure of change itself. "Day and night are one." Each thing is defined by the complementaries with which it is "continuous." "Eyes and ears are bad witnesses"; they tell us of separate existences which seem to be each by itself, but it is all as unreal, to use.a modern simile, as the patterns created by motion arrested in the flash of the stroboscope. The motion itself is the primary thing. "In changing, it takes its rest." "It"—what? We might say the process, but not in the modern ample sense—rather as exchange flickering between opposite extremes. There is indeed a certain electric quality about Heraclitus's fire, which is further confirmed by the idea that he forms of its main action:

"It is the thunderbolt which steers the course of all things."
The strong relativistic accent of previous Ionian thinking
is not lost on Heraclitus. He strikes in fact the aspect of it
which goes most against instinct and common sense, by
proclaiming, "The way up and the way down are one and
the same." This sentence, which in later times was to take
on mysterious overtones to initiates, seems meant here
quite physically. Fire not only leads change upwards, as
it would seem at first sight; it also closes the cycle downwards. The commanding image is the thunderbolt, which
is fire descending from heaven to earth. The waterspout or
whirlwind, the "burner," as he calls it, is the principal
agent, with its summit made of downward-whirling clouds,
its lower part a column of rising water and sea mist, and
its body shot through with lightnings. "The changes of fire
are: first sea, then one half of it earth, the other half whirlwind."

All this is physical enough, yet it remains a barely
sketched-out scheme. Heraclitus is impatient of consistent
explanation, even concerning the heavens. "The sun is new
every day," because it is nothing but the perpetual re-
kindling in some kind of "bowl" of the terrestrial exhala-
tions. As to size, it is "as big as it appears—about a foot."
Things are really unimportant except as manifestations of
what is beneath the surface. "Nature loves to hide." To the
attentive mind, the supposed definite outlines of things
blur, a quality changes into its opposite as we watch, its
nature comes and goes, that is, it possesses no nature, no
essence that remains; there is nothing, in any particular object, to know; only the whole makes sense. The true element is force, change, process, "ever-living Fire." It is
hidden in the air and causes it to be the warming "breath
of life," *pneuma;* it is present as the link between all things
as well as that which encompasses them. "As our soul, being air, holds us together, so do breath and air surround
the whole universe." This had been said by Anaximenes,
but it might have been said with greater force by Heraclitus, if we understand fire as the real active thing in the
breath. That fire also bears the consciousness which makes
the living aware of one another. It retreats from the sleeper
and leaves him cloistered in his own being. It rekindles
for him "the order of the waking."

The electric quality which flickers and sparks like summer lightning in Heraclitus's thought appears vividly in his great idea of the identity of opposites. To identify any one thing is also to name its opposite, "for day and night are one." "In the circle beginning and end are the same." Polarity is the great flywheel of nature. The process of coming-into-being and passing-away is a constant inter-transformation of opposites, one into the other. It is "the way up and the way down" along which things wander and cross each other unceasingly. The Anaximandrean justice "according to the order of Time" becomes here simultaneous, timeless, while still all-embracing; "immortals mortal, mortals immortal, living each other's death, dying each other's life." But there is an inherent tension in it all, which has made of Heraclitus the philosopher of unresolved strife. "War is father of all and king of all: some he made gods and some men, some slave and some free." Here is the ancient theme of conflict and balance, but in a new light. There are the great oppositions and polarities of nature, of which sex and war are only the too-visible symbols. But "men do not understand how that which draws apart agrees with itself; a fitting-together of counterten-sions, as in the bow and the lyre." Here is the true form of the idea. The arrow's flight, the warrior's honor, the music of the lyre, could not be without strife and the built-in tension of opposites, and Heraclitus plays deftly on the double meaning of the word *harmonia,* which means both the fitting together of the parts of the instrument and the tuning that results. "Opposition unites. From what draws apart, the best harmony. All things take place by contrast." It is so everywhere, even where we would not look for it, and to the mind that can grasp the complex music of the all, "hidden harmony is better than manifest."

Heraclitus has realized that Fire itself is far from being the ultimate thing. It is a power which is only the vehicle for measure, harmony, proportion. It operates as bearer of the *Logos,* the Measure, which makes all things one. "There is only one wisdom, to know that insight which steers all things through all things." The steering thunderbolt, then, was not as simple as it appeared. It has become, as it were, a carrier wave. But which, then, is the substrate? There is a saying of which Fränkel has suggested that the apparent nonsense we have quoted about the sun must be a detached fragment. The whole would run like this: the sun itself, giver of light and life, is a limited thing, it is held to its path, it appears in the whole circle of heaven no bigger than a man's foot, but "though you travel in every direction you shall never find the bounds of the soul, so deep is the *logos* of it." It is the *logos* of the soul, we note, which is deep and far-ranging to infinity, whereas everything else in nature is partial and limited. As living entities, sun and soul are really of the same kind and nature; what Heraclitus means is not the individual soul of a man (he did not even possess a word for "consciousness"; he had only "reason") but the "life" that man shares with everything in the world, sun and stars included. In that soul is the *logos* of *all* the measures. The Rational Fire is (to use another electrical term) a flashover to the regularity of nature from the infinity of Reason, which always "increases itself." The physical system makes sense in the light of an emergent metaphysics. The electrical similes that we have been led instinctively to use in our explanation show a profound change: the duality of substrate and appearance becomes one of carrier wave and message. A new dimension has entered our thinking. But there is more.

Together with the ruling *Logos* (a concept destined to have a fateful career in later thought), another word has appeared in the fragments of Heraclitus. We find for the first time, explicitly mentioned, a Law, *nomos*.

Those who use their mind should strengthen themselves with what is common to all, as a city does with its law, and even stronger, for all laws of men are fed by the one divine law; for this holds sway as far as it will, and suffices for all, and rules all over.

The historians who maintain that Anaximander's natural necessity was directly patterned after the law of the community seem to have overlooked this, which to Heraclitus appears as his own discovery, and rightly so. Who says "law" says "command"; the *Logos* steers things in a way which cannot be really immanent to their nature, since they have no individual nature to speak of. "The Sun shall not overstep his bounds; if he does, the Erinyes, ministers of justice, will find him out." This may be as allegorically and Homerically stated as we like. It still implies a command, a norm that has been set.

Everything else is challenged. "Time is a child playing draughts." * "The fairest order is but a heap of garbage emptied out at random." The steady gaze and self-possession of knowledge, which have been felt as natural by the preceding sages, yield to the flash of paradox. True wisdom has moved beyond man's estate. "Of all whose teachings I have heard, no one has gone far enough to know that the Wise is apart from all things." It is apart from man, too, who is caught inside things. "Man's way of being [ethos] has no insights, but the divine has them." Most men need not care, for "present they are absent, and their life is like a sleep," but even to the mind awakened wisdom does not come as discursive thought; it is the brief moment of intuition which reveals all opposites as one. As for that Wise itself, for whom "good and bad are one," who is "day night, winter summer, hunger surfeit," who is at the same time nature and beyond nature, we have no name for him; "it does not and does consent to be called by the name of Zeus."

Heraclitus remains in history as "The Obscure." Socrates, when asked by Euripides what he thought of him, is said to have remarked: "What I have understood is excellent; also, I think, what I have not understood—except that it needs a champion diver." To plunge into those dark waters remains forever a tempting enterprise. As various rationales are developed from a view which will hardly support them, as "dialectics" is brought in to expound it, we shall have the Reason of the Stoics, the intuitions of Nicholas of Cusa, as well as the mystic insights of the nineteenth-century *Naturphilosophen,* the dialectical treatment of Hegel and Marx.

As for us, it is enough to mark that we confront a Law which, even when it calls itself natural, has little to do with the laws of nature as we mean them. It is a far cry from

* The word for Time, however, is the old *Aion,* "aeon," and it is so clearly related to the "Rip van Winkle" motif of the Aion playing his game with the planets that it shows Heraclitus to have been mindful of whatever was left of archaic tradition.

the "necessity of things" or from what we called automatic control. It will be, however, for two thousand years, what people come to understand by natural law. It is born of the pantheistic outlook, which ties up the universe and man. The binding power of that law does not rest on its being "positive law," i.e., on having been regularly decreed; it rests on the "universal reason" it embodies. Heraclitus calls it simply the discipline of reason, and it applies both to nature and to society. It is only much later, in our own Renaissance, that our idea of "laws of nature" comes up explicitly, and of course it is quite paradoxical as it stands, seeing that it combines the concept of law, i.e., something "laid down" and imposed, with that of nature, that is, living, self-creating reality. If the paradox was not so keenly felt in the seventeenth century, it is because nature by then was understood to be not so much alive as controlled by an omnipotent deity.

Heraclitus had planted the seeds for a great misunderstanding. He is and remains an unscientific thinker. But he comes back at all times to haunt the thoughts of the scientist. He has focused attention on how mysterious and ambiguous the objects of nature really are, however familiar and obvious they may appear to be. Only through the *logos,* he says, can we make sense of them, and it is very deep. This realization has never been lost since, except in very dogmatic and simple-minded phases of thought.

Texts

Here are some of the fragments of Heraclitus, in addition to those already quoted in the text. The translation is that of John Burnet * (with slight changes). We have preserved his numbering, which follows that of Bywater.

4. Eyes and ears are bad witnesses to men, if they have souls that understand not their language.
5. The many have not as many thoughts as the things they meet with; nor, if they do remark them, do they understand them, though they believe they do.

* *Early Greek Philosophy,* translated and edited by John Burnet. London: Basil Blackwell.

7. If you do not expect the unexpected, you will not find it; for it is hard to be sought out and difficult.

17. Pythagoras, son of Mnesarchos, practised inquiry beyond all other men, and made himself a wisdom of his own, which was but a knowledge of many things and an art of mischief.

23. [The earth] is liquefied, and the sea is measured by the same tale as before it became earth.

24. Fire is want and satiety.

25. Fire lives the death of earth, and air lives the death of fire; water lives the death of air, earth that of water.

26. Fire will come upon and lay hold of all things.

27. How can one hide from that which never sinks to rest?

35. Hesiod is most men's teacher. Men think he knew very many things, a man who did not know day or night! They are one.

40. It scatters things and brings them together; it approaches and departs.

41, 42. You cannot step twice into the same rivers; for fresh waters are ever flowing in upon you.

43. Homer was wrong in saying: "Would that strife might perish from among gods and men!" He did not see that he was praying for the destruction of the universe; for, if his prayer were heard, all things would pass away.

46. It is opposition that brings things together.

48. Let us not conjecture at random about the greatest things.

49. Men who love wisdom must be acquainted with very many things indeed.

52. The sea is the purest and the impurest water. Fish can drink it, and it is good for them; to men it is undrinkable and destructive.

53, 54. Swine like to wash in the mire rather than in clean water, and barnyard fowls in dust.

59. You must couple together things whole and things not whole, what is drawn together and what is drawn asunder, the harmonious and the discordant. The one is made up of all things, and all things issue from the one.

60. Men would not have known the name of justice if there were no injustice.

64. All the things we see when awake are death, even as the things we see in slumber are sleep.

68. For it is death to souls to become water, and death to

water to become earth. But water comes from earth; and, from water, soul.

77. Man is kindled and put out like a light in the nighttime.

78. Quick and dead, waking and sleeping, young and old, are the same; the former are changed and become the latter, and the latter in turn are changed into the former.

79. Time is a child playing draughts, the kingly power is a child's.

80. I have sought to know myself.

81. We step and do not step into the same rivers; we are and are not.

92. Though wisdom is common, yet the many live as if they had a wisdom of their own.

93. They are estranged from that with which they have most constant intercourse.

97. Man is called a baby by god, even as a child by a man.

105–107. It is hard to fight with desire. Whatever it wishes to get, it purchases at the cost of soul.

108, 109. It is best to hide folly; but it is a hard task in times of relaxation, over our cups.

112. In Priene lived Bias, son of Teutamas, who is of more account than the rest. (He said, "Most men are bad.")

114. The Ephesians would do well to hang themselves, every grown man of them, and leave the city to beardless youths; for they have cast out Hermodoros, the best man among them, saying: "We will have none who is best among us; if there be any such, let him be so elsewhere and among others."

117. The fool is fluttered at every word.

119. Homer should be turned out of the lists and whipped, and Archilochos likewise.

122. There awaits men when they die such things as they look not for nor dream of.

CONCLUSION

Ionian natural philosophy seems to have thus reached the end of the road.

The mechanics of the whirlpool or of "felting" affords at best a limited explanation: opposites separate out of each other, the stuff packs up or vaporizes, the river of change carries all things in its flow. Beyond that one has to fall back on the capacity of the primal substance to organize itself according to some hidden spontaneity, whether it be the seeds of all things already contained in the Unbounded, or the flash "which steers all" of the Heraclitean lightning. The Wise, whatever it be, begins to be revealed above and apart from substance. Yet the conception has to be monistic, as all thought had been from the beginning. Substance and soul had ever been one. The Ionian *physis,* which was also "the divine," remains more than half alive, but its ways are becoming more difficult to organize intellectually. Ionian thought had set out to solve the central problem of the One and the Many, or why things are different. As it drives forward its dialectic, it finds it has no proper way of thinking of the separate Many; they dissolve under the intense gaze into flickering aspects of the One Thing. The paradox is only apparent. The Many are just what we see and sense, but they cannot be firmed by reason; either they are reabsorbed into what we would call a steady state, or they become Process itself. The elements of form, precision, and design which are apparent in nature are taken for granted; they are not accounted for. When Anaximenes suggests an analogy between the twists and turns of the planets in their courses and the gyrations of dead leaves falling through the air, he is using reasonable models to little purpose. The "beggarly elements" could go no farther. A new idea was needed, and it came from another quarter.

4

The Power of Number

PYTHAGORAS

IN THE ISLAND of Samos, about 590 B.C., was born the enigmatic character known to us as Pythagoras. When he was forty he removed to southern Italy, which was coming to be called Greater Greece because of the numerous Greek colonies on the coast, and there founded a brotherhood, with some monastic features, which lasted for about two hundred years and left a tradition which was still living in the early Christian centuries. Of his life we know little, and that for a significant reason. By his immediate followers, he was already recognized (like his near contemporaries, Zoroaster and Buddha) as one of those divine men who stand as mere names in history because their lives are at once transfigured into legend. He was, they said, the son of Apollo by a mortal woman. Historians recorded some of the miracles ascribed to his more than human powers. In fact, the later the story, the more wondrous. Here is one such transmission from late Antiquity; it is due to Hippolytus,* a Christian bishop.

[Pythagoras], . . . in his studies of nature, mingled astronomy and geometry and music and arithmetic. And thus he asserted that God is a monad, and examining the nature of number with especial care, he said that the universe produces melody and is put together with harmony, and he first proved the motion of the seven stars to be rhythm and melody. And in wonder at the structure of the universe, he decreed that at first his disciples should be silent, as it were mystae [adepts of the mysteries] who were coming into the order of the all; then

* Translated by Dr. Arthur Fairbanks in *The First Philosophers of Greece.* Quoted in *Selections from Early Greek Philosophy,* edited by Milton Charles Nahm (3rd ed.). New York: F. S. Crofts & Co., 1947. Reprinted by permission of Appleton-Century-Crofts.

when he thought they had sufficient education in the principles of truth, and had sought wisdom sufficiently in regard to stars and in regard to nature, he pronounced them pure and then bade them speak. He separated his disciples into two groups and called one esoteric [i.e., inner] and the other exoteric. . . . The early sect perished in a conflagration in Kroton in Italy. And it was the custom when one became a disciple for him to liquidate his property and to leave his money under a seal with Pythagoras, and he remained in silence sometimes three years, sometimes five years, and studied. On being released from this, he mingled with the others and continued a disciple and made his home with them; otherwise he took his money and was sent off. . . . And those of the disciples who escaped the conflagration were Lysis and Archippos and Zamolxis the slave of Pythagoras, who is said to have taught the Pythagorean philosophy to the Druids among the Celts. It is said [this comes straight from Herodotus] that Pythagoras learned numbers and measures from the Egyptians; astonished at the wisdom of the priests, which was deserving of belief and full of fancies and difficult to buy, he imitated it and himself also taught his disciples to be silent, and obliged the student to remain quietly in rooms underneath the earth.

Such accounts are weird mixtures of later wonder-mongering tales and the deadpan reporting of very early chroniclers, not devoid of sarcasm, which is echoed so delightfully by Herodotus. Take only Zamolxis, the slave of the Master, who gets unaccountably mixed up here with the Celts. The real connection belongs to another character of the tradition, carrying with him the aura of the Druids of Stonehenge, Abaris the Hyperborean, who was said to have been guided and led to Pythagoras by a golden arrow he held in his hand—the earliest version of the Three Wise Kings of Bethlehem. Now it is not clear whether Abaris was the name of a Druid or of the deity he represented, or maybe just an invention, but as far as Zamolxis is concerned we know that he would have been an uncomfortable companion to have around, for he was none other than the huge, lumbering bear-god of Thrace, a grizzly now extinct in Europe, who was first cousin to the Alaskan bear. The Thracian shamans or medicine men ruled the tribe in his name, and imitated his hibernation by retiring into caves for long periods of trancelike sleep whence they emerged with visions. If Pythagoras really imposed silence and obliged his students to remain quietly in rooms underneath the earth, it means (for the Egyptians had no such practice) that he was considered something of a shaman himself, no less than that other strange figure of a prophet before him, Epimenides the Cretan, the authority whom the Athenians once called in for consultation on rites about 600 B.C. during an epidemic, and who was rumored to have been asleep in a cave for years on end. One cannot but be reminded of Ezekiel lying stretched out in God-imposed penance for three hundred and ninety days in another cave. Pythagoras, we are told from a different source, went through the initiation rites of Cretan Zeus by lying for a month in a cave in Crete, and then being "purified with the thunderstone"; in other words, he became an embodiment of the god. We are told further by Aristotle that, at a solemn gathering in Olympia, he showed the crowd that he had a golden thigh. This must have been the ritual sign for his being one with the bull-god Atabyrios, or Tabor, another form of Dionysus, worshiped in Lydia and once unfavorably known to the Jews as the Golden Calf. As for that fire in which the early members of the sect perished, it is part of a somber political crisis, for it appears that Pythagoras and his companions seized control of the political machinery in Croton in alliance with the aristocrats, and drove the city to a successful war of extermination against neighboring Sybaris, only to be overthrown and destroyed in their turn by a rival faction. They were not so much meek ascetics as rigorous Puritans, and the open part of their teaching was a strong moral doctrine which was to cast its late glow over such different characters as Cato the Elder in Rome, Herennius the Samnite chieftain, and Epaminondas the hero of Thebes.

What we perceive here dimly is a complicated web of political ferment and religious revivals which tied together many of the archaic or protohistoric remnants, hitherto preserved only among the lower orders. Legendary masters like Epimenides and Pythagoras appear then as taking on the traditional figure of the initiatic teacher, but intent on transforming and reinterpreting the ancient rites. One such reinterpretation underlies a sophistic paradox which much later—in our time—was to provide the occasion for

Bertrand Russell to construct his own famous paradox, and out of it his theory of logical types. We all know from St. Paul the story of Epimenides the Cretan saying that all Cretans were liars. From this it followed obviously that he too must be lying, which meant that Cretans tell the truth. So he turned out again to be telling the truth when he said that they are liars; and so on. The historical core of this *jeu d'esprit* seems to be this: Epimenides told the Athenians that although the rites of the Cretan religion enacted a yearly death and rebirth of Zeus, this was not meant to deny the truth known in Athens, that Zeus is unchanging and everlasting.

These traditions, in turn, may tell us something of what this new divine figure of Dionysus could mean, which overran Greece at the time, with his cult of death and resurrection, of seasonal frenzies and new mystery plays. It must have been, as Rudolf Otto has suggested, a terrible awakening awareness of the contradictory and irreconcilable nature of our experience of life, in which pleasure and horror, life and death, light and darkness, are brought to us by the same ambiguous power—an awareness which had been firmly held in check by the aristocratic discipline of Homeric civilization, left to the countryside to be worked out in peasant rites, but which was moving now from silent acceptance to tormented consciousness.

It is this tension which gives power and significance to Pythagoras's endeavor—the search for new and higher means of purification, for a way to "justify the ways of God to man." The contemplation of the eternal, says Plutarch, is the aim of philosophy, as the contemplation of the mysteries is the aim of religion. Both contemplations, he might have added, involve also "things that are done": holy sacrifices in one case, music and ascetic discipline in the other. Through the many-faceted tradition which shimmers in the fog of the past, we may see that the several teachings of Pythagoras are part of a unifying vision of the universe.

The soul is of its own nature immortal—that is to say, divine. Its original body (for there is no soul without a body) is a star. It is a body of "intelligent fire" such as truly befits it, from which it lapses into earth, where it can enter only a mortal body. When that dies, the soul, according to its deeds, passes into other forms of life, of man or animal or plant. It is bound upon this wheel of reincarnation until it shall have become pure. It will then regain a place in a star in the company of the immortal gods and heroes. This is how the archaic idea of "going to heaven" re-enters Western thought, for it did not belong either to Hebrew or to Homeric tradition; and with it comes the beginning (only the beginning) of a dualism between matter and spirit. The body is no better than a temporary prison house or "tomb" of the living soul. But the incipient spiritualism here only accents the unity of all life: there is a bond of kinship uniting man to the gods above us and to the beasts below, for any soul may climb or descend to any rung in the ladder of existence. And the sin for which the fallen soul has been condemned to its round of mortal births was a mysterious breach of this unity, symbolized on earth by the shedding of blood.

HARMONY AND NUMBER

What emerges here is not completely strange to the Greeks, for reincarnation had been taught by the votaries of Orpheus, who were banded in mystical cult-societies everywhere, but more thoroughly in South Italy. It is also, certainly, a revival of archaic, Proto-Mediterranean motifs which had lain buried for centuries. Pythagoras, albeit son of Apollo, comes as a reformer in the tradition of prehistoric cults. It was recounted of him that "whenever he found someone who had a community of symbols with him, he went out to make him his friend." A new constellation of ideas was being drawn from the disintegrated beliefs of the dim past; it is the high point of what should be considered the "Greek Renaissance."

The Orphics, too, had abstained from killing animals or eating flesh, holding the same belief that the unity of life should be inviolate. Upon secret sympathy between all creatures had rested the legendary power of Orpheus, who had tamed animals and caused stones to rise into walls by the magic of his rhythms. Now, the myth of Orpheus contains a thought that took shape in the mind of Pythagoras. How can music possess this magical influence over the soul, and be the instrument of order already verified by the early legislators? There may be in the principle of life itself, and in the soul of man and of universal nature, chords that can answer to the touch of harmonious sound.

That is why Pythagoras taught that the soul is, or contains, a *harmonia*—the original word meaning not, as with us, a concord of several sounds, but the orderly adjustment of parts in a complex fabric, and, in particular, the tuning of a musical instrument. Now Pythagoras's one physical discovery, the original starting point of mathematical physics, was that the concordant intervals of the musical scale can be exactly expressed in terms of simple ratios. By changing the length of strings on a monochord stopped by a movable bridge, he found that the ratio of the octave is $1:2$, of the fourth, $4:3$, of the fifth, $3:2$. These are the fixed intervals common to all Greek scales. The numbers which occur in these ratios are 1, 2, 3, 4, the sum of which is 10, the perfect number. So perfect and potent, indeed, that Pythagoras worshiped it as the Divine Ungenerated *Tetraktys,* "The source having the roots of ever-flowing nature"—a symbol of the Higher Unity wherein the One is unfolded.

Thus was the theory born: "all things are numbers"; which meant, in the old terms, "The nature of things is number." No use asking what it could mean precisely, in the moment of creative insight. There were in it centuries of thoughts and feelings unknown to us; the precise delicate twanging of the lyre bursting like stars upon the soul, turned into stars in the all-enveloping darkness of heaven; the One, the Monad of intelligent fire alone in the dark of Unlimit, populating that dark in mysterious array with units of fire like itself, as "the One begat the Two, the Two begat the Three, and the Three begat all things. . . ."

"In approaching the moment of illumination," writes Cornford,

the soul must have reached out with every power intent. . . .
The final act of recognition must be overwhelming, because the truth, in such a moment of insight, is not presented as an intellectual formula, compact and comprehensible. It comes rather as an undefined mass of significance, fused in a glow of intense feeling. It may take years or generations for all the meaning and implications to be expressed in words. . . .
When the feeling has passed, the thought is felt, an intellectual content distilled into the language of prose.

Of what happened in the early years of the sect little has reached us. Numbers seem to have been mainly figured as rows of monads. One such construction became fundamental. Take the row of integers as in Figure 3, and construct successive squares on them: the carpenter's

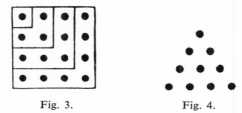

Fig. 3.   Fig. 4.

squares or "gnomons" indicated by the lines "build" the successive squares of numbers: here is shown the virtue of the Odd, for the gnomons are the progression of odds. The One alone is Odd-Even. The *Tetraktys* was a triangular number as in Figure 4, made up of the first numbers: $1 + 2 + 3 + 4 = 10$, the perfect number, generated by the Monad and in turn conceived as generating all the other combinations of number and figure which made up what was called the *kosmos,* or "good array."

What could number come to mean in all this fermenting of ideas? There is no doubt that the Pythagoreans thought originally of physical patterns, such as are those engraved on the dice. Hence also the rather simple idea among some that shapes might be given by successive layers of gnomons or carpenter's squares, a naive kind of crystallography. And with it went a simple arithmetic of numbers made up of units, separated by gaps. But let us not forget that the "true" power of number, that which united knowledge with purification, had been discovered in the vibrating string. There it was that the *Tetraktys* rules, through the first four integers. Now, if the musical scale depends simply upon the imposition of definite proportions on the indefinite continuum of sound between high and low, might not the same principles, Limit and Unlimit, underlie the whole universe? Of course ingenious theories were attempted to link those two principles with number theory by way of odd and even, and to extend them to the whole of reality by way of the table of contraries. But Limit and Unlimit seem to have remained above it all as the constitutive principles of number itself. The very words "to define" meant originally the setting of a term, the act of limiting. It was the act which gave birth to reality. How? It is the point we know least about. But never mechanically.

It is this stage of thinking that we find in the earliest written evidence, the fragments of Philolaus of Tarentum, an obscure and singular genius, difficult to gauge, who came over from Italy after the Croton disaster and settled in Thebes. He found it fit to put certain things in writing for the first time (about 460 B.C.); we have about twenty fragments from the book. Hypercritical critics have put the authenticity of the fragments in doubt, without much success. The book (of which we give the fragments hereafter *) was said to begin thus: "Nature in the cosmos was fitted together of Unlimit and Limit, the order of the all as well as all things in it." The point of departure is set. Each single shaped thing is such by the power of the One which is Limit-Unlimit; and that One is called Harmony, which means also the octave. This will be shown again in the monochord, if we note the successive partials of c:

$\frac{1}{1}$	$\frac{1}{2}$	$\frac{1}{3}$	$\frac{1}{4}$	$\frac{1}{5}$	$\frac{1}{6}$	$\frac{1}{7}$	$\frac{1}{8}$	$\frac{1}{9}$	$\frac{1}{10}$
c	c′	g′	c″	e″	g″	b″ᵇ	c‴	d‴	e‴
*		*		*		*		*	

The even tones show only higher octaves, whereas the odd provide the new tone individualities, just as the gnomonic series of the odds shape successive squares out of evens. We can see why Philolaus says that "even and odd take many forms, and each thing shows them by itself"; why he insists: "it is the dissimilar and the disparate and unequally ordered which need the attunement of the octave to keep them together, and it is through it that they are fitted into an order."

The quest may seem to lead through disparate objects

---

* This and subsequent quotations from Philolaus in this chapter are from *Ancilla to the Pre-Socratic Philosophers:* A Complete Translation of the Fragments in Diels, *Die Fragmente der Vorsokratiker,* by Kathleen Freeman. Oxford: Basil Blackwell & Mott, Ltd., 1948; Cambridge: Harvard University Press. Reprinted, with some changes, by permission of the publishers.

indeed, but then we must consider what a dizzy attainment these men themselves were hoping for.

The distinction between element and principle remains capital. The numbers are originally both elements and principles; that is why they tend to associate into numeric components *and* higher principles. Earth, water, air and fire are components; they are never really understood as principles. Anaximander's Unbounded is a principle, not an element. The word *archē,* "principle," implies origin, rule, control, "beginning and end," whereas the Greek for element, *stoicheion,* was used originally to indicate the letters of the alphabet. Our chemical elements of the pre-Rutherford era were also conceived of as simple components, "building blocks," which are put together. The energy of modern physics is more in the nature of a principle; it modulates itself into action, form, and structure; it is, in the ancient sense, "beginning and end."

After all that has been said, it becomes more and more difficult to define the nature of number. As usual, the answer is tied up with a cosmogony. This one is so fanciful that even Aristotle was baffled. Says he in his *Physics*:

> It is strange also to attribute generation to things that are eternal. There need be no doubt whether the Pythagoreans attribute generation to them or not; for they say plainly that when the one had been constructed, whether out of planes or of surfaces or of seed or of elements they cannot express, immediately the nearest part of the unlimited began to be constrained and limited by the limit. But since they are constructing a world and wish to speak the language of natural science, it is fair to examine their physical theories.

Let us come closer to the School's own thought. The elementary units of fire or monads are all equal, but each has in itself the power of Number, which manifests itself as it goes into composition with others, to form figures or series or classes. Monads will link up according to special angles, chief among them 30° and 90°, very much as we today think of the atoms doing in stereochemistry. Each of the angles is a power under the invocation of one or more gods. But numbers can multiply like the sands of the sea; they can assume structure in infinitely many ways. Hence one has to assume guiding principles to keep order.

The first four numbers, which provided the four dimensions (the point being the first one), became different in quality, in fact principles for all the others. They formed a higher unity of their own, the *Tetraktys*, which provided the model for the All. If we compare this with Anaximander's primal matter, we see how it has been rationalized: from the One are born four elements, for that is what the four numbers stand for (they are even called by that name); but here we have a clear rationale between unity and multiplicity, which rules further differentiation and growth into structures. The same One which began as simple unity reappears in complex form in that higher unity which is the Tetrad; and that in turn contains the laws of growth, the potential forms of all the universe; it *is,* implicitly, the universe. Numbers do have that capacity of determining infinite classes and regular expansions from the outset. Thus the four principles and their tetradic system are true "forms" and are rightly called such, *eide;* they are the "shaped charges" which create with irresistible power. Are they taken to be in themselves simple principles? Hardly, since their numeric composition is manifest, and is based upon two more general principles, Limit and Unlimit, which go beyond them. The numbers which make up real things may have been thought at the outset to be "nonseparable," qualitative entities, as we are told, physical structures (whence still comes our word "figure" for number); but when their virtue was seen to reside essentially in their prodigious analytical interrelationships which came forth to "greet the soul," in the words of an old poet; as they appeared and reasoned, as it were, of themselves, they soon became a hierarchy of pure ideal entities subsisting on their own level, whence they rule things by some mystic "participation." The design has been laid out for Plato's theory of Ideas.

Numbers may have been conceived at the outset as simply and materially as we like to imagine; in three intellectual steps they have led the mind to extreme heights of abstraction, in fact to a hierarchy of abstractions, from which comes the pattern of all Greek metaphysics. It is not the first instance in thought, to be sure. The cosmogony of the Egyptian Book of the Dead is of comparable subtlety: "I am Atum when I was alone in Nūn . . ." Atum,

like the Monad, stands for "that is all." But the built-in
guiding and corrective power provided by number carries
the Greek system on to developments that were beyond
the reach of archaic theory. The number principles are
halfway between the live and the inanimate, as would be-
fit Anaximander's Substrate. But they are such with full
right, for they represent also the laws of thought.

We can watch these laws of thought laying the foundations of theory. For when we have said of the monads that
they are "points having position," when we have created
out of them a framework of points, lines, and planes in
three dimensions, aiming, it may be, at first, for the closed
perfect frameworks of polyhedra but then moving into
more complex structures, we have created a system of
"positions" which alone give meaning to the points. What
had been conceived as Unlimit, the dark void, the emptiness "breathed in" by fire, the interval contained by reality,
is on the way to becoming a reality by itself. It is all very
well to define reality as geometrical body, the cosmos itself,
most perfect, Being imagined as enclosed in the dodecahedron as in a "hull," or bounded by the sphere of Olympian
fire, all of reality shaped by the Decad in unified form and
discrete structure; but when the indiscreet question arises:
"in what?" we find the great Archytas willing to face it.
"Supposing," he said, "that I came to the outer limits of
the universe, if now I thrust out a stick, what would I find?"
The vague stock answer, "nothingness," is invalidated, for
now there is a stick in that nothingness, it can at least be
contained in it. So there must be space, as here. Hence we
have gone back to what the principle of sufficient reason
had suggested—the Unbounded.

One can hardly imagine any thought less dogmatic, even
in its fervent affirmations about numbers. What is essential is that they are supposed to be alive and real, as nature
is. They are not a logical mechanism of abstractions. This
comes from the early concreteness of the Pythagoreans,
but also from the curious inductive bent which kept them
close to the facts, as can be seen in their theory of music.
This extraordinary, Renaissance-like, unbroken tension between the heights of abstraction and the nature of things
keeps Aristotle profoundly puzzled. Coming, as he feels,
to close the inventory of the past and settle all the differ-

ences, the Master of Those Who Know is able to deal with his predecessors in a few well-chosen words, but when he comes to the tangle of Pythagoreanism he is never finished thrashing and edging his way out, as can be seen from the last book of *Metaphysics*. It is from this, to him maddeningly primitive, complex that he has to extract his ordering ideas, for mathematics remains the model of his formal logic, and yet, at the same time, he infers in his curious way, these people who own mathematics never seem to have the proper answer to a proper question. Vast and far-reaching misunderstandings are bound to follow. For instance, what is substance itself?

Substance is thought to belong most obviously to bodies; and so we say that not only animals and plants are substances, but also natural bodies such as fire and water . . . and so the stars and moon and sun. But whether these alone are substances, or there are also others, must be considered. Some [i.e., the Pythagoreans] think the limits of body, i.e., surface, line, point and unit, are substance, and more so than body or solid. . . . And some say Forms and numbers have the same nature. . . .

The word "substance" is applied (by us) at least to four main objects, for both the essence and the universal and the genus are thought to be the substance of each thing, and fourthly the substratum. Now the substratum is that of which everything else is predicated, while it is itself not predicated of anything else. And so we must first determine the nature of this; for that which underlies a thing primarily is thought to be in the truest sense its substance. But . . . on this [Pythagorean] view, *matter* ends by becoming substance. For if this is not substance, it baffles us to say what else is; when all else is stripped off, evidently nothing but matter remains. While the rest are affections, products and potencies of bodies, length, breadth and depth are quantities and not substances (for a quantity is not a substance), but the substance is that to which these belong primarily. But when length and breadth and depth are taken away, we see nothing left unless there is something that is bounded by these; so that to those who consider the question thus matter alone must seem to be substance. But this is impossible, for both separability and "thisness" are thought to belong chiefly to substance.*

* Aristotle, *Works*, translated under the editorship of Sir William David Ross. Oxford: Clarendon Press, 1908–1952, 12 vols. *Metaphysica*, translated by W. D. Ross, Vol. 8.

In a flash of perception, Aristotle has seen what someone may do with *quantity of matter,* and refuses it utterly.
That someone will be Galileo and Descartes, no less. To
Aristotle, it is plainly absurd, for in this way we shall never
be able to account for the multitude and true variety of
substances. The science of nature, for many centuries to
come, will gradually become centered on "thisness." But
the cold outside appraisal is enough to show which way
Pythagorean thought is bound to tend, once its youthful
fever of fancies is over. It is only just that Galileo's natural
philosophy should have been denounced by his opponents
as "the Pythagorean doctrine."

THE BIRTH OF THEORY

It is here that certain fundamental concepts of science
arise, in full dress and in their own name. We should try
to catch them in the nascent state. Let us go back to the
Tetraktys which was the "root" of harmony, as principle
of all fourfold proportions. It was also the "root" of bodily
reality: the simplest solid, the tetrahedron, was its expression (6 edges $+$ 4 faces $=$ 10); the cube embodied
the "geometric harmony" (12 edges, 8 corners, 6 faces,
$12:8 :: 6:4$). Its power was again visible in the simple
succession of integers, where, through the virtue of the
odd, it brought forth, as we have seen, the "square numbers." The odd, under the aspect of the gnomon, became
the "building form" for squares. On such promptings, the
early Pythagoreans moved rapidly through elementary
number theory, uncovering wondrous properties at every
step. It was by means of gnomons and squares that they
discovered what we call the Pythagorean theorem, a formula for which had already been known to the Babylonians.

What they were inventing was a "geometry of numbers"
or arithmogeometry of a rather fanciful kind. It served
well to express their original idea of proportion as underlying everything. If "proportion" comes to take such a
vast importance in Greek thought, it is largely due to the
undefined mass of significance contained in its name.
Logos means "discourse," "reason," "argument," "inference," and also "proportion." The Latin *ratio* preserved
much of the total meaning, but in our language it ended
up by designating numerical proportion alone. If we go

back to the original complex, with its musical connotation, we see how the "right proportion" or "right *logos*" took on the aspect of the secret language of the gods, that which presided over the creation of things. The living bond thus established between numbers and their relations preserved Pythagorean thought from degeneration into mere number magic on the one hand or sheer intellectual mechanism on the other. Numbers were essences, but they had to be thought of relationally. The structured number is a *form* (*eidos*); the very act of thinking, *eidenai,* means representing forms (the German *vorstellen*); the unbroken tension between *eidos* and *logos,* "form" and "relationship," determines the whole development of Greek theory. The very word *theoria* is tied up with it, for it was used for the procession or ordered display of symbols in the mysteries; it characterizes the contemplative attitude; and it is a Pythagorean term. So is "philosophy" itself, "love" or "quest" of wisdom, that Pythagoras brings in to describe the way of life he intends for his sect. Intellectual activity is no longer embodied in the pronouncement of the *Sophos,* the sharp-minded sage; it is an unending search for the hidden truth of things, "following the track of the God." Thus, the strange dogmatic pronouncements of the early revelation are turned by the force of number into the discipline and the way of science.

A bridge—in fact, *the* bridge—had been thrown between the concreteness and abstraction. To the old question: "What is the nature, the *physis,* of things?" the answer was given: "It is not an element or a substrate in the material sense, it is the *eidos* and *logos* of Number." Many hard choices remained to be made before the answer became unambiguous, but the way had been set.

More light will come on this from the fragments of Philolaus which we give below. As we confront these few surviving testimonials of a lost thought, we should not dismiss what appears to be strange and obscure in them, but should try to decipher the message. The peculiar insistence in searching for mean proportionals springs from musical theory, but it goes far beyond. If reality is made of things which oppose each other, the theoretical answer is seen to lie in the musical instrument, in the *harmonia,* which is the old word for the tension between opposites. The mean proportionals do more than articulate the intervals; they are held to be the actual bond or *fastening* which holds together the disparate or unrelated elements of reality and welds them into a whole. All of Pythagorean and Platonic physics rest on that certainty. To expect "geometric harmonies" or mean proportionals to provide real, structural binding forces may seem to us a dreamy enterprise, but it was fair poetic justice that out of this quest there should spring, as we shall see, full-fledged and unexpected, that other great instrument of power for our times, the theory of conic sections, which allowed Kepler and Newton to conquer the heavens.

The Fragments of Philolaus

The translation is (with slight changes) that of Kathleen Freeman, which preserves the numbers of Diels-Kranz's *Vorsokratiker*.

1. Nature in the kosmos was fitted together from Unlimit and Limit, the order of the all as well as everything in it.

2. All existing things must necessarily be either limiting, or non-limited, or both limiting and non-limited. But they could not be merely non-limited (nor merely limited). Since, however, it is plain that they are neither wholly from the Limit nor wholly from Unlimit, clearly then the universe and its contents were fitted together from both Limiting and Unlimit.

3. For there could not even be an object set before knowledge to begin with, if all things were non-limited.

4. In truth, everything that can be known has a Number; for it is impossible to grasp anything with the mind or to recognize it without it.

5. Number has two distinct forms, odd and even, and a third compounded of both, the even-odd; each of these two forms has many aspects, which each separate object demonstrates in itself.

6. This is how it is with Nature and Harmony: the Being of things is eternal, and Nature itself requires divine and not human intelligence; moreover, it would be impossible for any existing thing to be even recognized by us if there did not exist the basic Being of the things from which the universe was composed, namely both the Limiting and the Non-Limited. But since these Elements exist as unlike and unrelated, it would clearly be impossible for a universe to be

created with them unless a harmony was added, in which way this harmony did come into being. Now the things which were like and related needed no harmony; but the things which were unlike and unrelated and unequally arranged need the fastening of the attunement, through which they are destined to endure in the order. . . .

The content of the Harmony (Octave) is the major fourth and the major fifth; the fifth is greater than the fourth by a whole tone; for from the highest string (lowest note) to the middle is a fourth, and from the middle to the lowest string (highest note) is a fifth. From the lowest to the third string is a fourth, from the third to the highest string is a fifth. Between the middle and third strings is a tone. The major fourth has the ratio 3 : 4, the fifth 2 : 3, and the octave 1 : 2. Thus the Harmony (Octave) consists of five whole tones and two semitones, the fifth consists of three tones and a semitone, and the fourth consists of two tones and a semitone.

7. The first composite entity, the One, which is in the centre of the Sphere, is called Hearth.

8. The One is the beginning of everything.

9. By nature, not by convention.

10. Harmony is a Unity of many mixed elements, and an agreement between disagreeing elements.

11. One must understand the activities and the essence of Number in accordance with the power existing in the Decad (Ten-ness); for it (the Decad) is great, complete, all-achieving, and the origin of divine and human life and its Leader; it shares. . . . The power also of the Decad. Without this, all things are unlimited, obscure and indiscernible.

For the nature of Number is the cause of recognition, able to give guidance and teaching to every man in what is puzzling and unknown. For none of existing things would be clear to anyone, either in themselves or in their relationship to one another, unless there existed Number and its essence. But in fact Number, fitting all things into the soul through sense-perception, makes them recognizable and comparable with one another as is provided by the nature of the Gnômôn, in that Number gives them body and divides the different relationships of things, whether they be Non-Limited or Limiting, into their separate groups.

And you may see the nature of Number and its power at work not only in supernatural and divine existences but also in all human activities and words everywhere, both throughout all technical production and also in music.

The nature of Number and Harmony admits of no Falsehood; for this is unrelated to them. Falsehood and Envy belong to the nature of Unlimit and the Unintelligent and the
Irrational.

Falsehood can in no way breathe on Number; for Falsehood is inimical and hostile to its nature, whereas Truth is
related to and in close natural union with the race of Number.

12. The bodies (physical Elements) of the [cosmic] Sphere
are five: the Fire in the Sphere, and the Water, and Earth,
and Air, and, fifth, the hull of the Sphere [i.e., the dodeca-
hedron].

14. The ancient theologians and seers also bear witness that
because of certain punishments the soul is yoked to the body
and buried in it as in a tomb.

15. (Socrates to Cebes in the *Phaedo:* [Philolaus's] *theory
that we are in a sort of watch-tower which we must not desert
is difficult; but I agree that we are one of the possessions of
the gods.*)

16. There are certain thoughts which are stronger than
ourselves.

17. The universe is one, and it began to come into being
from the centre, and from the centre upwards at the same intervals (of distance) as those below. For the parts above from
the centre are in inverse relationship to those below; for the
centre is to what is below as it is to what is above, and so
with all the rest; for both stand in the same relationship to the
centre, except in so far as their positions are reversed.

19. (Proclus: Plato, Pythagorean doctrine and Philolaus in
the *Bacchae* teach theology through mathematical figures.)

THE CRISIS OF THE IRRATIONAL

The early arithmogeometry of figured numbers was a
wonderful representational device. It led to an algebra of
sorts, dealing with integers and the ratios of integers. Lines,
surfaces, and volumes were thought of as composed of a
finite number of indivisible units, put together like pebbles
in a pattern. These must express all the geometric magnitudes which come up in the theory of proportions as
integers, i.e., as integral multiples of a sufficiently small
denominator. As more magnitudes were considered, the
common unit that could measure them became smaller
and smaller. The monad seemed to be shrinking painfully.

Then came a stunning surprise. Someone looked for the

ratio between the side and the diagonal of the square, and it turned out that there was no such ratio, expressible in rational numbers. It was found, indeed, that such a number, if it existed, would have to be both odd and even. This put it beyond the pale. No *logos*. It was a grievous blow. If numbers lose their reason, who shall save ours? But other such were discovered, in the golden section, for instance. They were mentioned in hushed tones as "unspeakable" numbers, nonrational. One great illusion was lost. The man who gave away the secret, Hippasos, was thrown out as a renegade and a traitor. After a while, the mathematicians turned to and incorporated the irrationals into their general number theory. By the time of Theodorus of Cyrene (c. 440) the crisis was over. But meanwhile, in order to minimize the scandal, it had been accepted as a lesser evil to produce rational solutions which could approximate to any desired degree the exact irrational one. This meant shrinking the original monadic point beyond any assignable limit, until it became a kind of infinitesimal that was not really one, for it did not tend to vanish, but was still taken as actually existent. This "actual infinitesimal" could not but be fraught with fearful confusions, as Zeno was to show. Number atomism had run itself into a dead end.

The way the crisis could be really solved was by going over into geometry, and having it cure the wound it had itself inflicted. This is what the later-generation Pythagoreans did with considerable courage.

It so happened that of such formulas as $\sqrt{2a^2}$—if not in their modern notation—there were plenty available in the arithmetical and engineering data which had reached Greece from the great reservoir of Babylonian civilization. Pythagoras's purported *Wanderjahre* through the Near East may or may not be true; communication had been established for some time in any case, as we have seen in connection with the engineering work of the Ionians. Far from detracting from Greek originality, it helps us understand the newborn quest for a logical structure. When the results of Oriental mathematics reached Greece, they belonged to a long-dead wisdom. They were a set of disconnected rules. Of theory, indeed, there had been hardly any, but at least there had been procedure. The very early phase of mathematics goes for results. One is occupied with such direct questions as how to calculate the area of a quadrangle, or the volume of a pyramid, or the length of a chord. Once the device had been found, no need was felt for a proof. But the Greek would get only the bare formula. The train of thought which underlay it was no longer known. From a Babylonian source he might hear that $\pi = 3.52/360$, from some others that $\pi = 3$ (it is so in the Bible), and in Egypt he might find that it is $4(8/9)^2$. In ordinary approximation they both worked. But which was the true one? The question was more important than any result. Out of it was born the logically connected system which leads to a *proof*.

Here, for example, was a basic algebraic formula: $(a + b)^2 = a^2 + b^2 + 2ab$. Translated into a figure, it carried its own proof. This is Proposition II 4 of Euclid.

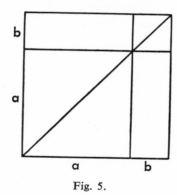

Fig. 5.

Now the whole of Book II of Euclid is a text of such a geometric algebra. Its peculiar aspect reveals its origin. The Babylonian treatment of problems of second degree consisted in reducing them to the "normal form," where two quantities, x and y, should be found from their given product and their sum or difference. In this way a quadratic problem was reduced to the simplest form of two linear equations. The geometric formulation leads precisely to the central problem of the geometrical algebra, which it is otherwise difficult to motivate. This problem is known as the "application of areas." In the simplest form, it is this: given an area A and a line segment b, construct a rectangle of area A such that one of its sides falls on *b* but in such a way that the rectangle of equal height and of length *b* is either larger or smaller by a square than the rectangle of area A. The identity of this strange problem with the

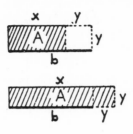

Fig. 6.

Babylonian "normal form" is at once evident once we formulate it algebraically. Let *x* and *y* be the sides of the rectangle in both cases. Then we are given

$$xy = A$$

In the first case a square y^2 should remain free, and we must require

$$x + y = b.$$

In the second case, a square should exceed the rectangle of side *b;* thus we should have

$$x - y = b.$$

These are indeed the Babylonian normalized equations, as Neugebauer has shown in his masterful study of cuneiform texts. Here, then, is the *geometric algebra* of the Greeks, the basic tool that later masters like Theaetetus, Apollonius, and Archimedes were to handle with such consummate virtuosity. The new thing is that the formulas are proved, and proved with all necessary rigor. For the Babylonians, segments and areas were simply numbers. They had no scruples about adding the area of a rectangle to its base. When they had no exact answer for a square root, they went by approximation. But the Greeks wanted to know "the diagonal itself," as Plato puts it, not an approximation. Now there is no number or ratio of numbers which will solve $x^2 = 2$, but "the diagonal itself" does it.

Hence geometry was needed; it provided a new kind of geometrical number which was accepted, along with the old *arithmoi,* as being of "the foundation of the universe." An important case of such is the "golden section," which is also constructed in Book II of Euclid: "To divide a segment in such a way that the rectangle formed by the segment and one of its parts is equal to the square of the other part."

The golden section was to remain a fundamental proportion in art up to and beyond the Renaissance. For the Pythagoreans, its importance was clearly signified by its role in the construction of the *pentagram* or star pentagon,

Fig. 7.

which was their symbol of recognition. Each one of the five lines divides every other in mean and extreme ratio. The great betrayal of Hippasos, it is said, was not so much that he revealed the existence of the irrational, as that he divulged the construction he had found of the "sphere with the twelve pentagons," i.e., the dodecahedron, one of the five Cosmic Bodies. Kepler, twenty centuries later, was to carry on the Pythagorean program by constructing the stellate dodecahedron.

Quite apart from these wondrous things, the technique of application of areas was to lead to one of the greatest systematizations. "Application" is called in Greek *parabolē.* "These," says Eudemus the historian, "are discoveries of the Pythagorean muse, the *parabolē* of areas, their *elleipsis* (deficiency), and their *hyperbolē* (excess)." We can already see how far it will reach. We shall find presently how it works out.

The whole of geometry known at this stage seems to

have covered approximately the first four books of Euclid, the Pythagorean theorem and the other important one, that the sum of the three angles of the triangle is equal to two right angles. The first work that carried the title *Elements of Geometry* was written by Hippocrates of Chios about 450 B.C. It is unfortunately lost, but we have a passage

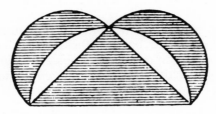

Fig. 8. The Lunules of Hippocrates. The sum of the lunules constructed upon the cathetes of the right-angled triangle is equal to the area of the triangle.

from it, dealing with the squaring of the lunules, which was copied by Simplicius (A.D. 500), according to his own statement, from the earliest history of mathematics, that of Eudemus, the pupil of Aristotle. Here is the original text of Eudemus,* as liberated by modern scholars from the additions of Simplicius.

The squaring of the lunules [i.e., crescents], considered as remarkable figures on account of their connection with the circle, was first formulated by Hippocrates and his explanation was considered to be in good order. Let us therefore attack the matter and study it.

He considered as the foundation and as the first of the propositions which serve his purpose, that similar segments of circles are in the same ratio as the squares of their bases. He demonstrated this by showing first that the squares of the diameters have the same ratio as the circles. For the ratio of the circles is the same as that of similar segments, since similar segments are segments which form the same part of the circle.

After having proved this, he raised first of all the question how to square a lunule whose exterior boundary is a semicircle. He accomplished this by circumscribing a semicircle about an isosceles right triangle, and by constructing on the

* B. L. van der Waerden, *Science Awakening,* translated by A. Dresden. Groningen: Erven P. Noordhoff, Ltd., 1954.

base a circular segment similar to the segments cut off by the right sides. Because the segment on the base is equal to (the sum of) the two (segments) on the other (sides), it follows, when the part of the triangle which lies above the segment on the base is added to both, that the lunule is equal to the triangle. Since it has now been shown that the lunule is equal to the triangle, it can be squared. Thus, by taking a semicircle as the external boundary of the lunule, he could readily square the lunule.

The text of Eudemus goes on to deal with the more difficult case of the external boundary greater than a semicircle, which requires fairly complicated constructions, and the knowledge of a good many fundamental propositions. But we can see the whole of the geometrical method present already in the section we have quoted. Hippocrates uses here the same concept of proportionality that underlies the Pythagorean theory of numbers: four magnitudes are proportional if the first is the same part or the same multiple of the second that the third is of the fourth. Strictly speaking, this definition is applicable only in the case of rational ratios. Hippocrates had not yet arrived at a rigorous treatment of irrational ratios.

ARCHYTAS

Archytas (c. 380 B.C.) seems to have been the lumbering, oxlike type of genius (there are such; Niels Bohr is one today) with a desperate inaptitude for making his thought clear, yet with unerring tread. The passage we give below is the only authentic piece of Pythagorean writing of some length that has reached us. In it Archytas plows his way patiently through all sorts of wrong inferences concerning the variable speed of sound to the correct conclusion that pitch is determined by frequency. The visible speeds of the rattle and the swinging rod provide a clue to the invisible speeds of the vibrating string.

He was a pupil of Philolaus, and in his turn had a profound influence on Plato. His relationship to the latter shows the contrast between the brilliant speculative literary mind and the man of action, for he seems to have been just the philosopher-ruler that Plato tried to theorize. He was elected seven years in succession to the post of commander in chief of his city, Tarentum (today Taranto, still a naval base); and during his long tenure he was never defeated. The powers granted to him by the city were virtually autocratic, but there is no record of his having abused them; all the anecdotes about him show a man trained in the rigid Pythagorean conceptions of justice and self-restraint. It is said that on finding his estate badly mismanaged, he told the workers: "It is your luck that I am angry with you, for otherwise I would have had to punish you." We are also told that he loved to play with children and invented for them a rattle and a wooden pigeon that could fly. His authority was accepted not only in Tarentum, but over a confederacy of Greek cities in Italy, of which he had come to be the elder statesman. When Plato found himself in dire straits in Syracuse, after his attempts at political reform, it was Archytas who negotiated his safety with the powerful tyrant Dionysius, and sent a naval ship to rescue him. His name remained a legend with the Romans, as that of the ancient sage. In one of Cicero's dialogues, Cato the dour Censor recites an "old speech" of Archytas on ethics that he learned in Tarentum "when I was there as a young man serving under the consul Quintus Maximus."

Notwithstanding his activities in public life, Archytas is the first figure that appears to us as a full-time scientist. He was outstanding both in number theory and in geometry. But if we try to find a thread to his many interests, it would seem to be musical theory. It is in him, in fact, that we see outlined the Pythagorean cosmos of thought that we could only infer in the previous generation. It is he who laid the number-theoretical foundations for Euclid's *Sectio Canonis* (The Divisions of the Monochord). He is also, as van der Waerden showed conclusively, the author of Book VIII of Euclid's *Elements*. The central problem of Book VIII is: Under what conditions is it possible to find one or more numbers in continued proportion between a and b? This problem leads us directly back to music, for in Archytas's mind numbers had a physical reality as "tone values." Any proportion that could be found was going to yield a harmony. Following this line, Archytas is led to distinguish between similar and nonsimilar plane and spatial numbers, and one of his main results is the proof that no

mean proportionals can exist between two numbers in the
ratio $(n + 1):n$. Now this type of ratio had been the object of passionate interest for the School over a long time;
it was called "epimoric," that is, "with a part added." It
had been defined originally as the case in which the difference $b - a$ is part both of a and of b. The importance of
this ratio comes from musical theory. The octave, fifth,
fourth, or whole tone are epimoric intervals. It appears

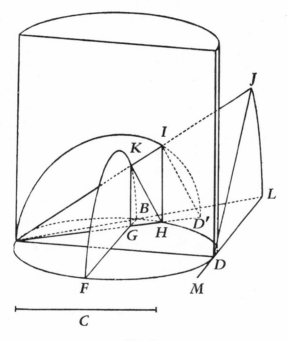

Fig. 9.

then that they cannot be split into equal intervals, and
Archytas had to look for other divisions by means of the
arithmetic or the harmonic mean. This is actually the
method that he used in constructing his very elaborate
scales.

But the problem of the two mean proportionals remains,
and arithmetic has been proved unable to solve it. Archytas
turns then in a highly creative way to the techniques of
geometric algebra, which had already given constructions

for irrationals. This is what led him to solve the so-called "problem of Delos," or duplication of the cube. Described thus, the problem would seem a rather artificial assignment, and indeed the later story and rationale was that the solution had been requested by the Delian Apollo, through the oracle, for his cubic altar. This shows how the Pythagorean policy of discretion worked. The pieces of the puzzle were kept artfully scattered, so that the interest of the curious should be led forward in different directions rather than work back towards the source. But Apollo had been acting clearly in his capacity as god of music, for the problem of Delos amounts to constructing two mean proportionals between two given line segments, just as the duplication of the square involves one mean proportional, $1 : x :: x : 2$, and the symbolic interest of the cube lies in its being, itself, a "geometrical harmony." The solution is marvelously ingenious, and is based upon a diagram in which segments move on fixed curves, as they would do in a mechanical model. We give here the diagram without Eudemus's explanation, as it would take us too far. This type of moving diagram is based upon the principle of continuity, as yet not clearly formulated. If a continuous variable is first greater than a given magnitude and later less, then at some time the variable equals this magnitude.

The duplication of the cube, this seemingly out-of-the-way problem, was really part of the enterprise of discovering the "bonds" of the cosmos, as we have tried to show previously. It was to prove of immense fecundity in a wholly unexpected direction, for, soon after Archytas, Menaechmus was to find that the search for mean proportionals

$$a : x :: x : y :: y : b$$

led to what we would write today as

$$x^2 = ay, \; xy = ab, \; y^2 = xb$$

That is, the point xy could be derived as the intersection of two parabolas, or of a parabola and a hyperbole. Menaechmus in fact constructed the curves as sections of the cone, and thus was born that *theory of conic sections* which was to be of such decisive importance from Apollonius to Newton.

The Fragments of Archytas *

1. Mathematicians seem to me to have excellent discernment, and it is in no way strange that they should think correctly concerning the nature of particular existences. For since they have passed an excellent judgment on the nature of the Whole, they were bound to have an excellent view of separate things. Indeed, they have handed on to us a clear judgment on the speed of the constellations and their rising and setting, as well as on plane geometry and Numbers (arithmetic) and solid geometry, and not least on music; for these mathematical studies appear to be related. For they are concerned with things that are related, namely the two primary forms of Being.

First of all, therefore, mathematicians have judged that sound is impossible unless there occurs a striking of objects against one another. This striking, they said, occurs when moving objects meet one another and collide. Now things moving in opposite directions, when they meet, produce a sound by simultaneously relaxing (i.e., checking each other's speed). But things moving in the same direction though at unequal speeds create a sound by being struck when overtaken by what is following behind. Now many of these sounds cannot be recognized by our nature, some because of the faintness of the sound, others because of their great distance from us, and some even because of their excessive loudness, for the big sounds cannot make their way into our hearing— just as, in vessels with narrow necks, when one pours in too much, nothing enters. Thus when things impinge on the perception, those which reach us quickly and powerfully from the source of sound seem high-pitched, while those which reach us slowly and feebly seem low-pitched. For if one takes a rod and strikes an object slowly and feebly, he will produce a low note with the blow, but if he strikes quickly and powerfully, a high note. Moreover, we can know (this) not only by this means, but also because when in speaking or singing we wish to produce a loud high sound, we employ strong exhalation as we utter. . . .

This happens also with missiles. Those which are vigorously thrown are carried far, those weakly thrown (fall) near; for the air yields more readily before those which are vigorously

* Kathleen Freeman, op. cit.

thrown, whereas it yields less readily to those which are weakly thrown. This is bound to happen also with the notes of the voice: if a note is expelled by a forcible breath, it will be loud and high, if by a feeble breath, soft and low. But we can also see it from this, the strongest piece of evidence, namely, that when a man shouts loudly, we can hear him from a distance, whereas if the same man speaks softly, we cannot hear him even near at hand. Further, in flutes, when the breath expelled from the mouth falls on the holes nearest the mouth, a higher note is given out because of the greater force, but when it falls on the holes further away, a lower note results. Clearly swift motion produces a high-pitched sound, slow motion a low-pitched sound.

Moreover, the "whirlers" which are swung round at the Mysteries: if they are whirled gently, they give out a low note, if vigorously, a high note. So too with the reed: if one stops its lower end and blows, it gives out a low kind of note; but if one blows into the middle or some part of it, it will sound high; for the same breath passes weakly through the long distance, powerfully through the lesser.

That high notes are in swift motion, low notes in slow motion, has become clear to us from many examples.

3. In subjects of which one has no knowledge, one must obtain knowledge either by learning from someone else, or by discovering it for oneself. That which is learnt, therefore, comes from another and by outside help; that which is discovered comes by one's own efforts and independently. To discover without seeking is difficult and rare, but if one seeks, it is frequent and easy; if, however, one does not know how to seek, discovery is impossible.

Right Reckoning, when discovered, checks civil strife and increases concord; for where it has been achieved, there can be no excess of gain, and equality reigns. It is this (*Right Reckoning*) that brings us to terms over business contracts, and through it the poor receive from the men of means, and the rich give to the needy, both trusting that through it (*Right Reckoning*) they will be treated fairly. Being the standard and the deterrent of wrongdoers, it checks those who are able to reckon (*consequences*), before they do wrong, convincing them that they will not be able to avoid detection when they come against it; but when they are not able (*to reckon*) it shows them that in this lies their wrongdoing, and so it prevents them from committing the wrong deed.

5

The System of the World

IT WAS the Pythagoreans who invented the astronomical system of the world as we understand it. This may seem unfair to the Babylonians, who knew the planets well and computed their positions with extreme accuracy. But for them it was really a matter of special positions, like heliacal risings and settings, whose recurrence when due was supposed to confirm the stable intentions of celestial powers. What those particular stars did in between was of little concern to them; it was simply represented by columns of figures on the tables. The Pythagoreans, true to their geometrical conceptions, thought of orbits on the celestial sphere, and imagined them, like the rest of the heavenly motions, as circular. They were proper motions, from west to east against the 24-hour rotation of the stars, not simply a "lag," as before imagined. The moving stars were then called "planets," or "wanderers." The different speeds suggested different distances, and it is thus that we have, with some occasional variants, the present order of the planets, with Mercury closest to the center and Saturn farthest off. The yearly period of the Sun put it in third place, between Venus and Mars. As for the nature of the Sun, which must surely be apart, there were many theories, as we shall see.

The Earth was for the first time declared to be a sphere, for reasons of symmetry, and also because its shadow on the moon during eclipses was observed to be circular. The author of this theory is said by some to have been Pythagoras himself; by others, more reliably, Parmenides.

As if this were not momentous enough, there follows in one or two generations another no less momentous development, for the abstract geometrical way of thinking in the School gave them a prodigious freedom of imagination. Once it had become clear that sun, moon, and planets describe orbits from west to east, it probably was felt as strange that the whole heaven should rotate so much more rapidly in the opposite direction. Would it be possible to account for this by still another motion from west to east?

Philolaus, who seems to have been the chief theoretician of the period around 450 B.C., came up with the bold idea that it was really that the Earth was moving from west to east which caused the apparent rotation of the heavens the opposite way. This was a stroke of genius: the immensity of the heavens became at once more natural in repose. But Philolaus did not imagine, as we might think, the Earth turning around its center. He imagined it on the model of the moon, revolving closely around a center while keeping always the same face outward. And then he imagined another Earth on another circle just below it, keeping pace with us, and called it the "Counter-Earth." The only reference we have is a brief and unsympathetic account by Aristotle:

> They also assume another earth, opposite to ours, which they call the "counter-earth," as they do not with regard to phenomena seek for their reasons and causes, but forcibly make the phenomena fit their opinions and preconceived notions. . . . As ten is the perfect number they maintain that there must be ten bodies moving in the universe, and as only nine are visible they make the counter-earth the tenth.

This may have been for Philolaus a good reason, but certainly not the chief one. We shall go into this later. But there is at least one more good reason which is very evident. The sphere of the universe was conceived of as defined and bounded by the outer envelope of fire, the Olympus.* It stood to reason that its center might be of the same nature, as suggested by pure geometry. Philolaus postulated a Central Fire of the same Olympian nature, a "unitary harmony" around which the Earth and Counter-Earth revolve, with all the other celestial bodies, and he called it "Hearth of the all, watchtower of Zeus, altar, bond

---

* This unconventional transformation of the abode of the gods may be prompted, as many other ideas of the sect, by relics of certain archaic images. A recurrent one is that of a mountain chain enclosing the course of the planets, called Elburs in Iran and Kwen Luen in China.

and measure of nature." In other words, the *archē* or principle must be at the strategic center. It is the only thing in the universe that does not move, while everything else does. The Central Fire remains then hidden, not only from us who always face "outward," but also from the antipodes, since it is screened by the Counter-Earth. But its light, some said, is visible on the moon as "ashen light."

As the Earth goes around the Central Fire in 24 hours, all the effects are produced that we expect of the Earth rotating on herself. A question which was sharply raised was that the daily motion of the Earth on her orbit would make the distance of the moon from the Earth vary considerably in the course of a day, with a consequent change in apparent diameter. It was answered that the orbit was small with respect to that of the moon—a few times the actual radius of the Earth, which would have to be considered anyway if the Earth stayed in the center. But the objection may have moved Hiketas of Syracuse, a later Pythagorean, and Heracleides of Pontus, who was a successor of Plato, to make the Earth rotate simply on herself, with the Central Fire placed inside it, and this was the beginning of other great developments.

Another even sharper question was asked of Philolaus: if the Earth swings around the Central Fire, should not the stars at the pole show a parallax, i.e., an apparent counterswinging against the celestial background? The answer was that they are so distant as to make the effect unobservable. This was the correct answer and went on being so until Bessel's refined measurements in 1838.* With this the dimension of the heavens becomes really "astronomical" and immense. There were still at the time naturalists who made the sun be "pushed off" by the trade winds; a century or so earlier some of the "wise men" of Ionia had still thought the earth a pillar founded on the "deep," and surmounted by a brazen dome, which contained the "waters above."

* Galileo, once he had invented the telescope, affirmed that we would find a stellar parallax as soon as we had sufficiently precise instruments. The time came in 1838, when Bessel gave the parallax of 61 Cygni by alignment with more distant stars. In the same year Henderson measured Alpha Centauri, and Struve Alpha Lyrae. Even the nearest stars give a fraction of a second of arc. The modern unit for stellar distances is the parsec (parallax of one second).

Now the Earth had become a "star" (a word which was still to arouse the ire of Inquisitors two thousand years later) moving like all other stars; the moon was "another Earth" and was supposed, as a matter of course, to have "trees and clouds and people on it."

One more idea of Philolaus's should be noted. He suggested a Great Year (i.e., a lunisolar period when positions return the same) of 59 years with 21 intercalary months. The total of months, he said, was as much as the number of days and nights in the year. This would make the year equal 364½ days, and we must assume that Philolaus had accepted the approximation of about a unit, since the year had already been measured by Oenopides with an error of only 30 minutes. But the idea of a Great Year in which the smaller intervals are combined remains in Greek thought.

RHYTHM AND MELODY

The idea behind these closed circling patterns of periods-within-periods is that of the "choral dance" led by heavenly bodies, or, as Hippolytus said, "rhythm and melody." The idea occurs consistently through the early works to link astronomy with music; it accounts charmingly for the "hesitating" curves described by the planets in heaven, with their stations and retrogressions which will give so much trouble to the later mathematical astronomers. The precision of the motions, then, is that dictated by the rhythm of music.

But the over-all rotation of the sky, the obliquity of the ecliptic carrying all planetary motions in the opposite sense, seem to have suggested very soon, certainly close to the time of Parmenides (480 B.C.), the idea of separate concentric spheres as bearers of the individual motion. The "dance" is becoming geometrized, but the musical preconception remains deeply anchored. The cosmos was an ordered system which could be expressed in numerical ratios and which had partly revealed itself in the connection between the length of vibrating strings and their notes. The different radii of planetary spheres must then have harmonic ratios; they become comparable to the lengths of the string, and the angular velocities to the frequencies of vibration. Thus was born the idea of the "music of the spheres." The ones that revolve faster give a higher note than the slow ones, and all make up a harmony. "It seems to some thinkers," reports Aristotle,*

that bodies so great must inevitably produce a sound by their movements; even bodies on earth do so, although they are neither so great in bulk nor moving at so high a speed. . . . Taking this as their hypothesis, and also that the speeds of the stars, judged by their distances, are in the ratios of the musical consonances, they affirm that the sound of the stars as they revolve is concordant. To meet the difficulty that none of us is aware of this sound, they account for it by saying that the sound is with us right from birth and has thus no contrasting silence to show it up; for voice and silence are perceived by contrast with each other.

Two thousand years after Philolaus, Kepler tried his hand at reconstructing the "harmony of the world," but, not realizing the original meaning of the Greek word, he set up with infinite labor, out of the observed planetary velocities, a modern harmonic canon.

All this, including Kepler, may look very "archaic" compared to the achievements of the hard-headed Mesopotamian computers who had come before. It is. It turned out also to be more creative, reviving as it did vast protohistoric schemes of thought, combining precision with fantasy.

The way in which the Pythagoreans understood the cosmos corresponds to an almost lost state of consciousness—and we say lost because although we have some information we have no real representation of what ancient Greece meant by *mousikē*. It stands for an intrinsic union of *logos,* melody, and motion. Our Western poetry is preceded by great stretches of prose culture. Dante presupposes the Latin authors, the Bible, and Aquinas. But in Greece philosophical thought comes of a background where technical prose was barely being born for the use of craft books and chronicles, and all serious thought still couched in the somewhat "poetic language" that Theophrastus notices in Anaximander. Even in the time of Cicero, the old laws were still chanted. The poetry of Homer or Pindar was essentially a "song," where the rhythm was dictated

* W. D. Ross, *op. cit.*

by the firm cadence and shape of the *logos* itself with its longs and shorts. The choruses of tragedy, like the religious hymns, were slow choral dances whose circling was marked by a subtle alternation of forward and back, a ripple and halting in the stance which brought out the free "numbers" of the song. The rhythm was not superposed, as is the metronome "beat" of modern music; the word and the act were as one body. To circle in the dance meant to experience in one's being the timelessness of first and last things, as expressed in the steady *logos* of the words. It all became, as it were, the substrate of speech, a direct ontological realization of the "divine" in immediate reality.

This is as much as to say that *mousikē* was not only an aesthetic experience as we mean it, but an activity closely tied to the poetic and the ethical side of man's being: something which affects and transforms the soul. An interchanging of tunes would make heroes out of cowards, as the story of Tyrtaeus in Sparta is meant to show, and the legend of Orpheus tells how the hidden melody of things can hold man and nature in its spell, once it is brought forth on the magic tones of the lyre. Apollo, the god of Pythagoras, is the power both of light and music, under whose strange song even stones had moved, "when Ilion like a mist rose into towers."

Towards the fourth century B.C., the old *mousikē* tends to fall apart into the more modern forms of music and poetry, and this may well be one of the causes for the eclipse of the Pythagorean school which supervenes at that time. Plato, in the *Republic* and then in the *Laws,* protests against the modern trend in the arts, which he calls a shameless mixing of styles and flouting of the laws, and advocates a system of education based on the pristine ways, right gymnastics and right music. The essence is, he adds, that harmony and rhythm should follow the "*logos* that is sung," and that the latter should be true, as the philosopher expects of the "*logos* that is not sung."

Against this background, the strict program of Pythagorean harmony stands out more clearly: silence, music, and mathematics. The soul must be kept clear to receive the true unspoken *logos,* "the secret language of the gods," in all its forms, from rhythm, number, and proportion to astronomy, and to grasp the connections between those forms which are inaccessible to discursive thought. The philosophical fragments of Philolaus and Archytas, in their fumbling, helpless style, make one think of men who would try to converse after a long sojourn in the region of silence. They lived among men, to be sure, they were versed in political counsel, they even taught theorems, but their own creative thinking they knew not how to talk about; it belonged to their search, their inner experience, and their unformulated intuitions.

6

A Universe of Rigor

Parmenides was born about 525 B.C. in the first generation of the new colony of Elea in southern Italy, where the Phocaeans had transmigrated a few years before. The story deserves telling.

When the free cities of Ionia fell one after another to Harpagus the Mede, there were only two, Phocaea and Teos, which refused to yield. Having asked for a twenty-four-hour truce, in one night they embarked the whole population on their ships and set out to sea. Then they took a solemn oath, throwing a red-hot iron wedge into the deep, and swore that they would never return to their enslaved land until the wedge should re-emerge from the waters of its own accord. After that they parted, the Teans going north to their colony of Abdera in Thrace, the Phocaeans sailing south to Italy. The oracle of Delphi advised them to go to Cyrnus, which was then the name for Corsica, and thither they went, and founded the city of Alalia. Then came difficult years of meager living in a land infested by hostile tribes. Alalia lay right athwart a Carthaginian sea route to Italy, and its men tried to eke out a living with an occasional bit of buccaneering. Soon they were deep in trouble, and had eventually to face the combined Carthaginian and Etruscan fleets. They emerged from the battle victorious but heavily damaged. They decided the oracle must have meant some other place, and moved to the Italian coast, where they founded, with the help of their fellow Phocaeans from Massalia (Marseilles), the colony of Elea. It was here that Parmenides was born a few years later, and he was in time to become its first citizen and to promulgate a code of laws which was much admired throughout Greece. For generations after him the

Eleans would gather once a year in their forum to renew their allegiance to Parmenides's constitution.

This is all we know about his life except for the fact that he was converted to the philosophical way of life by a Pythagorean, Ameinias, to whom he later dedicated a sanctuary in gratitude. This at least gives us his intellectual point of departure. We also happen to know, through fragmentary references, that he made important contributions to geometry and astronomy: he classified geometrical figures; he identified the morning star and the evening star as one and the same planet; he marked out on our globe the five zones into which it is divided by the tropics and the arctic circles; indeed, if we must stand by Theophrastus, our most reliable informant, it is he who first among the Pythagoreans taught the sphericity of the Earth, and that the moon shines by reflected light. Notwithstanding these scientific achievements, his glory comes from a different one: he is known as the inventor of logical implication.

He wrote only one work, entitled *On Nature,* of which almost one half has been saved for us by way of quotations from late commentators. It is a striking departure even in form, for while the Ionians wrote in sententious prose, this is a poem, in oracular and cryptic style, probably in the tradition of the lost Pythagorean "Sacred Discourses." It opens with the allegorical narrative of a voyage to the heavenly abode of the goddess of Truth, who then, speaking in the first person, proceeds to tell what the philosopher must hold onto as irrefragable, and where he can make intellectual concessions in order to account for the world of appearances. The poem thus divides into a "Way of Truth," which deals with the necessities of thought itself, and a "Way of Opinion," which seems to have been an ambitious cosmogony on the Hesiodic pattern, doubled with a physical theory, but of this second part we have such sparse fragments that it is difficult to reconstruct the plan. The poem has been described as "inspired by the rapture of pure logic" and as the first philosophical text in the modern sense of the word, but its direct relevance to scientific thought seems to have been overlooked. Yet it ties up very closely, not only in the title, with preceding speculation on nature, and it turned out to be decisive in the evolution of Greek mathematics. It is the novelty of the language which led interpreters astray. We shall first give the fragmentary text as we have it, and analyze it afterwards.

On Nature *

1. The mares that draw me have carried me on as far as ever my heart desired, since they brought me and set me on the much-heralded way of the goddess, which takes the man who knows unharmed through all things. On that way was I borne along; for on it did the steeds, exceeding wise, carry me, drawing my car, and maidens showed the way. And the axle shed sparks in the hub—for it was urged round by the whirling wheels at each end—and gave forth a shrill sound, when the daughters of the Sun, hasting to convey me into the light, threw back their veils from off their faces and left the abode of Night.

There stand the gates of the ways of Night and of Day, fitted above with a lintel, below with a threshold of stone. They themselves, high in the air, are closed by mighty doors, and Justice the Great Avenger keeps the keys that open and shut. Her did the maidens entreat with gentle words and skillfully persuade to unfasten without demur the bolted bars from the gates. Then, as the doors were thrown back, they disclosed a wide opening, when their bronze hinges swung alternately in the sockets fastened with rivets and heavy nails. Straight through them, on the broad way, did the maidens guide the horses and the car, and the goddess greeted me graciously, and took my right hand in hers, and spake to me these words:

Welcome, noble youth, you who come to my abode on the car that bears you tended by immortal charioteers! It is no ill chance, but all that is just and holy, that has sent you forth to travel on this way. Far, indeed, does it lie from the beaten track of man. Meet it is that you should learn all things, as well the unshaken heart of well-rounded truth, as also the opinions of mortals, in which there is no certain reliance; yet

* Translation by Giorgio de Santillana and Walter Pitts. The order of the fragments is that given by Diels-Kranz. Our reading departs from others on several important points. For justification we must refer to our forthcoming work on *Parmenides*.

this you shall learn too, how an explanation of things that appear must be considered valid when it goes through all that we know.

The Way of Truth

2. Come now, I will tell you—and do you hearken to my saying and carry it away—the only two ways of search that can be thought of. The first one, because it exists and because it is impossible for it not to exist, is the way of conviction, for it follows truth. The other, because it does not exist and because it is necessary that it should not, is, I tell you, a wholly unexplorable path. For you cannot know Not-Being—that is impossible—nor utter it.

3. For it is the same to be thought and to be.

4. Discern steadfastly with your mind the far and the near together. For Being does not divide from its connection with Being, not loosened up in arrangement everywhere, or compacted.

5. It is all the same to me from what point I begin, for I shall return to this same point.

6. One must say and think that there is Being; for it is possible for it to exist, and nothing is not. This is what I bid you keep in mind. For I hold you back from this way of inquiry, first of all, and from that other also, upon which people who know nothing wander in two minds; for helplessness guides the wandering thought in their breasts, so that they are borne along bewildered like men deaf and blind. Undiscerning crowds, in whose eyes the same thing and not the same exists and does not exist, and whose way goes back upon itself!

7, 8. For it shall never prevail that Non-Being exists; and do you debar your thought from this way of inquiry.

Nor let habitual experience force you on this track, using your eye unperceivingly or your ear full of noise or your tongue; but do judge the subtle refutation of (their) discourses proceeding from me.

One path alone is left of which we know, that exists. In it are very many tokens that Being is uncreated and indestructible, one all through, whole, immovable, and without end. It never was, nor is it ever going to be; for it exists now, all together, a single continuum. For what kind of origin for it will you look for? How, whence, could it have drawn its increase? Nor shall I let you say or think that it came from Non-Being; for the latter is neither thinkable nor speakable, because it does not exist. And, if it came from nothing, what need could have made it arise later or sooner? Therefore it must either exist all together or not at all. Nor will the force of truth state that anything can arise out of Non-Being beside it. Wherefore, Justice does not loose her fetters and allow it to come into being or pass away, but holds it fast.

So the decision about these (ways) lies in this: whether it is possible or not; and it has been decided accordingly, as was necessary, to suffer the one way to remain unthought on and nameless, for it is no true way, and that the other path is there and is genuine. How, then, can Being be going to be in the future? Thus is its becoming extinguished and passing away not to be heard of.

Nor is it separated, since it is all alike, and there is no more anywhere, to prevent it from being continuous, or lesser, but everything is full of Being. Wherefore it is all continuous; for Being adjoins Being.

Moreover, it is immovable in the bonds of mighty chains, without beginning and without end; since coming about and passing away have been driven afar, and true belief has cast them away. Remaining the same in the selfsame place, it abides in itself. And thus it remains steady in its place; for strong Necessity keeps it in the bonds of the limit that constrains it round. Because Being is not permitted to be incomplete; for it is not in want; while if it were, it would miss being all.

It is the same thing to think and that there is an object of the thought; for you cannot find thought outside Being, in which what has been said (i.e., the terms) exists. For there is not, and never shall be, anything outside Being, since Fate has chained it to remaining whole and immovable.

There will be a name for everything in it, as many (names) as men have assigned to things, believing them to be correct—coming into being and passing away, being and being not, change of place and alteration of bright color.

But since the last bound is defined on all sides, like a well-rounded sphere, it is equally poised from the center in all directions; for it is necessary that it should not be greater in one direction and smaller in another. Nor is there Non-Being to prevent it from reaching out to its like, nor is it possible for Being to be more here and less there, because it is all inviolable. For it is equal from everywhere, and fits equally in its limits.

The Way of Opinion

Here shall I close my trustworthy speech and thought about the truth. Henceforward learn the notions of mortals, giving ear to the tricky order of my words.

For they have resolved to name two forms, of which it is wrong [to name] one—in this they have gone astray.

They have assigned opposite characters to each, and marks separate from one another: on the one side the fire of heaven, light, thin, in every direction the same as itself, but not the same as the other. On the other, opposite to it, dark night, compact and heavy as it were. Of these I tell you the whole profitable disposition, in order that no mortal may surpass you in knowledge.

9. But now that all things have been named light and night, and the names which belong to the power of each have been assigned to these things and to those, all is full of light and dark night, together, which balance each other, since neither has anything to do with the other.

10. And you shall know the origin of all the things on high, and all the signs in the sky, and the secret works of the glowing sun's clear torch, and whence they arose. And you shall learn likewise of the wandering deeds of the round-eyed moon, and of her nature. You shall know, too, the heaven that encloses round, whence it arose, and how Necessity took it and bound it to keep the limits of the stars. . . .

11. . . . How the earth, and the sun, and the moon, and the Aether that is common to all, and the Milky Way, and the outermost Olympus, and the burning might of the stars arose.

12. . . . The narrower (crowns) are filled with pure fire, and those supporting with night, and between these rushes a portion of fire. In the center of them is the Daemon that directs the course of all things; for she rules over all dreaded birth and begetting, driving the female to the male's embrace, and the male to the female.

13. First of all the gods she contrived Eros.

14. (The Moon) Shining by night with borrowed light, wandering around the earth.

15. (The Moon) Gazing towards the rays of the sun.

16. For as each one holds the combination of his far-wandering parts, so Mind is present in men; for it is the same that thinks in all men and in each, a virtue of the components, for thought is the more.

17. On the right (of the womb), boys, on the left, girls.

18. When a woman and a man mix the seeds of Love together, the power (of the seeds) which shapes (the embryo) in the veins out of different blood can mold well-constituted bodies only if it preserves proportion. For if the powers war (with each other) when the seed is mixed, and do not make a unity in the body formed by the mixture, they will terribly harass the growing (embryo) through the twofold seed of the sexes.

19. . . . . Thus according to men's opinions, did these things come into being, and are now; and in time they will thus grow up and then pass away. To each of these men assigned the seal of a name.

THE INVENTION OF LOGIC

The Way of Truth is, without any doubt, one of the most impressively obscure statements in the history of thought. It became consecrated as the "foundation of metaphysics." But confronted with the straight text, recited solemnly as poetry had to be, many of Parmenides's contemporaries must have thought that this man must have been given the sight of things unspeakable, for all he could say was that Being is and Non-Being is not. Some, no doubt, must have wondered whether it was the case to interrupt the ruling deity of the universe at her work, to bespeak the service of "most intelligent" mares and of a cortege of daughters of the sun to carry him aloft, only to come back with a set of oracular tautologies.

It is a tribute to the intellectual maturity of the Greeks of the fifth century B.C. that they were able to discern in the close-textured argument the appearance of a new power of thought, that of pure logical implication. They saw the strength of the law of contradiction which had been established. The very name of the subject, Being, suggested a sunlike truth which dazzles the mind. Its invisible presence became obsessive: and, in fact, Parmenides is the one person of whom Socrates speaks with marked reverence, describing him in Homeric terms as "august and terrible in his greatness." He adds: "However, I am not sure we understand fully what he said." It is to the clarification and development of this central theme of Being that Plato will devote his greatest efforts and his most subtle dialectic. Thus, by way of Plato, Parmenides is enshrined in the realm of pure philosophy, as the First Metaphysician.

Yet there is evidence to prove that, taken on his own terms, Parmenides belongs at least as much to science. If we accept that word "Being," not as a mysterious verbal power, but as a technical term for something the thinker had in mind but could not yet define, and replace it by x in the context of his argument, it will be easy to see that there is one, and only one, other concept which can be put in the place of x without engendering contradiction at any point, and that concept is pure geometrical space itself (for which the Greeks had no word, but only such related terms as "place," "air," "breath," "emptiness"). Moreover, it is built up step by step, with the use of the principle of indifference or sufficient reason, that we have seen used by Parmenides's naturalist predecessors; it is here for the first time applied consciously as the fundamental instrument of scientific logic, while Plato and Aristotle discuss Being with different—and far from scientific—logical tools.

Geometry as the Greeks meant it put three requirements on its space: first, it must have continuity (in a sense somewhat stronger than the mere absence of gaps between points); second, it must be the same, homogeneous throughout, so that we can move figures freely from place to place without altering their geometrical properties; and, finally, it must be isotropic, or the same in all directions. In other words, if you are placed in geometrical space, it must be impossible to tell where you are or in what direction you are looking. In modern terms, we say that Euclidean space is invariant under the three-dimensional translation and rotation groups. This is implied by Euclid's axiom affirming the possibility of superposing any two figures, which is known to date from early times, since geometrical algebra depends on it.

Now it is also true that anything that satisfies these three conditions must be isomorphic with and intrinsically indistinguishable from Euclidean space. That is the fundamental reason why, when we find Parmenides stating repeatedly and emphatically that his Being satisfies his three conditions—as the reader can check by going over the text—we must conclude that whatever else his Being may have meant to him in addition, it was certainly the space of the mathematician (and physicist) that he had in mind.

We shall find further that when Zeno invented his paradoxes in order to defend Parmenides's doctrine, those paradoxes turn out to belong to the realm of mathematical logic and to deal with continuity and motion. We shall assume then, centuries of commentary notwithstanding, that we are on the right track.

Let us remember what it was that motivated the quest.

The great concern for science had been to find the common substrate of all things, the One that unifies the Many. The Pythagoreans had suggested that the substrate is Numbers, that is: "points having position." These points, Limit placed in Unlimit, it had been concluded, were the origin and as it were the substance of things. But here begin the difficulties with a doctrine still eminently poetic and magical. What is the single monad but a repetition of identity? Unlimit had been assigned the role of a field, or filling, but it carried within it all the determination of limit, since it was the field of all positions. The Pythagoreans had thought of the power of Number and Limit in a kind of imaginative intuition, but on the very grounds of arithmo-geometry the representation would hardly stand scrutiny, because, clearly, it is Unlimit which is the bearer of Position, and hence of Limit. Any logical thought on the idea of number brings forth a continuum underlying it. The Pythagorean School had taken its dualism without investigating it too deeply. But its mathematicians had to.

We have seen what happened to Pythagorean "number atomism." In the reduction of geometry to numbers, the expression of all the geometric magnitudes which come up in the theory of proportion necessitated a common unit to measure them all that became smaller and smaller. The universal common measure had to shrink to a smallness indeed beyond measure, and yet it had to remain a unit: a kind of *actual infinitesimal*. Such is the new monad. But the difficulties of defining the line as a row of pebbles remain, however far we shrink the pebbles. Either each monad is separated from the text by a tract of Unlimit, or it is not. Either conclusion leads to sacrificing a part of the doctrine. We can sacrifice the discreteness of units, or we can sacrifice precision. A wrongness will remain. Limit and Unlimit are crowded together at every point.

It is curious to note that the Pythagorean movement, which had aimed from the beginning at discovering the principle of form in nature, should have wrecked itself on a rock so much like the one the Ionians had struck. To have order, harmony, and form in the world presupposed a formal substratum which should have no form itself, but be the bearer of all form, exactly as the hydrodynamic universe of the Ionians had been a quest for a material substratum which should be sufficiently neutral in its own intrinsic properties to be modifiable into all the kinds of matter in the world.

It was Parmenides, standing at the confluence of the two traditions, who realized that the two problems were in fact one. The true conception of geometrical space, once formed, is equally well adapted to serve as a substratum for physical form, in view of its rigidity and impassibility, and for matter, if one adopts a view of matter which transforms it into an accidental and contingent property of the space it "occupies." As we shall see, that was the course taken by Parmenides, and later by Newton. It is not surprising that he should have ascribed such a master stroke to the inspiration of the deity. As was natural for one trained primarily as a Pythagorean, it was probably their form of the problem, the analysis of the continuum, which led him to his discovery. That continuum fulfills, then, the same role as the Anaximandrean Unbounded—and also as the Pythagorean numbers. It can no longer be visualized as a great Flow with its eddies, or as points of light in space radiating power. There is nothing to visualize this kind of substrate; we have to construct it mentally, by continuously passing to the limit. Whatever we can imagine between things or fixed points divides again and again without end; whatever substance we put there in imagination falls apart into points, and so on without end, until it becomes clear that what we have to comprehend is the texture, which is that of the continuum. "Grasp firmly with thy mind the near and the far together. . . ." This is truly the "Be-er" (*Eón,* a grammatical construction very similar to that of "filler") since it permeates all things and bears their properties. We have not been able to locate the Many in any "trustworthy" way, and the conclusion is that there are not many separate points of space but only the One. We have moved out of the magic of numbers and entered the realm of pure logical Necessity.

What Parmenides thought he could do to make his position unassailable was to formalize it so as to force total assent from the start. This was later to be the way of the metaphysician. Spinoza asks us to accept the conception of the All, and to deduce consequences therefrom. Parmenides asks: "Would you deny that Being is?" We cannot know at that point what is the "Being" he has in mind; hence later ontologists have been tempted again and again to see in it the pure verb *is* of the grammatical copula. The deduction from there can proceed only on the logico-verbal plane. But neither does Descartes, in his *Discourse on Method,* make it clear at the start that his procedure of enumerating and subdividing, by which he hopes to solve all and any difficulty, is described with simple geometrical operations in mind. From all that we have seen, this would seem to be the case with Parmenides.

In that newly conceived continuum, all of mathematics has its native ground and its abode. To it belong the surface lines, figures, numbers, proportions, and relations that the mind can bring forth. The realm of Truth is that of mathematics in its amplest formulation as our time has brought it forth: the domain of all the possibilities of rigorous thought. It is unalterable and unmoving, but the mind moves freely in it, for it is of the mind itself. It contains the life of reason. It *is,* even as reason *is.* Such is the true world beyond sense, whose existence has been revealed to Parmenides by something he felt to be divine inspiration.

There is, of course, for us, the difficulty that it is described as a sphere "resting within its bounds." The difficulty persists in whatever interpretation; in fact, the more "metaphysical" the worse. But the statements are quite compatible with a sphere imagined as stretching as far as the mind will go, i.e., of infinite radius. The image of the sphere would then express isotropy ("the same in all directions") as opposite to the uncharacterized Unbounded of Anaximander. And it seems singularly true, thinking of a dense continuum which is "all limit" at every point, that if it lacked a limit it would lack everything. There is no real contradiction here; we are following logic into a strange paradox that Parmenides did not have the means to solve. Some doubts of this order came to Galileo too, who yet had to consider Euclidean space as unbounded.

TRUTH AND REALITY

It is all a strange new world of thought. We might say that whereas his predecessors had been projecting intuitive symbols of eternity in their element, or life-stuff, or monad, or the like, Parmenides has reached the point where he has to try and project the abstract frame of timeless truth itself; but such an insight requires a new way of reaching it, a new method; and therein lies his fateful originality. His continuum cannot be visualized as an object; it is of the nature of the mind itself: "for it is the same to be thought and to be." Hence, says Aristotle, Parmenides is the first to speak of "the One" "according to reason" and he undeniably prepares the ground for Platonic ontology. But when Plato wants to turn the idea to his uses, and to put that being in metaphysical motion in the life of the soul, then he has to force it beyond its true nature. As he says himself apologetically, he has to "commit parricide" on his father Parmenides. Spiritual Platonism is surely not what that Eleatic Being was meant for. But what was it conceived as? The question remains in many ways a puzzling one.* "Being," or "that which is," cannot be physically real in any ordinary sense since it is of the nature of the mind, the result of a process of abstraction. But it is by itself a plenum, and, in some sense, bodily, dense, crystalline extension, as it were. Not concrete, not quite physical, yet existing and real in a way; a strange reality indeed, that Parmenides must have consid-

* It should be stated that the official interpretation, as found in practically all textbooks and histories of philosophy, is that the Being of Parmenides is purely a logical category, noncorporeal in any way, and not extended in space at all—in fact rejecting the full space as well as the empty space. This comes mainly from the fact that the Platonic *Parmenides* has been taken as a key to the historic character of that name. Burnet, it is true, considers Being as corporeal, but suggests no way of making sense of it.

ered as "real" as Anaximander his Unbounded, although neither could be perceived by the senses.

THE WORLD OF PHYSICS

Is this, then, the Truth? The poem answers with imperatorial absolutism that it is, for no other way is thinkable; and we can see why we are forbidden to think or speak of Non-Being. Nonspace is strictly nowhere, and not to be thought of. But then the goddess with "the tricky order of her words" takes us into the domain that Truth cannot guarantee, namely, physical reality, to show that if we want to give some coherent account of the order of the cosmos it can be done. The idea that this was the world of illusion as opposed to that of truth became consecrated in philosophical teaching, because of the idealist preconception of later interpreters. It is hardly compatible with the serious and detailed treatment of the physical cosmos which is indicated even by the few fragments that survive. "Parmenides," remarks Plutarch wryly,

has neither taken away fire nor water nor rocks and precipices, nor yet cities . . . for he has written very largely of the earth, heaven, sun, moon and stars, and has spoken of the generation of man; and being, as he was, an ancient naturalist, and one who in writing sought to deliver his own and not to destroy another's doctrine, he has passed over none of the principal things in nature.

In fact, we should rather take into account the way of speaking of Parmenides's immediate predecessors like Xenophanes, or even Alcmaeon, that other Pythagorean who wrote a book *On Nature:* "The gods alone have certainty. But as far as it is given to men to conjecture . . ." The illumination of the Way of Truth has given Parmenides an idea of what that certainty is, but in the matter of physics he is still left to reasonable conjecture.

A modern simile might help us understand this point of view. Suppose a newcomer, some kind of Noble Savage, with no idea of modern devices nor of optical machinery, were taken today into a dark theater where great shapes appear, moving as if by themselves to show action and life in familiar patterns. He would first believe it reality, then pronounce it illusion, then decide that they are phenomena taking place only on the surface of the screen: Light and Dark combining in various ways under some outside control. In the same sense, for Parmenides, physical reality is not illusion; it is what "takes place" in geometric space and occupies it in changing ways not rigorously to be accounted for:

"There will be names for everything in it, as many as men have assigned to things, believing them to be correct —coming into being and passing away, being and being not, change of place and alteration of bright color."

As the names are given conventionally by men, so will the explanation be supplied as rationally as can be. "They came to an understanding to set two forms," Light and Night, the airy and the dense. We are clearly back in Pythagorean dualism with its scheme of the table of opposites, and Parmenides is simply offering a new version of it, but a version on a strictly physical plane. Nietzsche once suggested that this system might have been constructed by Parmenides in his early Pythagorean days, before the great idea came to him which relativized all physical truth into opinion. This seems reasonable. The two contrary elements are two different states of reality whose interplay produces what we see. In the heavens they are sharply separated: the parts of Light move upon tracks of Night with rigid geometrical constraint, and this is what we call the turning of the heavens. But since the sun, moon, and planets change their positions and altitudes through the year, we are led to visualize their tracks as plaited "crowns" which occupy a whole band of the sphere north and south of the celestial equator. "In the middle," that is, at the pole of the world axis (or possibly at the ecliptic pole), sits again the goddess as "the Daemon who steers all things." The elements operate, apparently, not through any force of their own nature, but because, like the stars, they move upon paths which impose an external constraint on their motion. The spontaneity of Ionian matter has been quite abolished, and we have something which comes very close to our own "natural law."

It would also appear that on the terrestrial level the two elements are mixed up much more thoroughly than in the heavens to make up the texture of things, the different proportions accounting even for such differences as between male and female. But since the elements never blend, "neither having a part of the other," we must assume a kind of granular discontinuity, and here is the beginning of some very important theoretical developments. The whole system seems to have been carefully thought out, in such a way as would be enough to exclude that Parmenides's thought of reality was an inconsistent delusion. He seems to be stating simply that there has been and is always going to be a disagreement about physical opinions, whereas no one disagrees about mathematics; hence, let us define the zone of uncertainty. The forces and the order are real enough; but the words we use for them do not contain the logic of their necessity; they are merely countersigns. We are not speaking of "what is"; hence there remains an element of probability and choice in the construction. Einstein wrote once: "If it is certain, it is not physics; if it is physics, it is not certain." Twenty-five centuries earlier, Parmenides seems to have taken a very similar position.

ZENO

The discovery of a world of Truth led Parmenides to emphasize its difference from experienced reality, and to pronounce the latter logically insoluble and "unreliable." The added sharpness of his language brought about the scandal that he had probably been looking for, and caused him to be called a dogmatist, a "freezer" (*stasiotes*) of all reality, the man paradoxical enough to deny motion and change. His pupil Zeno came forward to challenge the scoffers, and, as Plato says, he gave them as good as he got, and more for good measure. His famous Paradoxes or "attacks," as he called them, are essentially polemical devices, in which he turned the tables on his opponents, by undermining assumptions which seemed obvious and showing the incoherence of current theories. That his polemic was aimed straight at Pythagorean geometric atomism can be seen from his classic "attack" against the Many:

If things are a Many, they must be a number of units. These may be either with or without magnitude.

(1) If they are without magnitude (that is, without size, thickness or bulk) then such a unit if added to another thing

will not make it larger. And so it will follow that that which was added was nothing. . . . [The same way about subtraction] so that it is clear that nothing is added to or subtracted from an initial nothing. That is, everything is infinitely small, so small as to have no magnitude.

(2) If the many things are units with magnitude, then the unit must have a definite size and thickness, and each part must be a definite distance from each other part; and if you take one such part, the same argument applies to its parts, and so on ad infinitum. There can never be a subdivision so small that it cannot be redivided, that is, so small that it will not have a "one part" and "another part," whose relations to each other can be stated in terms of the distance between them. Thus you get an infinite number of things each having magnitude, and this infinite number added together makes up infinite sizes. Thus things are infinitely great.

Generations of commentators were puzzled as to whether it was the One or the Many that Zeno was attacking in this argument; yet it is clear that he was simply reducing to absurdity the Pythagorean effort at saving the monad by contracting it to an actual infinitesimal. It cannot have a finite size; it cannot have a zero size; these were the horns of his dilemma. As a critique of real things it may appear specious; as applied to the actual infinitesimal it is rigorous. That last little monad cannot be "something"; it is simply a point having position inside the continuum.

The idea is restated in another "attack":

There must be a magnitude which is without part, that is, indivisible, because it is impossible to traverse an infinite number of positions in succession in a finite time.

Here we have time and motion coming upon the scene, and it will lead to the famous paradox of "Achilles and the Tortoise"; whereby Achilles can never catch up with the tortoise if it has a start of even one foot. It amounts to what is said in still another attack, that motion is impossible because it is impossible to pass through an infinity of positions in a finite time.

The problem of the "Arrow" concentrates on this aspect of motion. The arrow cannot get anywhere; or, in a different statement, "if it moves in the place where it is, then it stays put: if in the place where it is not, then how does it happen to be there?"

All these coruscating attacks show that Zeno was using the technique he had invented, that of the *reductio ad absurdum*, to very good purpose. Applied to ordinary reality, they looked like brilliant paradoxes which paralyzed the opponent without convincing him, and the Greeks seem to have found in the newly discovered art of logic, or dialectic as they called it, a source of unending delight. The search for the "catching" argument soon became the business of sophistry. Aristotle thought he had to refute Zeno's arguments gravely, and show how they could be brought back to sense. No doubt Zeno himself must have enjoyed his *succès de scandale,* and egged on some of his opponents to helpless anger. Others, as later Diogenes, would get up and walk about to show that motion was real. But of course Zeno had never denied in his mind factual reality and motion. He had simply shown that they were impossible to analyze rigorously. They were "phenomena," that is, appearances, which can only be taken as they are, in the rough, and given strictly phenomenological status. They are "happenings," a word which has its roots in hap and chance. If in order to "save phenomena" you introduce plurality into your ultimate cause, you are still unable to explain phenomena. The Many cannot have magnitude as their absolute property; it will end up in either infinity or zero. They cannot have motion as their own; to get motion, you have to have something fixed to start with, and your "explanation" of motion becomes a series of infinite positions, that is, relations, to that point of reference. If we ask for the natures of the Many, we get only a set of internal contradictions—or of external relations. If we try to understand their motion, we get only a set of relations, that is, again, nothing in itself. The logic of objects turns out to be a logic of relations. Everything shows up as inconsistent against the absolute background of the One, the locus of all relations, where all contradictions are solved.

The logical problems raised by Pythagoreanism had come to the end of a long road. The magical and qualitative aspects of individual number have been burned up in the flame of analysis; what is left is logical structure, implication, rigor, and continuity. A new science has been born which lasts to this day, that of the foundations of mathematics or metamathematics. On the side of philosophy, we have the same. Both ways, it is an irreversible change. The physics of the "substrate" will inevitably yield to metaphysics; the search for Being becomes ontology. Pure philosophy feels free to set out on its own way, with the new instrument of logic, disjoined from naturalistic speculation, in the direction of idealism. But philosophy, however great the virtuosity with which it plays with the new abstraction, will be singularly slow in coming to use the specific creation of Elea, which is relational logic. Hence, however official history may have crystallized opinion, it is to science that the greatest gain accrues from the Eleatic revolution.

The conventional view that we have mentioned is due to a misunderstanding still very much alive today, which has been analyzed by Bertrand Russell thus: "Mathematics and logic, historically speaking, have been entirely distinct studies. Mathematics has been connected with science, logic with Greek." Yet today the two have become one: "They differ as boy and man; logic is the youth of mathematics and mathematics is the manhood of logic." If we put it thus, then we understand why all of Greek logic was imagined as leading up to the Aristotelian "boyhood," and to be explained in such terms. It is only now that we begin to discern, in the Eleatic attempt, the early manhood of science.

Here we also have rationalism at the crossroads. The original rationalist position, that was present from the beginning of science, the faith that moves mountains, is nowhere more in evidence than in Parmenides: what can be deduced logically from a secure premise will be found to be so; in his own words: "It is the same to be thought and to be." To speak the rational becomes a momentous creation of Truth, hence fraught with solemn interdictions. If his Being be space as the body of geometry, as we suggest, we remain within the bounds of the certain. But what if the abstract word carry us beyond? In the word "Being" there is an incomparable and undecipherable richness which seems to touch all of our deeper certainties, and makes Non-Being unthinkable in more ways than one. What if the newly discovered power of implication could tie up all of reality in one truth, and steer our way through the uncharted seas of our total experience? That word "Being" may have seemed, to Parmenides himself, the miraculously found center of all thought, the source of a fulfillment stronger than sheer mathematics. He must have felt (for every man lives in his own past, in what he has learned to believe in) that he was transmuting the dark implacable archaic Order of Time into a timeless Present, into an order of space, clarity, and logical necessity. To explore it meant to him, as the exploration of Number had meant to the Pythagoreans, the "philosophical life." But he kept his own counsel, and never transgressed the bounds of rigor, remaining for posterity "august and terrible in his greatness." In modern times, the equivalent would be to prove successfully that the universe is certainly *one* (no small statement, if we consider it), and that beyond that one assurance many hypotheses are possible but no certainty. But it was natural for those who came after to think that the magic key of logic might unlock all doors, and that to be able to say of anything that it *is* would raise it to metaphysical status. From all that we can surmise, Parmenides himself would have remained, in his own words quoted by Plato, "wondrous hard to convince."

Two thousand years later, Descartes, laying the foundations of pure reason over the ruins of the Renaissance, was to start almost exactly at the same point. (And does not he, too, tell us of his heaven-sent revelation?) His "extended matter" is again the One Thing, like Parmenidean Being, and it coincides with the geometrical continuum; matter, space, and motion become again analytical relations. Sense perception is for him, as it was for the Eleatics, a source of obscurity, incapable of providing a base for true knowledge. We said at "almost" exactly the same point above, but not quite, for Cartesian space is also supposed to be real matter; motion is a real state, and thus the road is open for the natural philosophy of matter in motion. That "almost" stands for an intellectual compromise. Descartes was in a hurry to begin, and his new tool of analytical geometry provided an irresistible temptation; he identified space with substance, the way of Truth with that of Opinion. Out of that come the simple-minded aspects of materialism: simple location and misplaced concreteness.

7

Love, Strife, and Necessity

THOSE WHO came after Parmenides confronted a painful dilemma. Now that the One Substrate had been clearly specified, it could be shown to have exceedingly little to do with matter as we know it and as having utterly nothing to do with the Many. Could one, then, relegate any attempt at explaining the world to the "tricky" status of arbitrary opinion? The One was meta-physical, that is, it was not concretely "real"; the Many were real but not "true." The dilemma, in Burnet's words, came down to this, that one had to give up either corporealism or monism. That fateful word "Being" seems to have hypnotized the minds. It shows at least what it is that we expect of a scientific explanation. We want Being to be *in* events, not beneath or beyond them. We want it to be "reliably" there. And this turns out to be unexpectedly difficult. All the ways logically possible were explored to the end of the road.

ANAXAGORAS

One way was to suggest, as the severe Anaxagoras did (460 B.C.), that the One Being contains in itself all the qualities and differences of known things already inherent in it, but in a state of such extreme subdivision that made for dense uniformity. We are back in a sort of qualitative actual infinitesimal, although Anaxagoras tried to parry the difficulty by saying that "there is not a least to the small but there is always a smaller." It leads to an infinitely infinite number and variety of ultimate "seeds." The relation between substrate and phenomena he could define thus: "What appears is a vision of the unseen"—a vision which occurs, of course, when similars are aggregated together by the usual *deus in machina,* the vortex. Motion in a vortex preserves, at least formally, the idea of relative motion of the full-in-the-full. But then what brings it about? Anaxagoras, by answering: "a special whirling mixer called Mind," finds himself caught again in the old Ionian equivocation, although Aristotle compliments him highly for having at last brought Mind into the business.

EMPEDOCLES

A much more ingenious way was that attempted by Empedocles, who also imagined a universe satisfying both conditions, uniformity and multiplicity, but alternately, so that truth and reality could be, as it were, its warp and woof. We might call it the theory of Pulsating Being.

Empedocles of Acragas (Agrigentum) in Sicily (c. 450 B.C.) stands as a Pythagoras-like figure, fraught with legends of wondrous works and a wondrous end in the crater of Etna. He was in fact one of the great medical men of his time and the founder of the Sicilian school of medicine. But he was also credited with miraculous cures. A poet of considerable gifts (for he, too, wrote a poem which was meant as a counterpart to that of Parmenides) he displayed no less than the Elean an archaic loftiness, but not on the literary plane alone, for he gave clear intimations that he belonged to the race of gods and Orphic daemons.

Friends, who dwell in the great town on the city's heights, looking down on yellow Akragas, you who are occupied with good deeds, harbours (of refuge) to the foreigner, unacquainted with wickedness: greeting! I go about among you as an immortal god, no longer a mortal, held in honour by all, as I seem to them to deserve, crowned with fillets and flowing garlands. When I come to them in their flourishing towns, to men and women, I am honoured; and they follow me in thousands, to inquire where is the path of advantage, some desiring oracles, while others ask to hear a word of healing for their many diseases, long pierced as they have been with cruel pains.*

This may have been a deliberate rehearsing of the original character of Pythagoras, barely a century old but already lost in legend. If he comes to reform the scientific

---

* This and most of the subsequent quotations from Empedocles in this chapter are from John Burnet, *op. cit.*

doctrine, he remains withal a Pythagorean of the old observance who believes in reincarnation and the rites of purification, and holds it "a great shame to shed blood and devour the goodly limbs of animals whose life was reft from them"; he pays homage to Pythagoras as "a man of surpassing knowledge who, whenever he reached out with his whole intellect, easily discerned each one of existing things, in ten and even twenty lifetimes of mankind."

The system taught by Empedocles in his poem *Physika,* which often parallels closely that of Parmenides, is at first sight an elaborate consolidation of the Way of Opinion. Instead of two elements there are the old Four—Earth, Water, Air, and Fire. But this time they behave as passive matter, for there are also two opposite forces that move them around, positive and negative, Love and Strife. Their names are mythological but their nature is not. The first is what drives like to unlike; it is called, not Eros, but "Philotēs," Love in the sense of Friendship, Affection, and the urge of Eros is only a particular case of it (Empedocles does not go the way of Freud); Strife is what repels the unlike and draws like to like, so that contraries get massed together and separated out. This is all far more physical-minded than Heraclitus. Even the gods "who last over long spans of time" are made of the same substance. The world is an essentially unstable system which operates in great cycles. As Friendship predominates, everything is gradually compacted and fused together into a total mixture, "a god equal to himself and altogether eternal, a rounded Sphairos, complete, rejoicing in its aloneness." But when the time has come, "according to the oracle of Necessity," the ferment of Strife begins to stir, "the god quakes in all its limbs," the process of dissolution takes hold which does not cease until the world is dispersed in a vortex under the empire of Strife. At that point Love takes hold and brings all things together again.

As Parmenidean thought and turns of speech are very much present to Empedocles's mind, so it is clear that the Sphairos is meant to fulfill the requirements of Eleatic Being. It is, in essence, a continuous body in static repose, "the same at all points." It would stay such if Strife did not rend it asunder periodically. But its nature remains invariant:

From what in no wise exists, it is impossible to come into being; and for Being to perish completely is incapable of fulfilment and unthinkable; for it will always be there, wherever one may push it. . . . There is only mixing and exchange of what has been mixed; and the name "substance" [*physis*, "nature"] is applied to them by mankind.

The four elements and the two forces build up the Whole, for whose invariance Empedocles gives the Eleatic proof. Thus he feels he has produced a Way of True Opinion, since it has certain essential countersigns of the Way of Truth. In this world, such phenomena as coming into being and passing away are truly "opinion" and illusion, for in effect there is nothing but mixing and unmixing; these, remarks Plutarch, "are not the expressions of a man who denies those that are born to be, but rather of him who holds those to be that are not yet born or are already dead." The difference from Parmenides seems to be one of temperament rather than theoretical principles: Empedocles is very much a doctor with a biological imagination, while Parmenides's bent is mathematical, so that even his "probable" cosmos is a geometrical mechanism. Both are ultimately Pythagorean in their preconceptions. Starting from very similar invariantive conditions, Empedocles is preoccupied with a reality that has come alive in his mind, that of *process*. He finds it something as metaphysically important as Being itself, hence he has to imagine an inherently unstable universe, evolutionary, forever sliding into new conditions, which, being eternal, has to take on the form of a pulsating system. The intellectual guarantee that he needs is then sealed by the "mutual ample oath" through which the opposing forces are bound by the Oracle of Necessity. This is again a guarantee of invariance; it makes his "process" different from ours in that his time is not open at both ends, but forever cyclical, repeating itself in firm periodicity. What is eternal is the Sphairos itself through the cycles.

Obviously, what we call a world takes place only in the ascending and descending semicycles, since the terminal points are total mixture and total separation. On a 24-hour dial, we may imagine them respectively at noon and midnight. An approximate balance would occur at 6 A.M. and

6 P.M. There is a continuous interplay of Strife and Love in the shaping of life, since differentiation of parts leads to partial wholes, in a way which gives a first scheme of natural selection.

Many foreheads without necks sprang forth, arms wandered bereft of shoulders, eyes strayed alone, lacking brows. . . . As the two (opposite) divine forces clashed more extensively, these things fell together as they came upon each other . . . creatures were produced facing both ways, with double face and breast, cattle-kind with men's heads, and men-kind with heads of cattle. . . .

The fruit of the tree precedes the egg in the animal; hair, leaves, scales and feathers are the same, but they have developed in different ways; where the development helps survival, it is retained. The spine with its vertebrae was the result of an accidental turning of the neck and breaking it. This is the scientific imagination of genius, which will ever go against common sense. It had to go so far, even wildly, in order to eliminate purpose.

FUNCTION AND NECESSITY

But why has purpose to be eliminated? Just because common sense had to be thwarted, which shows us the world of things which change as a community of autonomous beings going each its own way. We have seen that in Parmenides's cosmos it is the Daemon who steers all things and drives the male to the female, even as she holds the stars to their courses. Here we have two opposite powers which in one respect are spatially extended as all reality is, in another respect are constant forces, attraction and repulsion, operating like the two electricities, in still another have a structural capacity which works at cross purposes, so that on all three levels they check off each other.

From the ruins of the text and a few muddled references, it is difficult to reconstruct the cosmogony; interpretations differ widely, and the one we are going to suggest is at variance with most of them, but it has a number of good grounds.

Let us take, then, as Time Zero, or, say, midnight on the dial, the uncontrasted reign of Strife. When Fire was gathered to Fire by Strife in the dispersion phase, it ap-

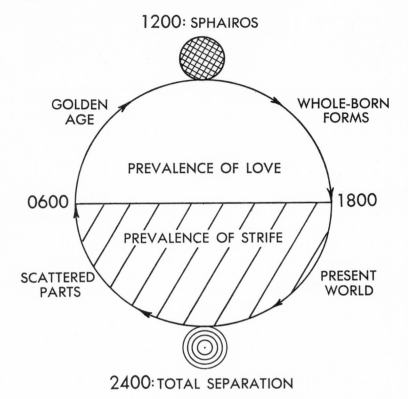

Fig. 10.

parently rose upward because it had nowhere else to go (the fullness of Being remains constant), driven by the pressure of Air. It collected inside the "glazed" outer-aether surface of a hemisphere. Hence its reflection concentrates into the burning spot of light that we call the sun (this classic Pythagorean explanation shows familiarity with curved mirrors). The elements were separated thus almost entirely into four concentric layers. But as Strife consolidated in the periphery, Love's wave by that time was moving out from the center of the whirl towards the middle.

Many things stand unmixed side by side with the things mixing—all those which Strife still aloft checked, since it had

not yet completely withdrawn from the Whole to the outermost circle, but was remaining in some places, and in other
places departing. But insofar as it went on quietly streaming
out, to the same extent there was entering a gentle immortal
onrush of faultless Love. And swiftly those things became
mortal which previously had experienced immortality (i.e., as
elements) and things formerly unmixed became mixed, changing their paths. And as they mixed, there poured forth countless races of mortals, equipped with forms of every sort, a
marvel to behold.

In the beginning it is the elements that seep into each
other, "the air sinking down with its tendrils into the
earth," then Love, working against odds, compounds the
earliest forms of life. Empedocles, like us, sees it beginning with fragmentary components. Where we are able to
think now in terms of asymmetric large molecules, amino
acids, viruses, and monocellular organisms he has to imagine separate parts, as we quoted previously, first bone
and flesh, then limbs wandering around and "eyes lacking
foreheads." These combine at random into monsters like
"creatures in dreams," oxheaded men and so on, which
are then selected out of existence, with only a few sur-
vivors, Strife still having the upper hand. As the hand
moves beyond 6 A.M., Love gains the ascendant, and a
harmonious world is produced. "For all were gentle and
obedient toward men, both animals and birds, and they
burned with kindly love." There is no shedding of blood,
the gods are honored with offerings of milk and honey, it
is the classic Golden Age. We are not told how all this
blends and vanishes ecstatically in the final stage under
the overwhelming force of Love, which is "like rennet in
milk," and then how things start again when the counter-
wave of Strife sets in, but it would seem that individual life
came up in this second half-cycle even before the skies
were made.* This is reasonable. In a substance still integrated and permeated by Love, the first stirrings of the elements at separation take an organic form. As fire tries to

* The reconstruction that follows of the second phase, as well
as of mixture and knowledge on p. 119f, has been worked out by
Dr. Harald Reiche of Massachusetts Institute of Technology in his
recent book on *Empedoclean Mixture, Eudoxan Astronomy and
Aristotle's Connate Pneuma*. Amsterdam: A. Hakkert, 1959.

rejoin fire upward, it pushes up trees from the ground. As earth strives downward, "Love kneads and bakes in its gentle crucibles" the first crawling things. Shell-backed creatures must be very early, for "they still have earth on top." The first objects to separate from the elemental mixture have a maximum of integration; they are "full-natured" or "whole-born" things. They have no sex or clear species, "neither the lovely forms of limbs, nor voice . . ."; they lead protozoan lives of torpor on the still-tropical earth. They are imagined as slow-growing foetuses incubated by the earth's heat; their life is a kind of chthonic pregnancy extending over hundreds of years. We may see one aspect of what Empedocles means if we think of the trees, left over from that era.

Then, as differentiation presses on under the growing power of Strife, beings become isolated from their earthy womb and diverge into opposite sexes, and animals bear their young. The earth has cooled down as fire concentrated above, so that birth has to take place in the enclosed warmth of the womb. Its cycle takes only weeks or months, leaving the parent free. Empedocles's leading idea here is that the growth of the embryo rehearses in a fore-shortened way the cosmogonic process. He suggests that the "whole-born" forms came to "birth" in 215 or 275 years, as many as there are days in the 7 or 9 months of present pregnancy. A day of ours corresponds then to a year of their dreamlike time. Embryology becomes a study of the "microcosm," and in it Empedocles made brilliant discoveries, among them that of the amnion that encloses the embryo, and of its function. He saw that prenatal life in that enclosed sac must be, in our terms, anaerobic, and hence that the soul with which the embryo is certainly endowed cannot be dependent on the outer pneuma or "breath" that Heraclitus and the medical thinkers before him had taken for granted as a universal principle of life. This change of views was adopted by Philistion, Empedocles's successor in the leadership of the Sicilian medical school, and had far-ranging consequences in the scientific thought of later times. The period of "articulation" of the foetus, representing another cosmic period of the previous era, is set by Empedocles between the 36th and the 49th day (6^2 and 7^2). The air-element that the fetus needs to be "complete" is supposed then to be borrowed through the placenta from the mother organism. That is the point where sex determination sets in, decided by the characteristics of the already functional heart, for it is the heart which is seen as the carrier of determination and individuality, for reasons which will become clear later on.

Articulation, differentiation, individualization, ever increasing, these are then the ruling characteristics of the present evolutionary period. It would almost look as if Herbert Spencer were already emerging from the mists of futurity. But Empedocles does not have a self-satisfied Victorian era around him to delude him into confidence. He remains clear-sighted. Creation, for him, still proceeds under the primordial force of Love, which is not all lost; but it has taken the shape of sexual attraction, which goes to increase possessiveness and Strife. Organisms close up into self-defense, self-love, aggression, and mutual destruction. Even the growth of consciousness in man, which might serve to redeem the whole, goes along the ways dictated by Strife; and that, we are told, is our present position in the cycle (about 10 P.M. on the dial), leading, as Empedocles might have said had he had modern terms of reference, towards a Thermonuclear Twelve.

THE REGULARIZING DESIGN

We can certainly trace this kind of thought back to the mystical Orphic doctrine of "escape from the wheel of rebirths," but it remains naturalistically consistent with the idea of Anaximandrian justice, whereby things "make mutual atonement in the order of time." The process is here carefully and imaginatively worked out, but the metaphysical constant remains, as it has been from Anaximander through Parmenides, an order of immanent justice which is also an order of Necessity, to be understood as physical, then logical, Necessity. With Empedocles, Necessity is the sum of the two contrary forces, together with the "contract" which ties them together. Between them, they build and destroy, each of them limited in its action by conflict with the other. Thus, Love brings forth at first partial harmonious assemblages with what it finds available at every point, and these assemblages undergo natural selection by virtue of Strife, which thus cooperates from the other side in creation; Love shapes forms out of drives caused by Strife, but also reabsorbs all varieties in the end, while later Strife sharpens, increases, articulates, the variety brought forth by Love, yet to a destructive end. The forces remain constant in behavior, but the fearful intrications of their interaction give the effect of chance. The pattern of this interaction weaves together the obvious "intentionality," or shall we say functionality, seen in the order of life with the mechanical causality which ensures the over-all pulsation. Everywhere elements of matter and elements of function, of purpose and no-purpose, so to speak, are locked together in the universal melee of process. (We shall see presently that Empedocles has his own way of resolving form and function into quantitative proportion, so that his discourse remains consistent.) The emergent labile forms are what we call beings, and may delude us by fettering our attention to their plane of existence: "Fools! for they have no far-reaching studious thoughts who think that what was not before comes into being. . . ." By concentrating on the invariant background of matter and force, Empedocles is led to treat events in a quasi-statistical manner, which draws on him from Plato and Aristotle the reproach of having brought in chance and eliminated purpose. From their point of view he may do so, but in reality his thought is subtler than that. What is dominant in his mind are the regularizing forces.

Empedocles sees a multitude of emergent partial purposes (the action of Love) which move on as soon as achieved to the side of Strife in order to preserve their individuality, until they are reabsorbed in the sovereign total oneness. Eros itself expresses this ambiguity, since its urge is towards mixture and its result separateness. Everything appears relative except the over-all balance which works itself out, inexorably in world cycles. The Anaximandrian equation is preserved in its canonic form.

The conflict between purpose and necessity, chance and design, runs so deep in scientific thought, and down to the present day, that it is important to see how it outlines itself at the very beginning. As we have noticed, Greek scientific speculation, from Anaximander on, stands under the sign of Necessity, since it is of the nature of reason, and provides the causal invariants. We may note that the tragic poets, so deeply concerned with human purpose, are in fundamental agreement, for their view is that any individual purpose, as soon as it becomes conspicuous or significant, and be it even that of Prometheus, is liable to be struck down by the gods, who are the guardians of the regularizing design of Necessity. To say design is to imply that it is not blind. Necessity, even if it appear to be blind, is never chance; what is properly chance or luck is bound to appear in the conflict of purposes. As we say: "It's an ill wind that blows nobody good." To grasp the inherent design is thus the way for man to become reconciled, or "at home," in the cosmos. Parmenides suggests one intellectual way, Empedocles another; both have recourse to the not entirely mythological form of claiming acquaintance with the Guardian Deity of that order; it translates into reason having become one with cosmic necessity. Empedocles, who as a Pythagorean believes in the transmigration of souls, has his own colorful way about it. He describes himself as a "daemon" punished for "thrice ten thousand seasons" by the elements bound to the pact of Necessity, for having once "trusted raging Strife." For remember, he says elsewhere, "all things have intelligence and a share in thought." They refuse to stay with us in our mind if we understand them badly. As we know "Love by Love and Hate by grievous Hate," so what we know by Mind, which is simply the integration of our perception, is some kind of Mind—it *is* out there, the "daemons" are participant with it on its universal level. Men can conjecture its ways, but its whole is a *phrēn hierē,* which we might perhaps translate as "Sacred Counsel," and "it darts through the whole universe with swift thought"—the Sphairos itself, obviously, whose consciousness goes on enduring through the alternations. To be sure, this is not the transcendent deity that we are wont to think of in our Platonic-Christian tradition. It is an awareness of itself that the integrated whole can feel "in its limbs," as Empedocles would say; the social pact of all beings, so to speak, become alive in Being, in a somewhat pantheistic way. As it "rejoices" in unity, the Sphairos must suffer in dismemberment, but it is held to its changes by Love, Strife, and Necessity, which take the names of gods but are really forces. Empedocles's favorite thought pattern is functional analogy between physiology and physics. It is clear that Empedocles's Necessity is, in natural terms, what a physicist would mean; it can even be statistical. Analogically, it becomes biological, then again metaphysical. In an Arab commentator, Shahrastani, we find amid much fanciful stuff something that looks like a real quotation:

In the Kalām of Empedocles it is said that the vegetative soul envelops the animal soul, this in turn the discursive soul, and the discursive soul envelops the rational soul; that the lower stands to the higher in the relation of mantle to core.

PERCEPTION AND MIXTURE

Empedocles, as befits a doctor, gave much thought to the way in which we perceive the outer world. To the principle that "we know like by like" he gave a strictly physical meaning, as his thinking is physical throughout. The air is full of "effluences" which reach us. This already poses the difficult problem of interpenetration, for Empedocles is very respectful of the continuum, and everything has extension as part of the continuum; even Love and Strife are said to be extended. How then do the components go through each other? Strict consistency cannot be maintained—it is not by Descartes either, who has to face the same problem. Empedocles's solution is fully as subtle as Descartes': he imagines all bodies to be full of invisible "pores" that the effluences traverse easily if they fit into them. There is no way here not to presuppose some forbidden mechanism of condensation and rarefaction (the lightning is fire "squeezed" out of clouds) but it is treated as circumspectly as possible. Each thing functions as active or passive in mixing in so far as it is a continuum shot through with holes, or a cloud composed of particles of (obviously) the right size for the holes. The two descriptions are hardly reconcilable—a singular early case of duality.

However that may be, it provides the universal mechanism for absorption. It explains, for instance, why deciduous trees lose their leaves: the absorbing pores of the roots are smaller than the emitting pores of the leaves. It also explains perception. We receive effluences by way of very fine pores which let in the particles of a specific mixture of elements, without letting the blood out. The mechanism is explained in the brilliant hydraulic analogy of the "water-catcher" or pipette, which we quote hereafter. It makes clear how things carried by air enter the body with the air itself. With sight the case is different. Light is Fire traveling with great (but finite) speed *through* the air. It meets the living Fire which issues from the eye, apparently in the pupil itself, to make for the shining of the eye, and vision is the result. We are dealing here with an idea which remained general and firmly anchored well into the Renaissance, that vision is an active function, something like visive antennae issuing from the eyes to touch the object, or, since we moderns now have a name for it, a kind of natural radar scanning the outside and bringing back shapes onto our inner scope. So Empedocles, too, has fire issuing from the eye, at least as far as the pupil; and how it gets through is again illustrated by a brilliant simile, that of the lantern whose plates keep out the wind but let the beams through.

The principle "like by like" remains axiomatic. But we must not think it is used simple-mindedly. If the fire outside were really able to meet directly the fire in us, it would draw and separate it out, i.e., we would be burned to death, which is, in fact, the unceasing attempt of Strife. Perception takes place only through similar mixtures, or, rather, through the *ratios* of those mixtures; it turns out to be a *resonance* of identical ratios. The transitory stability of the systems we call beings must be understood as a complex play of internal ratios responding adequately to an influx of ratios from outside.

Now, since intelligence is nothing but completer perception, and the blood is what sends the various mixtures to the organs of sense, Empedocles suggests that we think, or, shall we say, receive reality, chiefly through the blood: ". . . The heart dwelling in the sea of blood which surges back and forth, where especially is what is called thought by men. . . ." This theory is again accepted by Philistion, the medical successor. We see how thoroughgoing the explanation by mixture can be. It goes even farther. There is a well-worked-out analogy with the painter bringing out all forms from a few colors on his palette, which suggests

that the formative or organizing capacity of Love, shaping
the parts of animals, is not some unexplained principle of
form, or some organizational impulse, but simply her capacity to make harmonious mixtures. In fact, Empedocles
speaks of the "cement of Harmony" compounding the
bones out of eight parts of earth, two of water, and four
of fire. The dosage 4 : 1 : 2 would account, then, not only
for the substance, but for the shape and proportions of the
bones. Thus form is brought back to mathematical proportion, and the level of quantitative explanation re-established
throughout. It is hard not to see the Pythagorean idea in
the background: proportion is creator and builder. The
palette of Aphrodite needs the lyre of Apollo.

It is the *ratio* which provides the guiding thread through
Empedocles's theory, and resolves the physical mechanism
of his physiology into intellectual function. Perception,
cognition, are under the sign of Love, for they are based
on ratios and harmony; so is the *isonomia* which makes
the community of all things—the cosmos as such is ruled
by Love. Strife only attracts and breaks up; it operates on
the qualitative level of the elements; it has, we might say,
the purpose of no purpose. Love cannot even begin to
cope with separate substantial elements, only with mixtures, because it draws unlikes. Its power lies in the ratio
of unlikes. Only as a component part of some cognitive
mixture can an elemental particle "recognize," i.e., res-
onate to, its equal in another mixture; perception is bound
to be as universal as proportion itself is. That is how "all
things have a share of thought."

Love, then, operates only in terms of ratios and harmonies. But from what source does it draw them? To say
that they just *are,* in the candid Pythagorean way, is to
make them into magic entities. This could hardly be maintained after Parmenides had shown that "it is the same to
be thought and to be." The entities of reason are born out
of reason, as we remember; it is thought which is their native heath. But what thought can that be from which Love
is able to draw a world? The question is as old as time;
all civilizations try to give an answer as best they can. In
our own times Immanuel Kant, as he woke from his "dogmatic sleep" and put the question afresh, was led to conceive of an "archetypal intellect" which should harbor the

reason implicit in nature—whatever that reason might be. The question, like the universal reason it implies, is present in Greek speculation since Solon and Anaximander. The Pythagoreans present it in magical garb; Parmenides uncovers it in its logical form: "You cannot find thought outside Being, in which what is said exists." There is, then, Empedocles concludes, some sort of archetypal intellect identified with Being. It is what we have called the Sacred Counsel: its thoughts are "not to be uttered," but it is the fount from which Love draws the ratios and harmonies for its operations.

Different from it is human thought, identified with perceptions. "Each is convinced of that alone which he has chanced upon as he is hurried to and fro, and idly fancies he has found the whole. Thou, too, shalt learn no more than mortal mind has seen." Our thought is discursive, relative, timebound. Philosophically, it is approximate because the mixtures on both sides happen to be "coarse-grained." A finer mixture, as in the blood, gives the mobility of intelligence. But it remains in the nature of discursive thought not to reach "true insight."

We here see Empedocles using another traditional tool, that of *saphēneia,* sharpness, to discriminate between various forms of knowledge down to the subtle. As Anaxagoras said, "A way of seeing the unseen is the appearances." But he has managed to set up a new and very modern problem: what, at best, is man's intelligence worth, as the product of an evolutionary process? A current modern view is that, since our intelligence became a tool for survival, it must have supplied reliable knowledge. But of course that means reliable as far as survival goes. It ends up in a tautology. Empedocles is not so easily satisfied. For him our bloodbound intelligence, however reliable, however true the ratios it can reflect, as it arises from perception remains caught in the Way of Opinion. It is here that his religious tenets, far from being incongruous and not compatible with his science, as is often held, prove to be the completion of his thought. They allow him to throw a bridge across to the side of Truth, that Parmenides had postulated without justifying it further.

As sound beyond a certain pitch becomes inaudible, as a completely steady state which sends out no perturbations

is not perceivable, so, in a way, there is a point of exact
1:1 relationship where the mixture escapes the senses because it has become truly one, total, as it was in the
Sphairos. We are told that the four elements preserve their
identity, but it must be then as actual infinitesimals, uniformly compounded throughout in a state of harmony.
That is the harmony of the Sphairos; it is also the soul, or,
in the image provided by Orphism, the daemon *in* man,
which has nothing to do with his perishable intelligence
and consciousness of self. It is not anthropomorphic; it is
of the nature of the Sphairos and knows only the thoughts
of the Sphairos, which are not conscious thoughts as we
mean them. They are a kind of simultaneous awareness,
containing the analogical ratios and the life of harmony.
When Empedocles says that he (i.e., the daemon in him)
was born as bush and bird and dumb leaping fish, he cannot claim to have had such thoughts then as he has now.
But as man, what can come to consciousness in him, in the
form of intuition, is an extension of his intellect to universal conditions. This is nothing that can reach him
through touch or sight, "the main avenues of belief into
the heart," but only through inner light. He can grasp the
functional analogies relating all forms of life from the
lowest to the highest, illuminate his mind by direct understanding of the mathematical foundation, extend his awareness by identification with and compassion for all life; he
can, then, commit himself to the side of Love by ethical
purity and abstention from killing. "Empedocles," remarks Werner Jaeger, "speaks of all the various forms of
life with the loving inflexion of one who has felt their existence from within, and from whom none of these is any
more remote than he is remote from himself."

Through this, the unitive way, the great soul which has
become a leader of men, master of music, of healing, of
wisdom, may expect to step out of the wheel of rebirth and
be reunited—in a Spinozian sense, we might say—with
the consciousness of the all, or, as he says, to become a
god. The way of Truth is, he insists, "not utterable" (this
is what gave him the tag of a mystic by contrast with
Parmenides the rationalist), but this is mainly because it
contains all the ratios at once, all the laws of number and
harmony, disjoined from the mixtures. Theoretical cogni-

tion from there would again be discursive, bringing them out individually.

Empedocles has been presented too often as an incongruous two-minded figure, a kind of philosophical centaur, half Ionian scientist, half Orphic medicine man. This is hardly fair to one of the most complex thinkers of antiquity, who maintained the highest scientific standards of his time while respecting his religious insight. What he did was to develop unflinchingly the spiritual implications of the Pythagorean doctrine. The functional force of Friendship works itself out as Harmony, and tends to the total unification of all Being. The Parmenidean One is thus revealed, in its impassive rigor, to contain in itself all the infinite variety of nature, but with all its tensions resolved into concord. We might say it is the Heraclitean "hidden harmony" in a Parmenidean setting. Out of it emerges the physical world dominated by Necessity, to which Empedocles gives such a wealth of reasoned observation in zoology and botany as would make strong his claim to be the father of general biology (it is unfortunately the part of the text of which the least survives). He may seem to have revived the mythical and at times preposterous fantasy which went with early Pythagorean theory, but Lucretius, writing at a remove of four centuries, is not deceived by the appearance; he pays to Empedocles the same passionate respect that he considers due to his own atomist masters. He perceives the powerful intellect analyzing the dark ways of nature as it is, with its difficulty and intricacy and struggle and pitiless waste. Many writers in after ages will go on descanting profusely and wearisomely on the beauties of universal harmony, but none will have that profound cosmic sympathy which finds an echo in the strange words of Blake: "I look back into the Regions of Reminiscence and behold our ancient days before this Earth appeared in its vegetated mortality to my mortal vegetated eyes."

Aristotle on his side sniffs reproachfully at Empedocles for mixing up principles: "He identifies the good with love; but he makes of it a principle both as mover and as matter." For us, that is just his merit. The commitment that the soul has to make is at the very core of reality, in matter itself, where it encounters the adverse principle of disunion. It is a tragic choice because Strife is a stern imposition of Necessity, which breaks again and again forever the bonds of attraction to let a world arise. Strife has to be present, as live matter twists and forces its way into being, branches out irresistibly into variety in a vain struggle for completion. It is only the commitment to the side of Friendship, the animating but also the comprehending force, which can give man the theoretical insight, as well as the compassionate understanding, of things wandering forever, as he says, "their several ways along the breakers of the sea of life."

Texts

What has been saved of Empedocles is a hundred and fifty-three fragments totaling about seventeen pages. We give here a selection (with slight changes) from John Burnet's translation. The numbers are those of Diels-Kranz's *Vorsokratiker.*

12. For it cannot be that aught can arise from what in no way is, and it is impossible and unheard of that what is should perish; for it will always be, wherever one may keep putting it.

13. Nor is there any part of the Whole that is empty or overfull.

14. Nor is any part of the whole empty. Whence, then, could aught come to increase it?

16. For, of a truth, they (i.e., Love and Strife) were aforetime and shall be; nor ever, methinks, will boundless time be emptied of that pair.

17. . . . But come, hearken to my words, for it is learning that increaseth wisdom. As I said before, when I declared the heads of my discourse, I shall tell thee a twofold tale. At one time things grew together to be one only out of many, at another they parted asunder so as to be many instead of one; Fire and Water and Earth and the mighty height of Air, dread Strife, too, apart from these and balancing every one of them, and Love among them, their equal in length and breadth. Her do thou contemplate with thy mind, nor sit with dazed eyes. It is she that is deemed to be implanted in the frame of mortals. It is she that makes them have kindly thoughts and work the works of peace. They call her by the names of Joy

and Aphrodite. Her has no mortal yet marked moving among the gods, but do thou attend to the undeceitful ordering of my discourse.

For all these are equal and alike in age, yet each has a different prerogative and its own peculiar nature. And nothing comes into being besides these, nor do they pass away; for, if they had been passing away continually, they would not be now.

20. . . . this marvelous mass of mortal limbs. At one time all the limbs that are the body's portion are brought together into one by Love, and flourish in the high season of life; and again, at another time they are severed by cruel Strife, and wander each in different directions by the breakers of the sea of life. It is the same with shrubs and the fish that make their homes in the waters, the beasts that make their lairs in the hills, and the birds that sail on wings.

23. Just as when painters are elaborating temple-offerings, men whom Metis has well taught their art,—they, when they have taken pigments of many colours with their hands, mix them in a harmony, more of some and less of others, and from them produce shapes like unto all things, making trees and men and women, beasts and birds and fishes that dwell in the waters, yea, and gods, that live long lives, and are exalted in honour,—so let not the error prevail over thy mind, that there is any other source of all the perishable creatures that appear in countless numbers. Know this for sure, for thou hast heard the tale from a goddess.

27. In it is distinguished neither the bright form of the sun, no, nor the shaggy earth in its might, nor the sea,—so fast was the god bound in the close covering of Harmony, spherical and round, rejoicing in his circular rest, (i.e. the Sphairos).

42. (The moon.) And she scatters his rays away into the sky above, and casts a shadow on as much of the earth as is the breadth of the pale-faced moon.

45. It circles round the earth, a borrowed light, as on the track of a car.

56. Salt was solidified by the impact of the sun's beams.

57. It (Love) made many heads spring up without necks, and arms wandered bare and bereft of shoulders. Eyes strayed up and down in want of foreheads.

59. But, as divinity was mingled still further with divinity, these things joined together as each might chance, and many other things beside them continually arose.

60. Shambling oxen with undivided hoofs.

61. Many creatures with faces and breasts looking in different directions were born; some, offspring of oxen with faces of men, while others, again, arose as offspring of men with the heads of oxen, and creatures in whom the nature of women and men was mingled, furnished with sterile parts.

62. Come now, hear how the Fire as it was separated caused the night-born shoots of men and tearful women to arise; for my tale is not off the point nor uninformed. Whole-natured forms first arose from the earth, having a portion both of water and fire. These did the fire, desirous of reaching its like, cause to grow, showing as yet neither the charming form of women's limbs, nor yet the voice and parts that are proper to men.

73. And even as at that time Kypris (Aphrodite), plying her pleasant task, after she had moistened the Earth in water, gave it to swift fire to harden it.

74. The sea with its tuneless tribe of fertile fish.

76. This thou mayest see in the heavy-backed shell-fish that dwell in the sea, in maenae and buccinia and the stony-skinned turtles. In them thou mayest see that the earthy part dwells on the uppermost surface.

79. And so tall trees bear eggs, first of all olives. . . .

82. Hair and leaves, and the thick feathers of birds, and the scales that grow on mighty limbs, are the same thing.

84. And even as when a man, thinking to sally forth through a stormy night, gets him ready a lantern, a flame of flashing fire, fastening to it horn plates to keep out all manner of winds; and they scatter the blast of the winds that blow, but the light leaping out through them shines across the threshold with its unyielding rays inasmuch as it is finer; even so did love surround the elemental fire in the round pupil and confine it with membranes and fine tissues, which are pierced through and through with innumerable passages. They keep out the deep water that surround the pupil, but they let through the fire, inasmuch as it is finer.

93. The bloom of scarlet dye mingles with the gleaming linen.

100. Thus do all things draw breath and breathe it out again. All have bloodless tubes of flesh extended over the surface of their bodies; and at the mouths of these the uttermost surface of the skin is perforated all over with pores closely packed together, so as to keep in the blood while a free passage is cut for the air to pass through. Then, when the yielding blood recedes from these, the bubbling air rushes in

with an impetuous surge; and when the blood runs back it is breathed out again. Just as when a girl, playing with a water-catcher of shining brass, puts the orifice of the pipe upon her comely hand, and dips the water-clock into the yielding mass of silvery water,—the stream does not then flow into the vessel, but the bulk of the air inside, pressing upon the close-packed perforations, keeps it out till she uncovers the compressed stream; but then air escapes and an equal volume of water runs in. Just in the same way, when water occupies the interior of the brazen vessel and the opening and passage is stopped up by the human hand, the air outside, striving to get in, keeps back the water at the gates of the sounding strainer, pressing upon its surface till she lets go with her hand. Then, on the contrary, just in the opposite way to what happened before, the wind rushes in and an equal volume of water runs out to make room. Even so, when the thin blood that surges through the limbs rushes backwards to the interior, straightway the stream of air comes in with a rushing swell; but when the blood returns the air breathes out again in equal quantity.

106. For the wisdom of men grows according to what is before them.

109. For it is with earth that we see Earth, and Water with water; by air we see bright Air, by fire destroying Fire. By love do we see Love, and Hate by grievous hate.

110. For, if thou takest them (things and plants) to the close recesses of thy heart and watchest over them kindly with faultless care, then thou shalt have all these things in abundance throughout thy life, and thou shalt gain many others from them; for each grows ever true to its character, according as its nature is. But if thou strivest after things of a different kind, as is the way with men, ten thousand woes await thee to blunt thy careful thoughts. All at once they will cease to live when the time comes round, desiring each to reach its own kind; for know that all things have wisdom and a share of thought.

115. There is a decree of necessity, an ancient ordinance of the gods, eternal and sealed fast by broad oaths, that whenever one of the daemons, whose portion is length of days, sinfully pollutes his hands with blood, he must wander thrice ten thousand seasons from the abodes of the blessed, being born throughout the time in all manners of mortal forms, changing one toilsome path of life for another. For the mighty Air drives him into the Sea, and the Sea spews him forth on the dry Earth; Earth tosses him into the beams of the blazing Sun,

and he flings him back to the eddies of Air. One takes him from the other, and all reject him. One of these I now am, an exile and a wanderer from the gods, (because I was once) the bondsman of insensate Strife.

117. For I have been ere now a boy and a girl, a bush and a bird and a leaping dumb fish in the sea.

118. I wept and I wailed when I saw the unfamiliar land.

119. From what honour, from what a height of bliss, have I fallen to go about among mortals here on earth.

136. Will ye not cease from this accursed slaughter? See ye not that ye are feasting on one another in the thoughtlessness of your hearts?

8

Doctor vs. Medicine Man

THE DOCTOR WAS a well-defined figure in Greece from the time of Homer; the army surgeons in the *Iliad* are shown applying their skill without any admixture of magic. There is a strong religious element in medicine proper, but it is disciplined by a sect of priestly healers, the Asclepiads, whose famous temple hospitals in Epidaurus, Cos, Croton, and elsewhere remain the chief medical centers well into the Roman Empire. With the rise of Ionian science in the sixth century B.C., there emerges from the Asclepiad background the figure of the lay doctor, using the ideas of his scientific contemporaries to bring in new theories in his art. There is an Ionian school of medicine centered on the two islands of Cnidos and Cos; there is also in Italy a Pythagorean medical school of which we have already met the founder, Alcmaeon, the discoverer of the nervous system.

The interplay between medicine and natural philosophy never ceases. Empedocles, a doctor himself, we have seen, tries to found his art on elaborate physical theory. But with Hippocrates of Cos, who died around 377 B.C., the art is established on its own foundations, inductive skill, and mature clinical experience. Hippocrates is the molder of the figure of the *doctor* as it has been ever since, with its high ethical standards and its professional canons. As time goes on, we feel we know less and less about the historical Hippocrates, under whose name the work of a whole school established itself in tradition. The so-called Hippocratic corpus contains fifty-nine works of different epochs and trends. But the book on *The Sacred Disease,* i.e., epilepsy, which we give here, is generally considered authentic, and so are many of the *Aphorisms,* which became the vade mecum of doctors through the Middle Ages.

Some of them have become common proverbs: "Life is short, art is long, occasion fleeting, experience tricky, judgment difficult." The Hippocratic oath is still taken in our medical schools. The standard pharmacopoeia of a hundred years ago was still largely Hippocratic; and Greek remains even now the technical language of medicine.

The Greeks had a good knowledge of the bones and muscles, and knew how to handle them, thanks largely to the experience of the athletic trainers and surgeons, who were among the most highly paid specialists. Beyond that, their anatomy was hazy. As for their understanding of physiological processes, it could not but be hopelessly inadequate. Ours, too, went on being such until the nineteenth century. But since a theoretical rationale there had to be, they borrowed it from current physical conceptions about the universe. Health, accordingly, was seen as due to a correct balance between the four elements and their cardinal properties, hot, cold, dry, moist. To these corresponded the four "humors": blood, phlegm, yellow bile, and black bile. Our words "temper" and "temperament" still belong to the humoral language; they mean the individual's particular mixture, which could be phlegmatic, bilious, and so on. The four humors, so the theory goes on, are stirred and kept at the right simmer by the vital heat or inborn pneuma (a concept brought in by Empedocles),

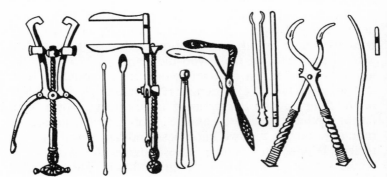

Fig. 11. Surgical instruments unearthed at Pompeii.

operating from the combustion chamber of the heart. Food, as well as pneuma, is brought to the body by arterial blood. The stomach, under the influence of inborn heat, digests or "cooks" the food until it is transmuted into the proper humors. The action of an injurious external agent, by ingestion, heat or cold, brings about an imbalance which is sickness. Whatever has badly coagulated or dissolved or gone wrong has to be brought back to the right temper by heightened "cooking" of the humors on the part of the pneuma, and this appears as fever. The doctor's main role is, then, to cooperate with the "healing force" of nature; his watchword is: "help, or at least do not hinder."

The circulation of the blood is as yet unthought of. The heart is seen as the central feeding chamber which is also the seat of the pneuma. It receives air directly from the lungs to sustain the vital heat, and sends out blood mixed with air and humors to the organism.

With such limited knowledge, there was little the doctor could offer except diet, symptomatic cures, and relief of pain. But, as Hippocrates remarks, right prognosis, that is, telling the patient ahead of time the course of his sickness, is in itself a great help to his morale. The wise clinical eye and the attention to essential symptoms were the doctor's greatest theoretical assets. But, as he insisted, his was not a science; it was an art, built up essentially from apprenticeship and experience. The doctor's chosen pupils were treated by him as his sons and heirs.

The doctor's sober attitude was in strong contrast with the usual luxuriant growth of quackery, magic, superstition, and other "illiberal practices," as Hippocrates calls them, which flourished around people's desperate concern. The old tribal faiths in medicine men and miracle-mongers, which have not died even today, were as strong then as were the old cults and the revived mysteries. The very word *pharmakos* meant the scapegoat which was magically laden with all the sins of the city in times of trouble and then shooed out of the gates. That was still "big medicine."

Of all illnesses, epilepsy, which strikes suddenly and inexplicably, was bound to look most like a visitation from the gods. It was called the "sacred disease." Yet it is on that terrain, where the doctor has no remedy to offer, that

Hippocrates carries the fight against superstition. His little treatise * is a memorable statement of what Nature and natural forces meant to the Greek scientist.

On the Sacred Disease

It is thus with regard to the disease called Sacred: it appears to me to be nowise more divine nor more sacred than other diseases, but has a natural cause from which it originates like other affections. Men regard its nature and cause as divine from ignorance and wonder, because it is not at all like to other diseases. And this notion of its divinity is kept up by their inability to comprehend it, and the simplicity of the mode by which it is cured, for men are freed from it by purifications and incantations. But if it is reckoned divine because it is wonderful, instead of one there are many diseases which would be sacred; for, as I will show, there are others no less wonderful and prodigious, which nobody imagines to be sacred. The quotidian, tertian, and quartan fever seem to me no less sacred and divine in their origin than this disease, although they are not reckoned so wonderful. As I see men become mad and demented from no manifest cause, and at the same time doing many things out of place; and I have known many persons in sleep groaning and crying out, some in a state of suffocation, some jumping up and fleeing out of doors, and deprived of their reason until they awaken, and afterward becoming well and rational as before, although they be pale and weak; and this will happen not once but frequently. And there are many and various things of the like kind, which it would be tedious to state particularly. And they who first referred this disease to the gods, appear to me to have been just such persons as the conjurors, purificators, mountebanks, and charlatans now are, who give themselves out for being excessively religious, and as knowing more than other people. Such persons, then, using the divinity as a pretext and screen of their own inability to afford any assistance, have given out that the disease is sacred, adding suitable reasons for this opinion, they have instituted a mode of treatment which is safe for themselves, namely, by applying purifications and incantations, and enforcing abstinence from

* From *World's Great Sciences in the Original Documents*. Vols. 1–10. Edited by Oliver J. Thatcher. University Research Extension, 1907. *The Greek World*, Vol. 2.

baths and many articles of food which are unwholesome to men in diseases. Of sea substances, the sur-mullet, the black-tail, the mullet, and the eel; for these are the fishes most to be guarded against. And of fleshes, those of the goat, the stag, the sow, and the dog: for these are the kinds of flesh which are aptest to disorder the bowels. Of fowls, the cock, the turtle, and the bustard, and such others as are reckoned to be particularly strong. And of potherbs, mint, garlic, and onions; for what is acrid does not agree with a weak person. And they forbid to have a black robe, because black is expressive of death; and to sleep on a goat's skin, or to wear it, and to put one foot upon another, or one hand upon another; for all these things are held to be hindrances to the cure. All these they enjoin with reference to its divinity, as if possessed of more knowledge, and announcing beforehand other portents; so that if the person should recover, theirs would be the honor and credit; and if he should die, they would have a certain defense, as if the gods, and not they, were to blame, seeing they had administered nothing either to eat or drink as medicines, nor had overheated him with baths, so as to prove the cause of what had happened. But I am of opinion that (if this were true) none of the Libyans, who live in the interior, would be free from this disease, since they all sleep on goats' skins, and live upon goats' flesh; neither have they couch, robe, nor shoe that is not made of goat's skin, for they have no other herds but goats and oxen. But if these things, when administered in food, aggravate the disease, and if it be cured by abstinence from them, then is God not the cause at all; nor will purifications be of any avail, but it is the food which is beneficial and prejudicial, and the influence of the divinity vanishes. Thus, then, they who attempt to cure these diseases in this way, appear to me neither to reckon them sacred nor divine. For when they are removed by such purifications, and this method of cure, what is to prevent them from being brought upon men and induced by other devices similar to these? So that the cause is no longer divine, but human. For whoever is able, by purifications and conjurations, to drive away such an affection, will be able, by other practices, to excite it; and, according to this view, its divine nature is entirely done away with. By such sayings and doings, they profess to be possessed of superior knowledge, and deceive mankind by enjoining lustrations and purifications upon them, while their discourse turns upon the divinity and the godhead. And yet it would appear to me that their discourse savors not of piety, as they suppose, but rather of impiety, and as if there were no gods, and that what they hold to be holy and divine were impious and unholy. This I will now explain. For, if they profess to know how to bring down the moon, and darken the sun, and induce storms and fine weather, and rains, and droughts, and make the sea and land unproductive, and so forth, whether they arrogate this power as being derived from mysteries or any other knowledge or consideration, they appear to me to practice impiety, and either to fancy that there are no gods, or, if there are, that they have no ability to ward off any of the greatest evils. How, then, are they not enemies to the gods? For if a man by magical arts and sacrifices will bring down the moon, and darken the sun, and induce storms, or fine weather, I should not believe that there was anything divine, but human, in these things, provided the power of the divine were over-powered by human knowledge and subjected to it. But per-haps it will be said, these things are not so, but, men being in want of the means of life, invent many and various things, and devise many contrivances for all other things, and for this disease, in every phase of the disease, assigning the cause to a god. . . . But terrors which happen during the night, and fevers, and delirium, and jumpings out of bed, and frightful apparitions, and fleeing away—all these they hold to be the plots of Hecate, and the invasions of the Heroes, and use purifications and incantations, and, as appears to me, make the divinity to be most wicked and most impious. For they purify those laboring under this disease, with the same sorts of blood and the other means that are used in the case of those who are stained with crimes, and of malefactors, or who have been enchanted by men, or who have done any wicked act; who ought to do the very reverse, namely, sacri-fice and pray, and, bringing gifts to the temples, supplicate the gods. . . . Neither truly do I count it a worthy opinion to hold that the body of man is polluted by a god, the most impure by the most holy; for were it defiled, or did it suffer from any other thing, it would be like to be purified and sanctified rather than polluted by the god. For it is the divinity which purifies and sanctifies the greatest of offenses and the most wicked, and which proves our protection from them. And we mark out the boundaries of the temples and the groves of the gods, so that no one may pass them unless he be pure, and when we enter them we are sprinkled with holy water, not as being polluted, but as laying aside any other pollution which we formerly had. And thus it appears to me to hold, with regard to purifications. But this disease seems to me to be nowise more divine than others; but it has its nature such as other diseases have, and a cause whence it originates, and its nature and cause are divine only just as much as all others are, and it is curable no less than the others, unless when, from length of time, it is confirmed, and has become stronger than the remedies applied. Its origin is hereditary, like that of other diseases. . . . And another great proof that it is in nothing more divine than other diseases is, that it occurs in those who are of a phlegmatic constitution, but does not attack the bilious. Yet, if it were more divine than the others, this disease ought to befall all alike, and make no distinction between the bilious and phlegmatic. But in them, the brain is the cause of this affection, as it is of other very great diseases, and in what manner and from what cause it is formed, I will now plainly declare. The brain of man, as in all other animals, is double, and a thin membrane (*meninx*) divides it through the middle, and therefore the pain is not always in the same part of the head; for sometimes it is situated on either side, and sometimes the whole is affected; and veins run toward it from all parts of the body, many of which are small, but two are thick—the one from the liver, and the other from the spleen. And it is thus with regard to the one from the liver: a portion of it runs downward through the parts on the right side, near the kidneys and the psoas muscles, to the inner part of the thigh, and extends to the foot. It is called vena cava. The other runs upward by the right veins and the lungs, and divides into branches for the heart and the right arm. The remaining part of it rises upward across the clavicle to the right side of the neck, and is superficial so as to be seen; near the ear it is concealed, and there it divides; its thickest, largest, and most hollow part ends in the brain; another small vein goes to the right ear, another to the right eye, and another to the nostril. Such are the distributions of the hepatic vein. And a vein from the spleen is distributed on the left side, upward and downward, like that from the liver, but more slender and feeble. By these veins we draw in much spirit for they are the spiracles of our bodies inhaling air to themselves and distributing it to the rest of the body, and to the smaller veins, and they cool and afterwards exhale it. For the pneuma cannot be stationary, but it passes upward and downward, for if stopped and intercepted, the part where it is stopped becomes powerless. In proof of this, when, in sitting or lying, the small veins are compressed, so that the pneuma from the large vein does not pass into them, the part is immediately seized with numbness; and it is so likewise with regard to the other veins. This disease, then, affects phlegmatic persons, but not bilious. It begins to be formed while the foetus is still *in utero*. For the brain, like the other organs, is depurated and grows before birth. If, then, in this purgation it be properly and moderately depurated, and neither more nor less than what is proper be secreted from it, the head is thus in the most healthy condition. If the secretion (melting) from the whole brain be greater than natural, the person, when he grows up, will have his head diseased, and full of noises, and will neither be able to endure the sun nor cold. Or, if the melting take place from any one part, either from the eye or ear, or if a vein has become slender, that part will be deranged in proportion to the melting. . . . But if the defluxion be determined to the heart, the person is seized with palpitation and asthma, the chest becomes diseased, and some also have curvature of the spine. For when a defluxion of cold phlegm takes place on the lungs and heart, the blood is chilled, and the veins, being violently chilled, palpitate in the lungs and heart, and the heart palpitates, so that from this necessity asthma and orthopnea supervene. . . . Such are the symptoms when the defluxion is upon the lungs and heart; but if it be upon the bowels, the person is attacked with diarrhea. And if, being shut out from all these outlets, its defluxion be determined to the veins I have formerly mentioned, the patient loses his speech, and chokes, and foam issues by the mouth, the teeth are fixed, the hands are contracted, the eyes distorted, he becomes insensible, and in some cases the bowels are evacuated. And these symptoms occur sometimes on the left side, sometimes on the right, and sometimes in both. The cause of every one of these symptoms I will now explain. The man becomes speechless when the phlegm, suddenly descending into the veins, shuts out the air, and does not admit it either to the brain or to the vena cava, or to the ventricles, but interrupts the inspiration. For when a person draws in air by the mouth and nostrils, the pneuma goes first to the brain, then the greater part of it to the internal cavity, and part to the lungs, and part to the veins, and from them it is distributed to the other parts of the body along the veins; and whatever passes to the stomach cools, and does nothing more; and so also with regard to the lungs. But the air which enters the veins is of use (to the body) by entering the brain and its ventricles, and thus it imparts sensibility and motion to all the members, so that when the veins are excluded from the air by the phlegm and do not receive it, the man loses his speech and intellect, and the hands become powerless, and are contracted, the blood stopping and not being diffused, as it was wont; and the eyes are distorted owing to the veins being excluded from the air; and they palpitate; and froth from the lungs issues by the mouth. For when the pneuma does not find entrance to him, he foams and sputters like a dying person. . . . The defluxion also takes place in consequence of fear, from any hidden cause, if we are frightened at any person's calling aloud, or while crying, when one cannot quickly recover one's breath, such as often happens to children. When any of these things occur, the body immediately shivers, the person becoming speechless cannot draw his breath, but the pneuma stops, the brain is contracted, the blood stands still, and thus the excretion and defluxion of the phlegm take place. In children, these are the causes of the attack at first. But to old persons winter is most inimical. For when the head and brain have been heated at a great fire, and then the person is brought into cold and has a rigor, or when from cold he comes into warmth, and sits at the fire, he is apt to suffer in the same way, and thus he is seized in the manner described above. And there is much danger of the same thing occurring, if in spring his head be exposed to the sun, but less so in summer, as the changes are not sudden. When a person has passed the twentieth year of his life, this disease is not apt to seize him, unless it has become habitual from childhood, or at least this is rarely or never the case. . . . But when it has gained strength from one's childhood, and become habitual, such a person usually suffers attacks, and is seized with them in changes of the winds, especially in south winds, and it is difficult of removal. For the brain becomes more humid than natural, and is inundated with phlegm, so that the defluxions become more frequent, and the phlegm can no longer be excreted, nor the brain be dried up, but it becomes wet and humid. This you may ascertain in particular, from beasts of the flock which are seized with this disease, and more especially goats, for they are most frequently attacked with it. If you will cut open the head, you will find the brain humid, full of sweat, and having a bad smell. And in this way truly you may see that it is not a god that injures the body, but disease. And so it is with man. For when the disease has prevailed for a length of time, it is no longer curable, as the brain is corroded by the phlegm, and melted, and what is melted down becomes water, and surrounds the brain externally, and overflows it; wherefore they are more frequently and readily seized with the disease. . . . And for these reasons, I say, they are attacked during changes of the winds, and especially south winds, then also with north winds, and afterwards also with the others. These are the strongest winds, and the most opposed to one another, both as to direction and power. For, the north wind condenses the air, and separates from it whatever is muddy and nebulous, and renders it clearer and brighter, and so in like manner also, all the winds which arise from the sea and other waters; for they extract the humidity and nebulosity from all objects, and from men themselves, and therefore it (the north wind) is the most wholesome of the winds. But the effects of the south are the very reverse. For in the first place it begins by melting and diffusing the condensed air, and therefore it does not blow strong at first, but is gentle at the commencement, because it is not able at once to overcome the dense and compacted air, which yet in a while it dissolves.* It produces the same effects upon the land, the sea, the rivers, the fountains, the wells, and on every production which contains humidity, and this, there is in all things, some more, some less. For all these feel the effects of this wind, and from clear they become cloudy, from cold, hot; from dry, moist; and whatever earthen vessels are placed upon the ground, filled with wine or any other fluid, are effected with the south wind, and undergo a change. And the sun, the moon, and the stars it renders blunter in appearance than they naturally are. When, then, it possesses such powers over things so great and strong, and the body is made to feel and undergo changes in the changes of the winds, it necessarily follows that the brain should be dissolved and overpowered with moisture, and that the veins should become more relaxed by the south winds, and that by the north the healthiest portion of the brain should become contracted, while the most morbid and humid is secreted, and overflows externally, and that catarrhs should thus take place in the changes of these winds. Thus is this disease formed and prevails from those things which enter into and go out of the body, and it is not more difficult to understand or to cure than the others, neither is it more divine than other diseases. And men ought to know that from nothing else but thence (*from the brain*) come joys, delights, laughter and sports, and

* In modern language, a "warm front" vs. the "cold front" above.

sorrows, griefs, despondency, and lamentations. And by this, in an especial manner, we acquire wisdom and knowledge, and see and hear, and know what are foul and what are fair, what are bad and what are good, what are sweet, and what unsavory; some we discriminate by habit, and some we perceive by their utility.* By this we distinguish objects of relish and disrelish, according to the seasons; and the same things do not always please us. And by the same organ we become mad and delirious, and fears and terrors assail us, some by night, and some by day, and dreams and untimely wanderings, and cares that are not suitable, and ignorance of present circumstances, desuetude, and unskillfulness. . . . In these ways I am of opinion that the brain exercises the greatest power in the man. This is the interpreter to us of those things which emanate from the air, when it (*the brain*) happens to be in a sound state. But the air supplies sense to it. And the eyes, the ears, the tongue, and the feet, administer such things as the brain cogitates. For inasmuch as it is supplied with air, does it impart sense to the body. It is the brain which is the messenger to the understanding. . . . But the diaphragm has obtained its name (*phrenes*) from accident and usage, and not from reality or nature, for I know no power which it possesses, either as to sense or understanding, except that when the man is affected with unexpected joy or sorrow, it throbs and produces palpitations, owing to its thinness, and as having no belly to receive anything good or bad that may present themselves to it, but it is thrown into commotion ["frenzy"] by both these, from its natural weakness. It then perceives beforehand none of those things which occur in the body, but has received its name vaguely and without any proper reason, like the parts about the heart, which are called auricles, but which contribute nothing towards hearing. Some say that we think with the heart, and that this is the part which is grieved, and experiences care. But it is not so; only it contracts like the diaphragm, and still more so for the same causes. For veins from all parts of the body run to it, and it has valves, so as to perceive if any pain or pleasurable emotion befall the man. For when grieved the body necessarily shudders, and is contracted, and from excessive joy it is affected in like manner. Wherefore the heart and the diaphragm are particularly sensitive, they have nothing to do, however, with the operations

* This theory of the brain opposes the Sicilian school of medicine, which placed thinking in the blood, in addition to holding the other beliefs mentioned below.

of the understanding, but of all these the brain is the cause.
. . . All the most acute, most powerful, and most deadly
diseases, and those which are most difficult to be understood
by the inexperienced, fall upon the brain. And the disease
called the Sacred arises from causes as the others, namely,
those things which enter and quit the body, such as cold, the
sun, and the winds, which are ever changing and are never
at rest. And these things are divine, so that there is no necessity for making a distinction, and holding this disease to be
more divine than the others, but all are divine, and all human.
And each has its own peculiar nature and power, and none
is of an ambiguous nature, or irremediable. And the most
of them are curable by the same means as those by which they
were produced. For any other thing is food to one, and
injurious to another. Thus, then, the physician should understand and distinguish the season of each, so that at one time
he may attend to the nourishment and increase, and at another
to abstraction and diminution. And in this disease as in all
others, he must strive not to feed the disease, but endeavor
to wear it out by administering whatever is most opposed to
each disease, and not that which favors and is allied to it. For
by that which is allied to it, it gains vigor and increase, but
it wears out and disappears under the use of that which is
opposed to it. But whoever is acquainted with such a change
in men, and can render a man humid and dry, hot and cold,
by regimen, could also cure this disease, if he recognizes the
proper season for administering his remedies, without minding
purifications, spells, and all other illiberal practices of a like
kind.

9

Atoms and the Void

WE COME NOW to what has been called by some the most "modern" aspect of Greek science, by others arbitrary and pointless speculation, both premature and immature, subversive of proper regard for the divine, and a foe of all sound philosophy. We mean the atomistic theory.

Leucippus is its inceptor. Tradition makes him born in Miletus, the city of Anaximander. It says that at one time he had belonged to the Eleatic school. This makes the double intellectual descent clear; but of him, beyond that, we know next to nothing, and the theory comes to us as it was worked out by his successor, Democritus (c.460–360 B.C.), surely one of the most original minds of antiquity.

Democritus was of Abdera in Thrace, but Abdera was a colony from the city of Teos, hence of purely Ionian culture. Teos was, in fact, the sister city of Phocaea, and their populations engaged together, rather than submit to the Persians, in the great migration overseas that we have recounted apropos of Parmenides. While the Phocaeans went south to Italy, the Teans went north to Thrace. It is only fair, then, that Democritus should have been Parmenides's worthiest successor, both men bringing into abstract thought the same ruthless decision which had distinguished their mother cities in their vicissitudes.

Aristotle, who is almost at the other pole from Democritus in his thinking, is generous enough to give him ungrudging praise. Democritus was the only one of his predecessors, he says, "who penetrated below the surface to make a thorough examination of the problems of coming-into-being and passing-away. He does seem, however, not only to have thought carefully about all the problems, but also to be distinguished from the outset by his methods."

Democritus was indeed a universal mind who embraced

the whole knowledge of his time, and the loss of his works
is a tragedy of history. We have of him only a few fragments and a group of ethical aphorisms.* Yet we know that
his varied accomplishments included pioneer work in
mathematics, in theories on biological and social evolution, geography, astronomy, meteorology, economics, even
scenography and the interjectional theory of language. He
spent his inherited wealth in traveling far and wide—some
say as far as India. He stopped in Athens, where he must
have met Socrates, who was only ten years older than he.
But as he says, "I went to Athens and no one knew me."
He came back to settle in his home town, honored by the
Abderites as their national "sage," and lived to be over a
hundred. From the stories circulated about him, he
emerges as a crisp, unconventional, sarcastic personality,
who did not suffer fools gladly, but was otherwise of a
cheerful disposition, "for he called Cheerfulness, and often
Confidence, that is a mind devoid of fear, the highest
good."

> Old Democritus under a tree
> Sits on a stone with book on knee;
> About him hang many features
> Of Cats, Dogs, and suchlike creatures,
> Of which he makes Anatomy
> The seat of Black Choler to see.
> Over his head appears the sky
> And Saturn, Lord of Melancholy.

These lines from Burton's *Anatomy of Melancholy* refer
to the story that Hippocrates, the great doctor, Democritus's contemporary, was called in by the Abderites, deeply
concerned about their sage, who seemed to be "acting
queer." After an ironic conversation on the foibles and the
absurdities of mankind, Hippocrates assured the townsmen
that their great man was quite sane, if anything a trifle too
sane for comfort. Such a tale might well be invented about
one who wrote that "he would rather discover one true
cause than gain the kingdom of Persia."

* The authenticity of these aphorisms was long in doubt, but
has been validated by Diels. (Hermann Diels, *Die Fragmente der
Vorsokratiker*, edited by Walther Kranz. Berlin: Weidmann, 1954.
See note B35.)

Leucippus's and Democritus's main idea, if we understand them aright, was, again, after the great intellectual
crisis brought about by Elea, to find a new base for a "reliable" or serious physics; and we mean serious in the
sense in which Anaximander would have meant it. Parmenides could not be ignored, he who was, says Diogenes
Laertius, "the person most talked of in their time"; hence
the need for a physics, if not necessarily certain in its de-
tails, at least "true" in the sense in which Parmenides had
defined Truth: that is, born of logical necessity. Parmenides, it will be remembered, had called his own physics
"opinion" because it could not be rigorously accounted
for. It needed by convention two contrary elements, and
in setting these, he remarked ruefully, we are bound to be
wrong. We have seen how Empedocles tried, with his
Pulsating Universe of four elements and two forces in a
vast biologico-religious construction. The One was there,
but only intermittently. Democritus tried another way,
more stripped and mechanical, but clearer. While Empedocles's attempt had been a desperate adventure with varying
"mixtures," Democritus's mathematical mind tries for a
mixture which should respect throughout the simple and
explicit requirement of "oneness." "If there were a Many,
they should be as the One." Such had been the Eleatic
conclusion. Very well, it could be achieved. In order to
rescue phenomena and have them reveal a rational reality, Democritus projects it, so to speak, on two levels.
Space is one, and matter is one, too, and events are due
to the changing dispositions of matter in space. Empedocles had apparently disregarded (if it had ever reached
him, for there is a question of dates, too) the sharp reasoning of Zeno, which led from total divisibility to the
irrelevance of physical matter. Democritus was mathematician enough to acknowledge its full impact. This led him
to dispose once and for all of the equivocations about particles going into the smaller and smaller, by positing firmly
a threshold of divisibility. Hence we must conceive of matter as composed of mobile elements, all of the same substance but of different forms and sizes; small enough to
bring forth the many things of this world only by aggregat-
ing and coming apart, and also small enough to remain
themselves unbroken or "undivided" in the turmoil, as are

the grains of sand on a wave-lashed beach. "Undivided" is in Greek *átomon,* and it is thus that the key image of modern physics makes its appearance.

Since atoms are the only reality, they move in what must be mere emptiness, and so that other key idea, the "void," has been brought in. The universe, until then, had always been thought of as full, were it only, as in Parmenides, "Being full of Being," the abstract density of the true continuum which was also in some way the body-of-the-world. Here the dichotomy is completed; we have the continuum become what it truly was from the start, geometrical empty space, and in it the one matter, conceived on its part as "wholly full" and compact; but that matter has nothing but geometrical properties itself, derived from space. It has "size, shape, position, and velocity." Nothing else is needed to describe the atom. And there is no more to nature. Atom and *physis* have become interchangeable words in this School. The reduction has been effected to sheer mathematical characteristics. Deduction is again secured from first principles. But this idea of the void is felt at the time as revolutionary. Democritus does not stoop to justifying it. He presents it, characteristically, in the form of a pun: *"Mēdén,* Naught, exists no less than *dén,* Aught," and lets it go at that.

The fact is that atoms and the void have been brought up for reasons which are strictly a priori. Says Aristotle: "Our predecessors . . . could not define reality or conceptual being. Democritus was the first to grasp the method, not, however, as necessary to physical investigation, but he was led up to it by the subject matter." This, considering Aristotle's own bent, is a fair statement, and solid evidence, in the absence of any direct statement from the atomists on the origin of their ideas. The extant scientific fragments of Democritus, as we have said, are miserably few. But each one of them goes straight to the heart of the matter:

Nothing comes about perchance, but all through reason and by necessity. [This is already attributed to his master Leucippus.]

Nothing can be created out of nothing, nor can it be destroyed and returned to nothing.

There is no end to the universe, since it was not created by any outside power.

By convention color, by convention sweet, by convention bitter; in reality nothing but atoms and the void.

Here is the end of the road for the starkest reduction possible to thought: the infinite variety of this world is "in reality nothing but atoms and the void." The mechanism of that reality is only motion and impact. We are told that the technical name for the atom in the School was *rhysmos,* "onrush," so little could it be thought at rest. It was, one might say with a bare transposition of words, an elementary quantum of action.

"Atoms have no weight, but they move by mutual impact in infinite space."

Such is the earliest statement of the inertial principle, a principle so abstract and unfamiliar to ordinary thought that the grasp of it was almost immediately lost. The words "no weight" means that the atoms are not all pulled down one way, but move freely through space any which way until deflected by elastic collision. That Democritus had a clear intuition of the difference between weight and inertial mass, but could not express it for lack of proper terms, is shown by the other, seemingly contradictory statement: "The more an indivisible exceeds, the heavier it is." Mass, in other words, is there and goes with volume; as to the "exceeding," it shows that by the principle of sufficient reason there is no assigned limit to the size of the atom, except for the action of impact, and Democritus is forthright about it: there is no reason, he remarks, why there should not somewhere be atoms as big as a world.

There is also in that compact statement about inertia, another startling novelty, brought in as a matter of course: space is for the first time formally and unequivocally infinite. The argument given is characteristic. "Democritus the Abderite," says Plutarch, "supposed the universe to be infinite because it had not been fashioned by any maker." This is straight sufficient reason, Greek style. Epicurus works out the proof in his own way:

The universe is boundless. For that which is bounded has an extreme point, and the extreme point is seen against something else. So that as it has no extreme point, it has no limit; and as it has no limit, it must be boundless and not bounded. Furthermore, the infinite is boundless both in the number of the bodies and in the extent of the void. For if on the one hand the void were boundless, and the bodies limited in number, the bodies could not stay anywhere, but would be carried about and scattered through the infinite void, not having other bodies to support them and keep them in place by means of collisions. But if, on the other hand, the void were limited, the infinite bodies would not have room wherein to take their place.

The reasoning which proves the infinite extension of space might well backfire into infinite divisibility of matter. But there is a pardonable disinclination to follow it where it might lead in that other direction, for fear, as Epicurus says, of matter melting away into nothingness. Even Descartes, committed as he is to divisibility by his inflexible logic, will have to try for a way around the difficulty.

THEORY OF CHANGE

The image that has been taking shape up to this point is exactly the modern one of the molecules of a gas in thermal motion. It has been, however, derived a priori. The problem is: how, out of this gas, does a world arise? Here Democritus has a device which corresponds, as it were, to a first level of stereochemistry, as we can understand from his commentators:

There are indivisible bodies, infinite both in number and in the varieties of their shapes (although all of the same nature), of which everything else is composed—the compounds differing from each other according to the shapes, positions, and groupings of their constituents. . . . The atoms have all sorts of shapes and appearances and different sizes. . . . Some are rough, some hook-shaped, some concave, some convex, and some have other innumerable variations. . . . The number of shapes among the atoms is infinite because there is no more reason for an atom to be of one shape than another. And this is the cause they assign for the infinity of the atoms. . . . Some of them rebound in random directions, while others interlock because of the symmetry of their shapes, positions, and arrangements, and remain together. This is how compound bodies were begun.

Aristotle, a century later, was able to characterize this type of thinking quite properly, if disapprovingly: "Generation for them is neither of many out of one, nor of one out of many, but consists entirely in the concurrence and entanglement of these bodies. In a way these thinkers too are saying that everything that exists is numbers, or evolved from numbers."

This is so true that Democritus, a brilliant mathematician himself and the originator of infinitesimal analysis, had written a (lost) book *On Pythagoras,* and Thrasyllus, his editor, calls him a straight Pythagorean.* The filiation from Pythagorean thinking is unmistakable, even if the numbers brought in are not connected with the Tetrad, and are all of them practically infinite, and there is no attempt at a mathematical physics. But what the effect could be on most contemporary minds is expressed by Aristotle himself, who does not hide his puzzlement.

They say there is always movement. But why and what this movement is they do not say, nor, if the world moves in this way or that, do they tell us the cause of its doing so. Now nothing is moved at random, but there must always be something present to move it; e.g., as a matter of fact a thing moves in one way by nature, and in another by force or through the influence of reason or something else.

We shall see how difficult it is for Aristotle to grasp, even vicariously, the idea of conservation of momentum, in fact any of the mechanical ideas on which atomism was based. His thinking starts from entirely different foundations and is deeply caught in its own mesh by the time it has to deal with the simplest fact of physics. Hence the difficulties he raises are all irrelevant. Democritus had countered them in advance with a definite statement to which Aristotle himself should have been unable to deny assent:

* There is evidence, which we cannot discuss here, that Democritus studied the problems of the "horn angle," i.e., of the tangent angle formed by one circle touching another from the inside. This takes us into infinitesimals of the second order. The range of his thinking must thus have gone far beyond the text on the volume of the cone that we quote below.

"Of that which ever is and has been there is no reason to inquire for the cause."

But Aristotle does, in fact, deny assent:

> Democritus does not think fit to seek for a first principle to explain this "ever"; so while his theory is right in so far as it is applied to certain individual cases, he is wrong in making it of universal application. Thus, a triangle has its angles always equal to two right angles, but there is nevertheless an ulterior cause of the eternity of this truth, whereas first principles are eternal and have no ulterior cause.

The metaphysician is showing his teeth. The issue is one of first and last things, and has not been decided to the present day. But we can see from the very next sentence how Aristotle has blithely incorporated his opponent's thought:

> Let this conclude what we have to say in support of our contention that there never was a time when there was not motion, and never will be a time when there will not be motion.

As we shall see later, this particular kind of motion is conceived of in the "higher sense," and derived by proper channels from the proper principles. Democritus, in his statement, shows no need for further principles. "What is," here, is purely and simply the one solid matter of which the atoms are composed. It just goes on being. The whole question of "what really is," later to become among philosophers the high science of "ontology," has been put to rest right then and there, with the simple answer: *rhysmos,* matter-in-motion. It may be "ontic" delusion; it may, as Whitehead put it, be "misplaced concreteness," but it will hold in classical physics from Galileo until the advent of electromagnetism, and thus allow investigators to devote their curiosity and their efforts to what that matter *does*. Since the properties of that matter are purely mathematical, it must be investigated by way of mathematical conceptions.

All the rest of phenomenal reality is purely secondary and derivative: color, texture, smell, taste, do not exist in themselves; they are the response of the sense organs to the "inflow" or onrush of atoms. At this point some contemporaries must certainly have made the objection that Aristotle voices later on: Can this account for the variety of combinations in which the components are seen to lose their identity and to become a new substance? Democritus has recourse to the analogy of the alphabet. To quote again from Aristotle:

> The differences among the elements, they say, are three— shape and order and position. For they say the real is differentiated only by "rhythm," and "inter-contact," and "turning"; and of these rhythm is shape, inter-contact is order, and turning is position; for A differs from N in shape, AN from NA in order, H from H in position.

This is excellent use of analogy in constructing physical theory, and it is natural to a Greek for whom *stoicheia* meant both letters and elements in a general sense. Syllables, of course, show the way to molecules, and just as a word is more than the sum of its letters, so the association of atoms can give more than its geometrical base combination, namely, qualities. Aristotle is so impressed by the simile that he adds: "Indeed Tragedy and Comedy are composed of the same letters." But, needless to say, he cannot accept it; his whole thinking is against it, based as it is on different complete substances, on the words without the letters, as it were. Moreover, the phenomena of change in this world seem to him to prove that coming-into-being and passing-away involve true changes of nature. He has therefore to attack the opposite view at its very foundation, that of compounds arising as a mixture of invariant particles:

> Components that have been mixed in particle form cannot be called a true mixture [what we would call a compound], for each part of the result (if we divide far enough) will not show the same proportion between the components as the whole substance. . . . But we maintain that, if combination has taken place, the compound must be uniform in texture throughout—just as any part of water is water; whereas, if combination is juxtaposition of small particles, the constituents will be combined only relatively to perception; the same

thing will be "combined" to one percipient, if his sight is not sharp, while to the eye of Lynceus nothing will be combined.

Let us note, *en passant,* this mention of Lynceus, the Argonaut who could see farther than other men. The challenge will be picked up two thousand years later by Galileo's circle, the founders of the Lyncean Academy.

But Aristotle, who represents here what we might call the point of view of the chemist, has no doubt a very strong point, and his criticism is taken up again by Theophrastus, who has in mind the change of juices in plants and such things as fermentation:

It is not clear how Democritus would have us conceive the creation of different kinds of juices from one another . . . since it is impossible for atoms to change their shape, there remain two possibilities: either some enter while others go out, or some remain, while others depart.

Since Aristotle believes in matter as a continuum, he has to have recourse to his distinction (of which more later) between "potential" and "actual" existence:

Since some things exist actually and others potentially, it is possible that the components of the true mixture exist in this latter sense, without actually existing. Actually, the mixture will be different from its components, whereas potentially each one of them will be just as it was before the mixing and both will exist indestructibly.

What Aristotle supposes, as set forth in his book, *On Generation and Corruption,* is that the components act on each other, each making the other somewhat like itself, and that true mixture is this kind of unification. His fundamental conception, still Empedoclean, is that things act on one another only because they are "other," whereas for Democritus, he remarks, "it is not in so far as they are other that this happens, but in so far as they are the same." The possibility of an "otherness" represented by pure motion escapes him, for he has his own theory of motion that he considers as much more advanced, as we shall see. It would lead to a not uninteresting way of approaching the problems of chemical reaction, were it not that Aristotle shows that he cannot get his mind away from ordinary mixture, such as wine and water. If there is a preponderance of water, he says, "the result is not a mixture, but the increase of the dominant component. . . . Hence a drop of wine does not mingle with ten thousand pitchers of water; instead, it loses its identity and merges with the whole volume of water."

This kind of thinking is obviously inspired by homely common sense and the social analogy, for it is fairly true that a compact group of a million people may obliterate a lone foreign element. But it does not belong to physics. Aristotle might have heeded Anaxagoras's dictum that "appearances are a way for seeing into the invisible." Democritus had taken care to distinguish: "There are," he said, "two forms of knowledge, the genuine or legitimate, and the obscure or illegitimate." This last comprises the sense data. "The other, legitimate form, is wholly distinct from those." It is, clearly, the mind's eye, which discerns only atoms controlled by necessity: "When the illegitimate way can no longer see or hear or taste or feel, and we have to go into the finer and subtler, then it is replaced by the legitimate, which possesses sharper instruments of knowledge."

Here is no deflection, no concession made to the sensuous world in which we live and breathe or to the many ways we cope with it in words and intuitions. The intellect pierces relentlessly down "towards the finer" in search of the invariants, the true objects of thought. The gradualness that people *saw* in water coloring itself with wine is an illusion, as is the color itself. The molecules of wine are pursued in their discreteness "with the eye of Lynceus" below the threshold of the sensible.

"No experimental proof of that discontinuity was possible, hence we are dealing here not with science, but with philosophy." This has been the too-oft-repeated judgment of historians of science who ought to know better. On the other side, curiously enough, we have philosophers denying Democritus's admission to their guild, because he was not interested enough, it seems, in the complexity of things; and this stricture is echoed in the late legend according to which the Abderite put out his eyes in order not to be diverted from his abstract speculation.

One wonders what both camps, but more especially the historians of science, would make of Galileo's straightforward acceptance of that philosophy:

> I never was thoroughly satisfied about this substantial transmutation whereby a matter becomes so transformed that it is necessarily said to be destroyed, so that nothing remains of its first being, and another body quite differing from it should be then produced. If I fancy to myself a body under one aspect, and by and by under another very different, I cannot think it impossible but that it may happen by a simple transposition of parts without corrupting or engendering anything anew.

When Galileo wrote this, Dalton and Avogadro were two centuries away, and yet another century was to pass before the first experimental confirmations of the atom. It is hard to deny, then, that such *is* the way of science— and by "way" we do not mean *method,* certainly not what is understood now as such, but what in the old Biblical phrase is "the way of a man with a maid." Or shall we call it by its good old name, natural philosophy, meeting with Democritus her first road block, and hence soon to be abandoned by the minds in quest of "ampler" comprehension. It only needed instruments to help her penetrate "into the finer." With a hawk eye and a free mind, one could already guess the mountains of the moon, and Democritus did it.

Another right intuition, if on the wrong scale, is the interpretation of the dancing motes in a sunbeam as showing the underlying "Brownian motion" of the air particles. That visible motion is due, as we know, to small convection currents, but in 1906 the ultramicroscope was to bring confirmation on the right scale (after all, even in the nineteenth century, the existence of atoms became established only through inference). And finally comes the right idea on the right scale, as shared by Democritus and Anaxagoras: The Milky Way is an assemblage of stars, but "owing to the distance they seem to be one, as when grains of salt are thickly sprinkled." Then the demon of Sufficient Reason drives them on to more chancy generalizations: the sky would all look like that, were it not that the sun's beams spreading into space from below the earth obliterate the weaker stars, and what we see as the Milky Way is only the track of the earth's shadow. Such are the pitfalls to be expected. We should not omit, on the other hand, Democritus's striking theories concerning the solid state. Why is lead softer than iron and yet heavier? Because iron is a lattice of strong but lacunar structure, while the atoms of lead are evenly packed.

When it comes to chemistry and biology, atomism is brought down inevitably to a game of blind man's buff. The prickly taste of acids is supposed to show the angularity of their atoms, and so on. We recognize here Democritus's principle that touch is the basic sensation, but it can be worked out only on a level which is close to mere common sense. In this reality which had been imagined as statistical (without knowing the word, or even the idea), there was little point in asking for particular explanations. It was enough that one could imagine a multitude of ways equally plausible for something to happen, so long as the principle stood: only out of atoms and the void.

Where atomism regains full scope and power is in cosmological speculation. Atoms collide, some of them become entangled, a whirl is born, which grows in size, with the massive agglomeration at the center. This persists until some heavier impact scatters it. As to how differentiation takes place within the mass, Democritus explains it with the old principle, "like to like," but taken mechanically. He points to the uniform sizes of pebbles on the shore, of grains coming from a sieve. These components are separated by the whirl into groups of similars; what was confusion becomes an order. Such was the manner of the creation of our world, and of innumerable others which arise in infinite space.

The worlds differ from one another in size and structure. Some have no sun and no moon, others have them larger than ours and more numerous. Some worlds are without animals, plants, or moisture. Some are close together in space, others widely scattered. Anything can arise out of the same components, according to what we call the laws of chance.

CHANCE AND NECESSITY

It is significant that in dealing with this, which we would call random disposition, Democritus makes no concession to chance. Statistical probability is implicit in his thinking, but it never comes into focus. "Chance" for the Greek, as we saw, means what is capricious, arbitrary, without reason, like luck; whereas the atoms move only "by reason and necessity." Mechanical determinism leaves no leeway to chance, even if it is impossible for us to predict any particular occurrence in the multitude of motions. What we can say is simply that the whole is bound to remain as it is: a steady-state physics.

The origin of our world system is conceived along the lines of the Anaximandrian vortex, but with the added freedom of molecular motions. The Earth was small at the beginning, and tossed around freely in the whirl, then as it gained weight it stayed in the center. The Sun grew in the same way by sweeping up fiery atoms projected to the periphery until it became a glowing mass; the moon is like the Earth but smaller; its nature is shown by the shadows thrown by its mountains; it has glens and valleys also. As for the origin of life, Democritus, like Anaximander, saw it arise out of the primeval slime. His theory is still perforce arbitrary, but he does not shun the detailed issues. The part of water in maintaining life; the growth of teeth, horns, and quills; the spider's ability to weave a web; the "wavelike" locomotion of caterpillars; the bones of the eagle; the crowing of cocks before dawn; the owl's ability to see at night—many such features were discussed by Democritus in a book of which Aristotle was to make use, albeit critically. It must have been far less comprehensive than his own, since it concentrated on explaining (or trying to explain) particular phenomena instead of describing the whole context. But it remains as the first treatise on biology.

What Democritus underlined, true to his monistic presupposition, was the continuity between animal and man. He characterized instinct as a truer guide than man's appetite, and reminded us that we are the pupils of the animals in the most important arts: spinning, building, singing. What was more difficult to explain, in his scheme, is what to other philosophers has seemed so simple: whence intel-lect, logic, moral feeling? How is it that we, an assemblage of atoms caught in the universal flow, can form an idea of truth and freedom?

MAN AND COSMOS

Democritus's answer is unafraid and consequent. The organism is a self-preserving system, "a little world," closed, tight-knit in its internal vibrations and circulations, in which highly mobile "soul-atoms" insure the liaison. It opposes to the outside a consistent surface, which receives the confused outer rush through the pores and the senses. These are as it were a screen, a breakwater between the open sea and the port enclosure. The outside waves set up smaller waves inside. These are the reactions, in prin-ciple just as confused; as they combine with our "disposi-tion," we have an inner "changing pattern." The outside impacts, by themselves, may set up resonances strong enough to disorganize us and tear us apart. But the or-ganism must know how to react and behave coherently; the one sense which guides the others is the sense of touch, since it apprehends large-scale reality directly in its spatial context. So far, this applies to all animals. Then comes the specific activity of man in decoding the sense messages and filtering out the "noise." Health, physical and mental, might be described then as the result of a moving, maneu-verable balance of impacts on both sides of a semiper-meable screen.

Here again, while dealing with an unpredictable game of "changing patterns," Democritus is scornful of chance and luck:

Men have fashioned themselves an idol out of Chance as a cloak for their lack of counsel. For chance opposes good judgment; most of life's tangles a keen and intelligent penetra-tion straightens out.

The Christian writer to whom we owe the quotation, Bishop Dionysius, adds this bewildered comment:

He starts from an empty principle and an erroneous hypoth-esis . . . and considers the observation of vain and random occurrences to be the highest wisdom; so he enthrones Luck as queen of divine things and of things in general, declaring that all things occur by her command; but he denies that she governs the lives of men.

There was more in another fragment which could well have puzzled the worthy Bishop:

For the gods grant to men all that is good, now and ever; what is bad, wrong, and useless they give not, but men blunder into it through delusion and ignorance.

What may have been the role of the gods in a nature defined as "ruler of herself" we are left to guess. So is Aristotle: "There are some to whom chance seems to be a cause, but a cause obscured from human understanding as something divine and mysterious." Maybe so, or maybe it had been only a manner of speaking. We know that Democritus thought that mind and soul are the same, that they are atoms of identical nature as fire and light, and that there is a kind of "seeding" of souls around in the air, a conception very much akin to the Universal Fire of Heraclitus, and which has its roots in the hylozoistic past. We also know that he took the existence of gods and demons for granted, since people have visions of them; and in his absolutely objective world this implied the emission of *eidola,* or real images. Such visions, he said, can be good or bad, and some are known to predict the future. He for himself prayed that he should never meet with any but good visions. All this can be explained by a unitary theory of perception spread from high to low throughout the universe, as a property of the fiery atoms. The mirror which reflects an image "sees" in its own way, but it has no consciousness to register its seeing; other more complex entities may "see" more than we do. We have here an elementary prefiguration of Leibniz's monadic theory, which was revived in our time by that other adventurous and very modern mind, C. S. Peirce. As far as Democritus's thought goes, all of this would hardly give the gods any cosmothetic role, but it suggests a universe populated with soul, and "soul and mind are one." Because his thought was clear, there is no reason to assume that it was also flat, and that a Greek of the fifth century B.C. could be a materialist on our eighteenth-century pattern.

One certainty, in any case, stands firm with him, that he shared with all his great predecessors: Truth is not otherworldly but is of this world. Wisdom does not lie in turning away from appearances but in mastering them. Good and bad are not in things, for they can act on us in different and even contrary ways, according to the manner they are "passed through" in the organism. What counts is the correct selecting and tuning, which adjusts outward influences to our good and ensures the autonomy and the impassive peace in which the intellect has free play to "reflect" outside reality. If there is an invariant reality underlying change, the subtle or "legitimate" knowledge able to penetrate to it will reflect its invariance in us, and its many aspects too. "Happiness does not reside in strength or money; it lies in rightness and many-sidedness." Such is the physicist's garden of Eden.

The advice that Democritus gives to his readers stresses generosity, high-mindedness, good sense, and the golden mean. It is willing to go down to homely realism and to astringent simplicity:

If you build a wall around your estate, it may cost more than the estate can bear.

He that contradicts and keeps on talking is unfitted to learn what he should.

Water can be both good and bad, useful and dangerous. To the danger, however, a remedy has been found: learning to swim.

But where the sage is concerned, his advice becomes rigorous. "It is godlike ever to think on something beautiful and on something new." It is not enough to abstain from evil; one should abstain from thought or word about it, for "words are the shadows of action." The penetration of thought requires an ethic of perfection. The edifice of knowledge is not based for him, as for us, on experimental conquests common to all; it relies only on that initial insight which shows us the One in time and space, an insight attained only by the impassive intellect organized for clarity and disdaining illusion. True wisdom is, if not self-blinding, certainly ascetic.

This may lead us to reverse somewhat the first impression generated by Democritus's crusty wisdom and by the character fastened on him as the "laughing philosopher." The point deserves attention, for it is with him that the idea of the "hard-boiled scientific mind" enters the commonplaces of culture. But if we are not carried along by his gruff affectation, we may discern in many of his sayings a sensitive perception, an aching awareness of the evils and sufferings of this world, which may have driven him to steel himself and to seek refuge in the intellect.

THEORY OF KNOWLEDGE

Democritus's explanations may be at times simple-minded in an archaic way, as when he explains visions by material "images," floating molecular layers, as it were, which detach themselves from bodies and enter the eye. But his position in the theory of knowledge, if uncompromisingly monistic, is also restrained and critical to a point which makes him sound strikingly modern. One of his aphorisms has become a classic tag: "Truth is at the bottom of a pit." At least we know where it is. The time may come for its "exantlation," as Sir Thomas Browne calls it; that is, for pumping it out of the deep. There is no radical distinction between mind and matter, truth and phenomena, no spiritual transcendence in the act of knowledge, for reality is all one. Atoms are real; so are the sense messages elicited by their impact, which are the appearances; the opinions that we derive are real, too. They can only be more or less misleading. There is no problem of what we know, but of how much we know. In an ironic statement that has been preserved by Galen, Democritus makes the senses put the mind in its place: "You poor judgment; you get your evidence from us and want to overthrow us with it? Your victory would be your downfall." But the senses give us messages that are understandable only by convention; they have to be decoded in our code. What they do receive directly is only the vast outside cosmic noise, the "ever-changing pattern."

Man must know that he is far removed from how things really are.

And it will be clear that it is most difficult to know how each thing is in reality.

There is an undertone of sadness here, unmistakably, as the tireless encyclopedist reviews his past effort. But it is not despair. For there remains the foundation of "legitimate" knowledge, which does not come from the senses, and pierces to the ultimate reality. (Whence does it come? Democritus does not tell us, any more than does Parmenides. Perhaps from the atoms of soul, "like to like.") But it is a priori, abstract and categoric; it answers the problem of the One and the Many, by showing them to us in space and matter.

There shines through all this the old rugged Ionian simplicity, of which Democritus is the last late representative. He did not care to ask, any more than did Parmenides: "How, by what means, do we know the One?" The old idea of "reflecting" the truth becomes strained. He left it to the work of atoms, in some recondite way. One misses in him the firm ratios and the distinct forms of Empedocles, the articulation of reality and design which makes things be and stay different from each other. But then he knew how far this kind of search would take him into the equally undemonstrable.

As things stand we perceive nothing that is reliable, but only what changes according to our constitution and to the onrushing or counteracting patterns.

This pronouncement might be taken up again, at the new subatomic level, by today's physicist. It is quoted from a lost late work entitled *Confirmations,* which would be enough to show the difference between this kind of critical *skepsis* and the radical skepticism of later times. Democritus may well emphasize his agnosticism, but if someone like John Donne were to echo his thoughts in the melancholy spiritual key: "Poor soule, in this thy flesh what wouldst thou know?" he would probably reply, in his brusque way: "If you'd keep that messy soul of yours in good trim, quite a lot; in fact, all that you really need to know."

From the *Aphorisms*

1. Culture is an adornment for the fortunate, and a refuge for the unfortunate.

2. Neither their bodies nor their wealth make men happy, but rectitude and much contemplation.

3. It is a great thing in misfortunes to think as one ought.

4. Repentance for shameful deeds is the salvation of life.

5. The envious man inflicts pain on himself as though he were an enemy.

6. The rearing of children is full of pitfalls. Success is attended by strife and care, failure means grief beyond all others.

7. Nature and instruction are similar; for instruction transforms the man, and in transforming, creates his nature.

8. More men become good through practice than by nature.

9. A year without feasts is like a long road without inns.

10. Man is a universe in little (*microcosm*).

11. The wrongdoer is more unfortunate than the man wronged.

12. Magnanimity consists in enduring tactlessness with mildness.

13. Many much-learned men have no intelligence.

14. Life is not worth living for the man who has not even one good friend.

15. It is proper, since we are human beings, not to laugh at the misfortunes of others, but to mourn.

16. (Inside, we are) a complex storehouse and treasury of ills, with many possibilities of suffering.

17. . . . wranglers and noose-twisters . . .

18. In a shared fish, there are no bones (i.e., what is shared in friendship is wholly good).

19. The cheerful man, who is impelled towards works that are just and lawful, rejoices by day and by night, and is strong and free from care. But the man who neglects justice, and does not do what he ought, finds all such things disagreeable when he remembers any of them, and he is afraid and torments himself.

20. . . . Images conspicuous for their dress and ornament, empty of heart.

21. People are fools who hate life and yet wish to live through fear of Hades.

22. Imperturbable wisdom is worth everything.

23. People are fools who live without enjoyment of life.

24. Freedom of speech is the sign of freedom; but the danger lies in discerning the right occasion.

25. Do not say or do what is base, even when you are alone. Learn to feel shame in your own eyes much more than before others.

26. To a wise man, the whole earth is open; for the native land of a good soul is the whole earth.

27. Poverty under democracy is as much to be preferred to so-called prosperity under an autocracy as freedom to slavery.

28. Democritus advised to learn the statesmanship and political wisdom of men like Parmenides and Melissus as the highest achievement, and to take on the labor from which come the great and splendid things for men.

29. One must not respect the opinion of other men more than one's own; nor must one be more ready to do wrong if no one will know than if all will know. One must respect one's own opinion most, and this must stand as the law of one's soul, preventing one from doing anything improper.

30. There is no means under the present constitution by which magistrates can be prevented from wrongdoing, however good they may be. For it is not likely for anyone else (any more) than for oneself, that he will show himself the same man in different circumstances. But we must also make arrangements to see that if a magistrate does no wrong, and convicts wrongdoers, he shall not fall under the power of the latter; rather, a law or some other means must defend the magistrate who does what is just.

31. A woman is far sharper than a man in malign thoughts.

32. I alone know that I know nothing.

The works of Democritus having been lost, we have to depend on references, of which those of Aristotle and Theophrastus his pupil are the most reliable. Some approximation to the detailed treatment of Democritus himself may be had from Theophrastus's paraphrase of his theory of vision and color. Theophrastus maintains a critical attitude throughout, but he is a true historian of science, the earliest in date, and usually more respectful of the texts than Aristotle, who often forces their meaning to make them serve as steppingstones to his system.

Scientific Texts *

1. [This is the first challenge to infinitesimal analysis.] If a cone were cut by a plane parallel to the base, what ought one to think of the surfaces resulting from the section: are they equal or unequal? If they are unequal, they will make the cone have many steplike indentations and unevennesses; but if they are equal, the sections will be equal, and the cone will appear to have the same property as a cylinder, being made up of equal, not unequal, circles, which is most absurd.†

2. . . . Posidonius the Stoic and Dionysius say the inhabited earth is shaped like a sling, but Democritus asserts it is oblong.

3. . . . From the autumnal equinox to the winter solstice is by Eudoxus' calculation 92 days; Democritus makes it 91. From the winter solstice to the spring equinox, both Eudoxus and Democritus count 91 days, Euctemon 92.

4. As the snow in the north melts under the summer sun and flows away, clouds are formed from the vapour. When these are driven south toward Egypt by the monsoons, violent storms arise and fill the lakes and the Nile.

5. (From Proclus.) . . . Pythagoras says it is not any chance person who can give names to things, but only he who sees mind and the nature of things. Names, therefore, exist by nature. But Democritus by four lines of argument develops the conclusion that names are conventional. First, equivocation, where different things are called by the same name, hence the name is not by nature. Second synonymy. For if different names apply to one and the same thing, they would also apply to each other which is impossible. Third, the exchange of names; for if names were by nature, why did we call Aristocles Plato and Tyrtamus Theophrastus? Fourth, missing derivatives; for why is it that the verb "to think" comes from the noun "thought," while from the noun "jus-

---

* Translated by Dr. Gordon H. Clark in *Selections from Early Greek Philosophy,* edited by Milton Charles Nahm, *op. cit.* Reprinted by permission of Appleton-Century-Crofts.
† Archimedes tells us that Democritus gave the volumes of the cone and pyramid; see p. 240.

tice" no verb is derived? Hence names exist by chance and not by nature. . . .

6. (From Aristotle.) . . . But not entirely like Democritus. For he held that soul and mind are absolutely the same and that appearance is truth. Therefore Homer did well in making "Hector prostrate thinking other thoughts." So he does not use mind as a potentiality for truth, but affirms that soul and mind are the same. . . . To some it seemed to be fire, for this is the finest and least corporeal of the elements, and further it excels in being moved and in causing motion. And Democritus has spoken very elegantly in explaining each of these phenomena; for soul and mind are the same. And this is that group of the primary, indivisible bodies which produce motion by their minute parts and shape. Now the most mobile of shapes is the sphere, he says; and such is mind and fire. . . . He said fire was incorporeal, not strictly incorporeal (for none of them said this), but corporeally incorporeal on account of the fineness of its parts. . . . Some say the soul moves the body in which it is as it itself is moved, for example when Democritus uses the same idea as Philippus the comic poet who said, Daedalus made the wooden Aphrodite move by pouring in mercury. Democritus speaks in a similar vein when he says, the indivisible spheres are in motion because by nature they can never be still, and so they draw along and set in motion the whole body.

7. (From Lucretius.) On this point, do not accept the theory of the reverend Democritus that the body atoms and soul atoms alternate and so bind our members together.

8. . . . How many senses are there? Democritus says that the senses are more numerous than the sensibles, but since the sensibles do not correspond to the number of senses we are not aware of the fact. . . . Because they are so fine, the mind cannot perceive them clearly, unless it makes a decided effort.

9. Brutes, sages, and gods have more than five senses.

10. Democritus says all things possess a soul of some sort, even corpses, because they clearly always share in a certain warmth and power of sensation, though the greater part disperses in air. . . . Dead bodies perceive, as Democritus thought.

11. (From Aristotle.) When Democritus says that it is water by which we see he speaks well, but when he thinks that sight is the reflection, not so well——However, in general, it seems nothing much was made clear on the subjects of re-

fraction and reflections. And it is strange that he did not think of asking why the eye alone can see, but not other things in which the reflections appear.*

12. (From Theophrastus, *On the Causes of Plants.*) When Democritus explains that straight plants bloom and die sooner than crooked ones because of the same necessary processes (for the nourishment on which the blossom and fruit depend is more quickly diffused through the straight plant, while in the other case more slowly because its tracheal tubes are constricted, and the roots themselves get the benefit, for the roots of these plants are both long and thick) he does not seem to be correct. For he says that the roots of the straight plants are weak and for a double reason they break and the plant is destroyed; for both cold and heat descend quickly from the top to the roots because of the easy progress, and since the roots are weak they cannot withstand the shock. In general many plants of this type begin to age from the bottom on account of the weakness of their roots. And further, the aerial parts because they are so slim are twisted by the winds and so disturb the roots. This results in harm and breakage and so decay attacks the whole tree. This, at any rate, is his account of the matter.

13. (From Alexander of Aphrodisias.) (Why the lodestone attracts iron.) Democritus himself asserts that emanations arise and that like moves toward like, although everything moves toward the void also. On this basis he holds that the magnet and the iron are composed of similar atoms, the magnet however of finer atoms, more widely spaced, and inclosing more void than the iron. Therefore, since its atoms are more easily moved, they move faster to the iron (for motion proceeds toward the like), and entering the pores of the iron they set its component bodies in motion by slipping through them on account of their fineness. The bodies so set in motion leave the iron as an efflux and move toward the magnet, both because of the similarity in particles and because the magnet has more void. Then by reason of the wholesale egress of the bodies and their motion, the iron itself follows them and is also carried to the magnet. But the magnet does not move toward the iron because the iron does not have as many void spaces as the magnet. But granted that iron and lodestone are composed of like particles, how about amber and chaff? When

* This last is a typical misunderstanding of Democritus's position, as we tried to show in the text; see p. 156.

anyone offers the same explanation for this case also, it must be recalled that amber attracts many things. Now if amber is composed of the same particles as all these, then the latter also are composed of similar particles and should attract each other.

14. The simple colours, he says, are four. What is smooth is white; since what neither is rough nor casts shadows nor is hard to penetrate—all such substances are brilliant. But brilliant substances must also have open passages and be translucent. Now white substances that are hard have the structure just described—for instance, the inner surface of cockle shells; for the substance here would be shadowless, "gleaming," and with straight passages. But the white substances that are loose and friable are composed of round particles, yet with these placed oblique to one another and oblique in their conjunction by pairs, while the arrangement as a whole is uniform in the extreme. With such a structure these substances are loose because their particles are in contact only over a small portion of their surface; friable, because their composition is so uniform; shadowless, because they are smooth and flat. But those substances are whiter, compared with one another, in which the figures are more exactly as described above and are freer from admixture with other figures and whose order and position more nearly conform to the given description. From such figures, then, is white derived.

Black is composed of figures the very opposite to those of white—figures rough, irregular, and differing from one another. For these cast shadows, and the passages amongst them are not straight nor easy to thread. Their effluences, too, are sluggish and confused; for the character of the effluence also makes a difference in the inner presentation, as this emanation is changed by its retention of air.

Red is composed of figures such as enter into heat, save that those of red are larger. For if the aggregations be larger although the figures are the same, they produce the quality of redness rather than of heat. Evidence that redness is derived from such figures is found in the fact that we redden as we become heated, as do other things placed in the fire until they have a fiery colour. Those substances are redder that are composed of large figures—for example, the flame and coals of green wood are redder than those of dry. And iron, too, and other things placed in fire become redder. Those are most luminous, however, that contain the most fire and the subtilest, while those are redder that have coarser fire and less of it. Redder things, accordingly, are not so hot; for what is subtile is hot.

Green is composed of both the solid and the void—the hue varying with the position and order of these constituents.

Such are the figures which the simple colours possess; and each of these colours is the purer the less the admixture of other figures. The other colours are derived from these by mixture.

Golden and copper-colour and all such tones, for instance, come from white and red, their brilliance being derived from the white, their ruddiness from the red component; for in combination the red sinks into the empty spaces of the white. Now if green be added to white and red, there results the most beautiful colour; but the green component must be small, for any large admixture would not comport with the union of white with red. . . .

Woad hue is composed of deep black and golden green, but with the major "portion" black. Leek green is of crimson and woad, or of golden green and purplish. . . . [For sulphur colour is of this character, with a dash of brilliance.] Indigo is a mixture of woad and fiery red, with round figures and figures needle-shaped to give a gleam to the colour's darkness.

Brown is derived from golden green and deep blue; but if more of the golden green be mixed, flame-colour is the result; for the blackness is expelled because the golden green is shadowless. And red, too, when mixed with white, gives almost a "pure" golden green, and not a black; which accounts for the fact that plants at first are of such a green before there is a heating and dispersion.

Many other aspects of atomistic theory are preserved for us intact, and with passionate belief, by Lucretius (c. 60 B.C.). Three centuries have passed, in which the Epicurean school has taken over the doctrine. Some of the scientific principles, like inertia, have been lost, the materialistic issue has been sharpened, but the mode of explanation remains remarkably consistent.

> The winds are sightless bodies and naught else—
> Since both in works and ways they rival well
> The mighty rivers, the visible in form.
> Then too we know the varied smells of things
> Yet never to our nostrils see them come;
> With eyes we view not burning heats, nor cold,

Nor are we wont men's voices to behold.
Yet these must be corporeal at the base,
Since thus they smite the senses: naught there is
Save body, having property of touch.
And raiment, hung by surf-beat shore, grows moist,
The same, spread out before the sun, will dry;
Yet no one saw how sank the moisture in,
Nor how by heat off-driven. Thus we know,
That moisture is dispersed about in bits
Too small for eyes to see.

Why what was black of hue an hour ago
Can of a sudden like the marble gleam,—
As ocean, when the high winds have upheaved
Its level plains, is changed to hoary waves
Of marble whiteness: for, thou mayst declare,
That, when the thing we often see as black
Is in its matter then commixed anew,
Some atoms rearranged, and some withdrawn,
And added some, 'tis seen forthwith to turn
Glowing and white. But if of azure seeds
Consist the level waters of the deep,
They could in nowise whiten: for however
Thou shakest azure seeds, the same can never
Pass into marble hue.*

* From *On the Nature of Things;* A Metrical Translation by
William Ellery Leonard. London: J. M. Dent & Sons, Ltd.; New
York: E. P. Dutton and Co., Inc. (Everyman's Library, D-7.)
Reprinted by permission of the publishers.

10

Man the Difficult Measure

NO GREATER CONTRAST can be imagined than that between Empedocles, the Orphic prophet, and the other Sicilian, Gorgias, who listened to him in order to learn the true art of presentation. For Gorgias moved to Athens in 427, the year when Plato was born, as ambassador of his city to the rising Athenian empire, and soon he became the undisputed master of rhetoric and disputation. But there was no thought in his mind about the Universe and its fate. Or rather, there was the decision not to be hypnotized by such problems. What he taught was public speaking and how one could, if needed, make "the weaker argument succeed." About the same time another visitor was causing a stir, who came from Abdera and was known to disagree vividly with Democritus; it was Protagoras, who professed to teach to ambitious young men the art of political leadership. His fees, like those of Gorgias, were stiff: over $1,000 for the course. Clearly the times had changed. One could hardly imagine the old masters of natural philosophy taking money in exchange for wisdom.

Yet the evolution was natural enough. Athens, after her victory in the Persian wars, was the "leading nation" in Greece, and fast outstripping her rivals in greatness and variety of achievements. Something like it happened in the Renaissance, when England went through the Elizabethan transformation that made of her a great sea power. Educated talent was at a premium in all ranks of the Athenian citizenry. The forensic bent which went with city-state politics was being offered an alluring new instrument in the logical techniques invented by Zeno, which were bewildering enough to leave the opponent without a comeback, and seemed particularly effective in dealing with encrusted prejudice or privilege. It was natural, then, that the new philosophical problem should arise: what type of education leads to excellence? In modern times, too, the democratization of public life, the growing economy, have raised the same urgent questions once again. Only at this stage of development are such problems as those of freedom and authority, of education for citizenship and education for leadership, conceived and answered. The power of reason was made manifest through eloquence, and the "excellence" that seemed most desirable was the power of persuading. Intellectual power and oratorical ability appeared interchangeable. A new type of intellectual, the "sophist" or skilled teacher, arose in answer to the demand. The old ideal of aristocratic excellence, *aretē,* had been understood as virtue; hence conservative-minded citizens, of whom Socrates was one, were asking scornfully whether virtue could be taught. But words had been changing their meaning. *Aretē* had come to mean political effectiveness.

Political education holds, then, the center of the stage. There is no denying that the great thinkers of nature could look somewhat remote, and even quaint, to the public mind of a modern city. They seemed to take pride in their remoteness. Pythagoras, asked why he lives, replies: "To look at heaven and nature." Anaxagoras is accused of caring nothing for his kin and his own city, but points at heaven and says: "There is my country." These men seemed only to care for the *meteora,* the "things above the air." They must be strange, too proud, "odd" (*perittoi*). This was said with respect. But when public opinion was upset, that respect could wear thin. The rude fun that Aristophanes poured on the lay figure of a Socrates perched in a basket midway, if not to heaven, at least to the ceiling, was really aimed at Anaxagoras, the first Ionian scientist who resided in Athens and who was befriended by Pericles and Euripides. Anaxagoras eventually had to leave Athens under the accusation of impiety, for having said that the Sun was a flaming stone as big as the Peloponnesus. But the impersonation stuck to Socrates viciously, and was revived by Meletus in his death trial:

"By Zeus, gentlemen of the jury, it is because he says the Sun is a stone, and the Moon earth." "Do you imagine, friend Meletus, that you are accusing Anaxagoras, and do you despise the jury, that you think them so illiterate as not to know that the rolls of Anaxagoras of Clazomenae are packed with such theories? The young, I suppose, learn these things from me— things that you can buy around for a drachma. . . ."

There is a great and tragic irony in Socrates, the opponent of the physicists no less than of the Sophists, being hounded to death as one of them. Anaxagoras had been, if anything, and a generation earlier, an exponent of "fundamental research," as it is being described rather hesitatingly even in our time. But it was by then 400 B.C., the panicky aftermath of a great national defeat, and if the man on trial was not a physicist, then he should be hanged for being an intellectual; all those Sophists were of one breed anyway; they spread impiety and warped the minds of young people. As it happened, Socrates was the chief opponent of the Sophists, but he could not be that without being a Sophist too in the public eye. The Sophist is, then, simply the new type of teacher who has replaced the old one. All of them are philosophers, all of them convincing talkers, all of them have a "science"; it is a matter of seeing which.

Seen as the end of a line, Gorgias is, no less than his master Empedocles, establishing a new Way of Opinion. The real difference lies in Gorgias's trenchant way of putting an end to the attempt to prove it also "true." It reminds one a little of the way in which, later, German philosophers disposed of the "thing-in-itself." With sound tactical instinct, Gorgias aims the offensive at the heart of the enemy position, and entitles his most celebrated piece of sophistry, *Concerning Nature, or What Is Not.* The gibe at Parmenides is unmistakable. If alone the One can be said to "be," and the Many are left out in the limbo of Opinion, let us get rid of Being, which is of no use whatever, and rejoin with new assurance the sensible people who are happy that the world should be full of a number of things—in fact are concerned only with these, whether or not they are "the same and not the same." Gorgias does not take the trouble to validate his Way of Opinion. For him, as for Protagoras, opinion is the only form of knowledge. What he attacks is the Way of Truth itself, turning against it a Zenonian dialectic of sorts, and the plan is well conceived. He is going to prove that: (a) Being cannot be said to exist, whether we try to conceive of it as everlasting, as created, as both, as One, or as Many; (b) if it existed, it would be incomprehensible; (c) if it existed and were comprehensible, it would be incommunicable.

Some of Gorgias's points may appear to us muddy and preposterous quibbles, but they must have left his listeners agape. Moreover, his text (of which we give hereafter a condensed version) is important not only as the first anti-scientific manifesto, but because, apart from some ingenious nonsense, it provides an arsenal of logical subtilities not easy to untangle, and so tempting indeed that Plato will be glad to borrow several of them (we always steal weapons from our enemies) and give them the status of "philosophical" logic. We are thus at the parting of the ways between scientific and unscientific (but by no means primitive) reasoning. The word "sophisticated" would apply to it by rights, if it still retained the old meaning of "adulterated," as it does in French.

We have indeed moved into the ambiguous world of sophistication, which carries with it the unjust appraisal of simple-mindedness for whatever came before. Nothing has really been overcome, but a choice has taken place. From the shadows of a lost text comes to us the angry snap of Democritus: ". . . wranglers, noose-twisters. . . ." But Democritus might insist on being old-fashioned; he still was a contemporary. He, too, as we saw, had to provide encyclopedic information; he, too, had to examine critically the value of knowledge. The times were ripe for a change.

The old order had known only isolated masters, who seemed to stand out like so many statues of Memnon in the landscape, each sending out his own note, announcing his own comprehensive *diakosmos,* his own truth of things. The disciples were fed that truth, to echo it in their turn. If there is one immutable nature of things to reflect, you can "build up" a man to reflect it in his own being, and that is all. That is what it means to be "instructed." Suppose that we want the "nature of number" to come to us and mold us in its image; we become a peculiar sect such as the Pythagoreans, somber and unkempt, living their own weird segregated discipline. Or, again, if we follow Parmenides and let our mind grasp unmoved Being, we may be safe with the Truth; we may raise a school of subtle

logicians, we may sally out to disorganize others with our
Zenonian attacks, but then we go back to our citadel, and
there is nothing much more that we can do.

But there is now that surprising novelty—education. If
one had to consider the mind an organized activity whereby
our tastes and judgment can be modified, something which
can be taught to "think for itself" in the many contingencies
of life, opposing its own structure to the reality outside—
then one must take deliberate distance from cosmic nature,
push off from it, so to speak. It is in this sense, we submit,
that we should understand Protagoras's famous pronouncement: *"Man is the measure of all things, of those that are,
that they are, of those that are not, that they are not."*

"A very renowned doctrine, my friend," says Socrates
wryly to Theaetetus,

whereby nothing is in itself a whole: you are unable to give
a correct name to a thing or to one of its qualities; as for
instance if you were to call it big, it might appear small, if
small, big, if heavy, light, and so on . . . for something always becomes with respect to something else, never by itself
. . . and as a thing acting on me at a given time is relative
only to me, so the truth of it is my sensation, which is a given
moment of *my* being. So that, as Protagoras says, I am judge of
what is for me, that it is, and what is not, that it is not.

There is, of course, a physical support for the doctrine,
namely the "changing pattern" of sensations as explained
already by Democritus, and there is also Heraclitus in the
background, but it is only a first-level meaning. On the
other hand, the word "measure" and the word "things"—
in the original *chrēmata,* "the goods"—would be enough to
show that this is in no way an existential statement about
"being." It simply relativizes our knowledge. Maybe, if we
translate into modern terms: "the measure of all values,"
the complex meaning becomes clear. Man, collectively, is
the new corporate entity which replaces the cosmos; it
provides its own measures.

There is also a new "nature"—not the nature of things,
but that of Man. When the Sophists oppose what is by
nature to what is by law or convention, they do not mean it
quite in the sense of Democritus. "You all present," says
Hippias of Elis, addressing the crowd at the Olympian

games, "I consider as relatives, brothers, and fellow citizens according to nature, not according to convention." Man is seen as a cosmopolitan, mobile, enfranchised, resourceful free agent. There is a striking similarity here, no doubt, to our own Era of Enlightenment, or, as the French called it, the "Siècle des Lumières," in its fight against prejudice, superstition, constricting old customs and superannuated ideas. Protagoras, like the Encyclopedists, does not hesitate to tackle the entrenched force of conservatism, the old local gods and godlings. He does so with characteristic restraint. "Concerning the gods," he says, "it is not given to me to know whether they are or are not, or what they are like; for there is much to prevent me from knowing, the difficulty of it and the shortness of man's life."

This was circumspect but clear enough. Protagoras was promptly accused of impiety by the pillars of society, who, as usual, connived with the rabble against anything that disturbed the old ways. But interest had been too strongly aroused among the young elite to be kept in check. Plato in the *Philebus* gives a delightful description of them:

The young man who has drunk for the first time from that spring is as happy as if he had found a treasure of wisdom; he is positively enraptured. He will pick up any discourse, draw all its ideas together to make them into one, then take them apart and pull them to pieces. He will puzzle first himself, then also others, badger whoever comes near him, young and old, sparing not even his parents, nor anyone who is willing to listen. He would not spare even the barbarians, if only he found an interpreter. . . .

This is the mind at last in free play. "Antilogies" and "double discourses" flourished, setting up a point and pulling it down. The play had to be with words, since there was little else available, and the young were naturally tempted by the teachers of pure sophistry, a branch which was properly called "eristics" and falsified the techniques of Zeno. But this was not the aim of the real masters, however different among themselves. Says Protagoras of the eager student:

If he comes to me he will not experience the sort of drudgery with which other Sophists are in the habit of insulting their pupils, who, when they have just escaped from the arts, are taken and driven back into them by these teachers, and made to learn calculation, and astronomy, and geometry, and music (he gave a look at Hippias as he said this); but if he comes to me he will learn that which he comes to learn. And this is prudence in affairs private as well as public; he will learn to order his house in the best manner, and he will be able to speak and act for the best in the affairs of the state. . . .

These various ways could be summed up in one new word—culture. Grammar, rhetoric, dialectic, the mathematical sciences, the structure of reason and language— all these were organized in the general order of disciplines which form the cultivated man, and this order was to last into our Renaissance.

The Sophists were intelligent enough to see that if this is a world that man makes for himself, technology becomes important; they were the first to speak openly of Progress, that magic word, and to stress the role of the crafts. Hippias proudly showed his tunic, his belt, his ring, his inkhorn, as made by his own hands. New applied sciences sprang up, which went from town planning (Hippodamus) to the theory of the social contract (Lycophron) and psychoanalysis (Antiphon). One might even say that, by and large, the personage of the intellectual specialist, as we have it now, comes upon the scene. Specialized craftsmen there had been since always, but in the field of the theoretical intellect, which was supposed to grasp things as a whole or not at all, it was felt as a disturbing innovation. The Sophists deliberately tied up with the specialized crafts to define what was their art, *technē,* such as medicine or shipbuilding could be. Each specialty had its own principles and method. Even Hippias, who in his multiple achievements is a fair predecessor of the *uomo universale,* presents himself as a poly-technician. His philosophy, for he also has one, is a nominalism of a well-reasoned kind. A matrix has thus been created for the succeeding centuries, in which that new figure, the professional scientist, can fit his activities with a minimum of philosophical presuppositions. The inevitable process of fragmentation which leads from philosophy into the "sciences" as we know them takes place largely under these auspices.

It was the status of the old fundamental sciences, if any-thing, that was becoming less clear. It would be unfair to say that the early Sophists as such were against mathematics. Hippias invented the first transcendent curve, the "quadratrix," which was applied to the trisection of the angle; Theodorus of Cyrene, the master of Theaetetus, studied the irrationals; Bryson carried on the Zenonian speculation on the continuum. But there is, on the part of most others, an outspoken tendency to discount the problems connected with abstraction and rigor, and to bring back the whole of science to practical concerns. Protagoras insisted that we need not think of the tangent as touching the circle at one point only, since it never does so in reality; nor is there any evidence that his friend Theodorus, who knew better, came out to oppose him. Antiphon explained that the problem of squaring the circle is practically solved as soon as we have an inscribed polygon with a sufficiently great number of sides. We can see the point of dangerous weakness: the lack of foundations.

The Sophists taught what was useful. This is an ambiguous word, for it involves also catering to the needs of customers indiscriminately. Then as now, degradation was sure to ensue. If we disregard the small fry and consider only leading minds like Protagoras, Gorgias, or Hippias, we can see that their aim was intellectual culture at its best. That culture, however, had a *social* bent. It was meant for the good of society, and of the person as a social being. That was said to be true which was conducive to that social good. It may not be easy for us to evaluate the novelty of the Sophistic approach because we ourselves happen to live again in a Sophistic era. All that we call progressive, pragmatistic, or social-minded education, all that calls itself the constructive attitude, or the positivistic theory of science as economy of thought, or the empirical approach to a growing world, or education for life, or adjustment to a mature outlook, or sociological anthropology or anthropological sociology and such like double-ended catchwords— all are Sophistic. They may mean some of the best and much of the worst. "Positive thinking" is one such term that Gorgias would have delighted in, and played with as a cat with a mouse, for he knew what he was doing. A difference, of course, stands out. Modern pragmatism professes to include all of science in its confines, and it will call itself scientific. The ancient Sophists did not. But we should consider that modern science has paid off in spectacular results. Its cash value, to use a pragmatistic term, is legal tender. We know that Scientific Method will invariably pay off. Yet even today, under the Sophistic ministration, the status of pure science, as distinct from applied, has become progressively dim and uncertain, if not ancillary, in the eyes of the average public.

This goes back a long way. Even in the halcyon days of pure science, in the last two centuries, the spectacular expansion of the specialized disciplines made a possible synthesis appear ever more remote and unattainable. Pure science lost, so to speak, its philosophical footing in the measure in which its methods and limitations were clarified. The result was a resigned but no less unfeigned indifference towards events in the universe. When Comte, the founder of Positivism, announced about 1850 that science should disregard such things as the spectroscope and the microscope for objects too far or too small, to concentrate on the good of Society as its supreme concern, he was reenacting as a faintly absurd joke what had been the essential tragedy of the Sophistic position.

We call it an essential tragedy because it is the Greek Sophists who also can be said to have invented humanism; if not the word (which is Roman) certainly the idea. It has gone through so many redefinitions and amplifications since that its meaning is somewhat blurred at present. It carries with it many and richer meanings picked up through time. But its foundational text is undeniably the word of Protagoras on Man the Measure of Things. There has remained something self-contradictory in its very essence.

It is only when we have met the Sophists, so frighteningly modern in many ways, that we can distinguish in retrospect the characteristic features of archaic thought that preceded them, and was truly and directly concerned with reality above all. In the original Greek conception of physics two subjects were confused: the old question as to the origin of the universe, the quest for comprehension and acceptance, which had formerly been answered by the cosmogonic myths, and still required feats of pure abstract imagination—and the other, proceeding from a new curiosity about all the things that are to be found in the world, and how they can be explained. This latter was called "investigation," in Greek *historiē,* and required all the information that one could get. It required Herodotus to survey the whole known world, its countries, its men and its gods; Megasthenes the doctor to travel to India; Pytheas to explore the North Sea; Anaximander to construct his maps and study fossil deposits. But it was felt that no empirical wealth of facts could make sense without an inquiry into the *why,* into the nature of the whole, and so men were led back to the question of how it came about, and from *what.*

Whence the search for invariants, for enduring patterns and sequences, for a chain of actions and reactions which can be described and foretold, both in society and nature. Solon and Anaximander, as we have noticed, are really of one mind about the point of relevance; natural science, history, and political theory come at about the same time from the same source. They have to go from observed regularities into the unseen causes, and are hence led back to the early metaphysics of myth, forward into its abstract developments. As Jaeger wrote, adapting a classic phrase of Kant's, mythical thought without the formative *logos* is blind, and logical theorizing without living mythical thought is empty. This is actually the way science was born, the first and only time when it happened. We have therefore to mark the inobjective and imaginative elements at least as much as the factual; although the former may look less new than the latter, in reality it is all one new thing.

When that unity is broken, something is lost irretrievably. The two texts that follow might be an indication of what happens: in the first, man establishes the autonomy of his discourse; in the second, he applies it to himself in his own inimitable way.

We are giving Gorgias's text from Sextus, *Adv. math.* VII, but abbreviated and also revised in the first part, for we know from another partial, but more ancient, version in *De Melisso Xenophane et Gorgia* that this section was strictly anti-Eleatic and therefore couched in the language of "being," whereas the other two parts are against the Pluralists, and thus deal with "existent things." By keeping the terms separate we avoid the "double take" that Sextus, as a radical skeptic, would have liked to effect. The first part—the attack against rationalism—is a piece of scandalous quibbling. Yet it is that fateful sophism about the verb *is* as implying a statement of existence which will be taken up by Plato and made into his very own.

The second and third parts deal not with "being" (i.e., truth) but with our knowledge of things. Gorgias attacks the physicists, those who believe in a reality which imprints itself directly in our cognition, so that our discourse reflects that reality. He shows it to be naive materialism. The second part is damaged in transmission, but its main point is clear: if we claim to think what is so, we have no criterion for distinguishing between truth and error. The third part is paradoxical only in appearance. It presents for the first time our modern correspondence theory of truth. What men can communicate to each other is not reality, but their own *discourse* about it, which may or may not be correct, but remains a discourse. Thus, Gorgias is the founder of nominalism. Brother Gaunilo (twelfth century A.D.) uses an image of arbitrary thought similar to Gorgias's "chariots on the sea," the "island of all perfections," to refute rationalism. As nominalism takes on importance again in our time for the theory of the scientific language, Gorgias stands out as an early and unpathetic Wittgenstein.

Concerning Nature, or What Is Not

1. . . . If being is, it is either eternal or created or at once both eternal and created; but, as we shall prove, it is neither eternal nor created nor both; therefore being does not exist. For if being is eternal (the hypothesis we must take first), it has no beginning; for everything created has some beginning, but the eternal, being uncreated, had no beginning. And having no beginning it is infinite. And if it is infinite, it is nowhere. For if it is anywhere, that wherein it is is different from it, and thus being encompassed as it is by something, will no longer be infinite; for that which encompasses is larger than that which is encompassed, whereas nothing is larger than the infinite; so that the infinite is not anywhere. Nor, again, is it encompassed by itself. For, if so, that wherein it is will be identical with that which is therein, and what is will become two things, place and body (for that wherein it is is place, and

that which is therein is body). But this is absurd; so that being is not in itself either. Consequently, if being is eternal it is infinite, and if it is infinite it is nowhere, and if it is nowhere it is not. So then, if being is eternal, it is not even existent at all. . . .

Moreover, if it is, it is either one or many; but, as we shall show, it is neither one nor many; therefore being is not. For if it is one, it is either a discrete quantity or a continuum or a magnitude or a body. But whichever of these it be, it is not one; but if it be a discrete quantity it will be divided, and if it be a continuum it will be cut in sections; and similarly if it be conceived as a magnitude it will not be indivisible, while if it is a body it will be threefold, for it will possess length and breadth and depth. But it is absurd to say that being is none of these; therefore being is not one. Yet neither is it many. For if it is not one, neither is it many; for the many is a sum of the ones, and hence if the one is destroyed the many also are destroyed with it. . . .

2. In the next place it must be shown that even if anything is, it is unknowable and inconceivable by man. If the things thought are not, the existent is not thought. And this is logical; for just as, if it is a property of the things thought to be white it would be a property of white things to be thought— so, if it is a property of things thought not to be existent, it will necessarily be a property of things existent not to be thought. Consequently, this is a sound and consistent argument—"If the things are not existent, the existent is not thought." But the things thought (for we must take them first) are not existent, as we shall establish; therefore, the existent is not thought. And, in fact, that the things thought are not existent is plain; for if the things thought are existent, all the things thought exist, and in the way, too, in which one has thought them. But this is contrary to sense. For if someone thinks of a man flying or of a chariot running over the sea, it does not follow at once that a man is flying or a chariot running over the sea. So that the things thought are not existent. Furthermore, if the things thought are existent, the non-existent things will not be thought. For opposites are properties of opposites, and non-being is the opposite of being; and because of this, if "to be thought" is a property of the being, "not to be thought" will most certainly be a property of the non-being. But this is absurd; for Scylla and Chimaera and many non-existent things are thought. Therefore the existent is not thought. And just as the things seen are called

visible because of the fact that they are seen, and the audible termed audible because of the fact that they are heard, and we do not reject the visible things because they are not heard, nor dismiss the audible things because they are not seen (for each object ought to be judged by its own special sense and not by another)—so also the things thought will exist, even if they should not be viewed by the sight nor heard by the hearing, because they are perceived by their own proper criterion. If, then, a man thinks that a chariot is running over the sea, even if he does not behold it he ought to believe that there exists a chariot running over the sea. But this is absurd; therefore the existent is not thought and apprehended.

3. And even if what is should be apprehended, it is incommunicable to another person. For if the existent things are objects, externally existing, of vision and of hearing and of the senses in general, and of these the visible things are apprehensible by sight and the audible by hearing, and not conversely—how, in this case, can these things be indicated to another person? For the means by which we indicate is speech, and speech is not the subsisting (underlying) realities; therefore we do not indicate to our neighbors the existent things but speech, which is other than the underlying realities. Thus, just as the visible thing will not become audible, and *vice versa,* so too, since the existent subsists externally, it will not become our discourse; and not being speech it will not be made clear to another person.

The discourse, moreover, is formed from the impressions caused by external objects, that is to say the sensibles . . . And if this be so, it is not speech that serves to reveal the external object, but the external object that proves to be explanatory of speech. Moreover, it is not possible to assert that speech subsists in the same fashion as the visible and audible things, so that the underlying and existent things can be indicated by it as by a thing subsisting and existent. For even if speech subsists, yet it differs from the rest of subsisting things, and the visible bodies differ very greatly from spoken words; for the visible object is perceptible by one sense-organ and speech by another. Therefore speech does not manifest most of the underlying things, just as they themselves do not make plain one another's nature.*

* From Sextus Empiricus, Vol. II, *Against the Logicians.* Translated by R. G. Bury. Cambridge: Harvard University Press. (The Loeb Classical Library.) Reprinted, with some changes, by permission of the publisher and The Loeb Classical Library.

The previous discussion about Being is an intellectual exercise. The dialogue that we give now is written in blood. Gorgias would not have willed this. He said once that victories over barbarians should be greeted with songs of joy, but that a victory of Greeks over Greeks should bring forth only songs of sorrow. But pragmatism was bound to spawn an evil brood, all the theories of pure power that Plato attacks so devastatingly in the persons of Thrasymachus and Callicles. There is nothing very new in the Athenian attitude as portrayed here. From King Lugal-zaggisi of Erech to the days of the atom bomb, international policy has presupposed such behavior. The unphilosophical Romans summed it up in one tag: Spare those who submit and break those who resist. But what had been hitherto practical and instinctual behavior has taken on a new meaning which is laid out and accepted in the clear light of the theoretical intellect. Thucydides, too, was fully aware of the influence of sophistic culture on political thinking. In his usual impassive way, he gives to the final negotiations of Athens with the Melians (416 B.C.) the form of a philosophical dialogue. We can spot in the argument the fine hand of Alcibiades himself, who had promoted the expedition: a cold, brilliant, scientific cruelty, not of the passions but of the rational intellect, the devilish element which runs through history isolated in its pure form. Melos chose to make a stand: the city was destroyed, its men slaughtered, the women and children sold into slavery.

The Death Dialogue of the Melians
from Thucydides's *History* *

Athenians. . . . Make no set speech yourselves, but take us up at whatever you do not like, and settle that before going any farther. And first tell us if this proposition of ours suits you.

. . . .

Melians. To the fairness of quietly instructing each other

* *The History of the Peloponnesian War.* Translated by Richard Crawley. Revised by R. Feetham. London: J. M. Dent & Sons, Ltd.; New York: E. P. Dutton and Company, Inc. (Everyman's Library 455A.) Reprinted by permission of the publishers.

as you propose there is nothing to object; but your military preparations are too far advanced to agree with what you say, as we see you are come to be judges in your own cause, and that all we can reasonably expect from this negotiation is war, if we prove to have right on our side and refuse to submit, and in the contrary case, slavery.

Athenians. If you have met to reason about presentiments of the future, or for anything else than to consult for the safety of your state upon the facts that you see before you, we will give over; otherwise we will go on.

Melians. It is natural and excusable for men in our position to turn more ways than one both in thought and utterance. However, the question in this conference is, as you say, the safety of our country; and the discussion, if you please, can proceed in the way which you propose.

Athenians. For ourselves, we shall not trouble you with specious pretences—either of how we have a right to our empire because we overthrew the Mede, or are now attacking you because of wrong that you have done us—and make a long speech which would not be believed; and in return we hope that you, instead of thinking to influence us by saying that you did not join the Lacedaemonians, although their colonists, or that you have done us no wrong, will aim at what is feasible, holding in view the real sentiments of us both; since you know as well as we do that right, as the world goes, is only in question between equals in powers, while the strong do what they can and the weak suffer what they must.

Melians. As we think, at any rate, it is expedient—we speak as we are obliged, since you enjoin us to let right alone and talk only of interest—that you should not destroy what is our common protection, the privilege of being allowed in danger to invoke what is fair and right, and even to profit by arguments not strictly valid if they can be got to pass current. And you are as much interested in this as any, as your fall would be a signal for the heaviest vengeance and an example for the world to meditate upon.

Athenians. The end of our empire, if end it should, does not frighten us: a rival empire like Lacedaemon, even if Lacedaemon was our real antagonist, is not so terrible to the vanquished as subjects who by themselves attack and overpower their rulers. This, however, is a risk that we are content to take. We will now proceed to show you that we are come here in the interest of our empire, and that we shall say what we are now going to say, for the preservation of your country;

as we would fain exercise that empire over you without trouble, and see you preserved for the good of us both.

Melians. And how, pray, could it turn out as good for us to serve as for you to rule?

Athenians. Because you would have the advantage of submitting before suffering the worst, and we should gain by not destroying you.

Melians. So that you would not consent to our being neutral, friends instead of enemies, but allies of neither side.

Athenians. No; for your hostility cannot so much hurt us as your friendship will be an argument to our subjects of our weakness, and your enmity of our power.

Melians. Is that your subjects' idea of equity, to put those who have nothing to do with you in the same category with peoples that are most of them your own colonists, and some conquered rebels?

Athenians. As far as right goes they think one has as much of it as the other, and that if any maintain their independence it is because they are strong, and that if we do not molest them it is because we are afraid; so that besides extending our empire we should gain in security by your subjection; the fact that you are islanders and weaker than others rendering it all the more important that you should not succeed in baffling the masters of the sea.

.   .   .   .

Melians. You may be sure that we are as well aware as you of the difficulty of contending against your power and fortune, unless the terms be equal. But we trust that the gods may grant us fortune as good as yours, since we are just men fighting against unjust, and that what we want in power will be made up by the alliance of the Lacedaemonians, who are bound, if only for very shame, to come to the aid of their kindred. Our confidence, therefore, after all is not so utterly irrational.

Athenians. When you speak of the favour of the gods, we may as fairly hope for that as yourselves; neither our pretensions nor our conduct being in any way contrary to what men believe of the gods, or practise among themselves. Of the gods we believe, and of men we know, that by a necessary law of their nature they rule wherever they can. And it is not as if we were the first to make this law, or to act upon it when made: we found it existing before us, and shall leave it to exist for ever after us; all we do is to make use of it, knowing that you and everybody else, having the same power as we have, would do the same as we do. Thus, as far as the gods are concerned, we have no fear and no reason to fear that we shall be at a disadvantage. But when we come to your notion about the Lacedaemonians, which leads you to believe that shame will make them help you, here we bless your simplicity but do not envy your folly. The Lacedaemonians, when their own interests or their country's laws are in question, are the worthiest men alive; of their conduct towards others much might be said, but no clearer idea of it could be given than by shortly saying that of all the men we know they are most conspicuous in considering what is agreeable honourable, and what is expedient just. Such a way of thinking does not promise much for the safety which you now unreasonably count upon.

11

The Care of the Soul

COMES NOW a momentous turn in the history of Western thought. Socrates (470–399 B.C.) can hardly be understood except as a personality formed in the Sophistic movement, and still engaged in it at the time when Aristophanes lampooned him vividly as a versatile one who taught for a fee the art of measuring the earth or that of dodging one's debts, according to demand. This is, of course, a composite caricature. Even then, Socrates the ex-stonecutter must have been somewhat apart from his intellectual confreres, asking direct questions in his obstinate way and trying to puzzle out what his inner voice might have meant when it whispered to him to "make music." He must have been getting on to fifty when he had a religious illumination which showed him the meaning of his quest. Following that, he became a new kind of Pythagorean, trying to work out the "invariants" behind changing reality.

The high point of Athenian culture, in which the strong virtues of the past still lived in a vastly expanded intellectual horizon, had been the age of Pericles. Thucydides, a man not given to illusion, had tried to fix that fleeting perfection in Pericles's Oration for the War Dead in 430.

. . . The gates of our city are flung open to the world. We practise no periodical deportations, nor do we prevent our visitors from observing or discovering what an enemy might usefully apply to his own purposes. For our trust is not in the devices of material equipment, but in our own good spirits for battle. . . . We are lovers of beauty without extravagance, and lovers of wisdom without unmanliness.

These were gravely considered words. But the course of Sophistic enlightenment had moved beyond that point, with its relentless critique, its scorn of intellectual restraint, its pragmatism, its relativizing of all frames of reference. The frivolousness of word play at one end of the spectrum, the cynical earnestness of wanton power-seekers at the other, the war losses and recriminations which gradually shook the community to pieces, were to be climaxed by defeat, surrender (404), and the rule of the Thirty Tyrants.

By the time Socrates met young Plato, he was deeply engaged in the search for the lost foundations of common reason. The Pythagoreans had Numbers; they might be enough for the archaic dreaming absolutism of the Brotherhood, but what the living body of the City needed was far different: it needed an analysis of the motives of men in their ordinary behavior, a clarification of the right and wrong, a guide to moral action. The Sophists had created the issue, by pretending to "teach virtue," that is, capacity to influence one's fellow citizens towards desirable ends, but they had left the definition of "desirable" tangled up in a soft-minded relativism and scattered through a multitude of points of view.

Take, for instance, the central problem of justice. Thrasymachus provides the gambit in the *Republic,* by thinking he knows all about it.

He was most anxious to speak, in order to gain applause, reckoning that he had a mighty clever answer to make. . . . "Hear, then," said he, "for I say that the just is nothing else but what is expedient for the strongest. But why don't you commend my answer?"

Socrates asks in mock puzzlement whether he means that the just diet for us would be the one which suits a heavyweight wrestler. Of course not, says Thrasymachus impatiently, I am talking of the state, and what I say is that in all states the same thing constitutes justice, viz., what is expedient for the established government.

From here on the argument unwinds quietly but implacably through the first books of the *Republic,* until Socrates gets the other interlocutors to agree (Thrasymachus having retired into a sulk) that if we understand justice in its true implications, the man who is undeviatingly just can have little hope of power in the state as it is, but rather ought to be prepared, as had been said in the

Gorgias, "to have his eyes put out, and to be crucified." There has been no affirmative position on the part of Socrates at any point in the long argument, but a patient probing of the minds of his collocutors until they discovered that what they really mean when they speak of justice is not what they thought they meant. In other words, it is the proper usage of the term, checked and analyzed through its many accepted connotations, which will reveal to us the truth of the thing behind it. It is, again, in a way, the search for an unvarying substrate, but that substrate is present only in men's souls.

In this way Socrates was led to take up again the Pythagorean concern with definition. "Having turned his attention to moral virtues," says Aristotle, "he tried for the first time to define them in universal terms." He did not stop at defining in the old way, by enumeration and subdivision, which had provided the Sophists with a tool for their tricky purposes. He was trying to find his way to the invariants by working out the true kind of species, under which several similar entities could be subsumed. This is, undeniably, the inductive method, and he went at it with scientific scrupulousness.

The logic of Socrates has, inevitably, a Sophistic tinge, dealing, as it does, with the subject matter of the Sophists; what is nonsophistical about it is the avoidance on his part of the affirmative position, which would turn the dialogue into the usual fencing of the set debate. He is really asking questions. He professes "to know only that he does not know"; he is trying to find out, and it is the other man who must gradually work out the truth that is in him, with Socrates acting only as "midwife." To be sure, there is a goodly amount of irony in the procedure. "There we are, Socrates," says young Meno,

I had been warned, and indeed you are leading me along and binding a spell over me, so that I too have begun to doubt what I thought I knew very well. If you will take it in good turn, you seem to me exceedingly similar in the face, as well as in the rest, to those torpedo fishes which stun whoever comes in contact with them. . . .

This is, at least, the Socrates that we know from the writings of Plato and, in a lesser measure, of Xenophon;

for he never wrote a line himself. But there are passages in which his own voice seems to come through. Such are the autobiographical remarks in the *Phaedo,* a dialogue which deals with Socrates's last day in prison. In this passage * (95C–98D) he explains why he turned away from physics which had once fascinated him. The unpremeditated historical sketch is also the earliest critical description by a Greek of the course of thought of his predecessors. The perspective of twenty centuries is lacking; this is how the problems may well have looked to a man still caught in their midst:

"Listen, and I will tell you. When I was a young man, Cebes, I was most amazingly interested in the lore which they call natural philosophy. For I thought it magnificent to know the causes of everything, why it comes into being and why it is destroyed and why it exists; I kept turning myself upside down to consider things like the following: Is it when hot and cold get some fermentation in them, as some said,[1] that living things are bred? Is it the blood by which we think,[2] or air[3] or fire;[4] or whether it is none of these, but the brain is what provides the senses of hearing and sight and smell, and from these arise memory and opinion, and from memory and opinion in tranquillity comes knowledge; again I considered the destructions of these things, and what happens about heaven and earth. At last I believed myself as unfitted for this study as anything could be. I will tell you a sufficient proof: I found myself then so completely blinded by this study that I unlearned even what I used to think that I knew—what I understood clearly before, as I thought and others thought—about many other things and particularly as to the reason why man grows. I used to think that this was clear to all—by eating and drinking; for when from his foods flesh was added to flesh, and bones to bones, and in the same way the other parts each had added to them what was their own, then what was the little mass before became great later, and so the small man became big. That is what I believed then; isn't it a natural opinion?"

* *Great Dialogues of Plato,* translated by W. H. D. Rouse. New York: The New American Library of World Literature, Inc. (Mentor Books), 1956, pp. 500–4. Reprinted by permission of J. C. G. Rouse, London.
   [1] Anaximander, Anaxagoras, and others.
   [2] Empedocles.
   [3] Anaximenes.
   [4] Heracleitos. [Heraclitus.]

"I think so," said Cebes.

"Look next at this, then. I believed that when a big man stood by a small man, it was correct enough to suppose that he was bigger by the head, and so horse and horse; more clearly still, I thought ten was greater than eight because two was added to it, and the two-cubit bigger than the one-cubit because it overreached it by half."

"But now," said Cebes, "what do you think about them?"

"I'm very far, I swear, from thinking I know the cause of any of these things, for I can't agree with myself, even when one is added to one, either that the one to which it was added has become two, or the one which was added has become two, or that the one added and the one it was added to become two, by the adding of the one to the other; for I am surprised that when they were apart from each other each was one and they were not then two, but when they approached each other this was the cause of their becoming two, the meeting, their being near together. Or again, if a one is cut in half I cannot be convinced any longer that this, the cutting, was the cause of its becoming two; then it was because they were brought close together and one was added to the other, now because one is taken away and separated from the other. Nor can I even convince myself any longer that I know how the one is generated, or in a word how anything else is generated or perishes or exists; I can't do it by this kind of method, but I am muddling along with another of my own[5] and I don't allow this one at all.

"Well, I heard someone reading once out of a book, by Anaxagoras he said, how mind is really the arranger and cause of all things; I was delighted with this cause, and it seemed to me in a certain way to be correct that mind is the cause of all, and I thought that if this is true, mind arranging all things places everything as it is best. If, therefore, one wishes to find out the cause of anything, how it is generated or perishes or exists, what one ought to find out is how it is best for it to exist or to do or feel everything; from this reasoning, then, all that is proper for man to seek about this and everything is only the perfect and the best; but the same man necessarily knows the worse, too, for the same knowledge includes both. Reasoning thus, then, I was glad to think I had found a teacher of the cause of things after my own mind in Anaxagoras: I thought he would show me first whether the earth is

[5] The logical method.

flat or round, and when he had shown this, he would proceed to explain the cause and the necessity, by showing that it was better that it should be such; and if he said it was in the middle of the universe, he would proceed to explain how it was better for it to be in the middle; and if he would explain all these things to me, I was prepared not to want any other kind of cause. And about the sun too I was equally prepared to learn in the same way, and the moon and stars besides, their speed as compared with one another, their turnings, and whatever else happens to them, how these things are better in each case for them to do or to be done to. For I did not believe that, when he said all this was ordered by mind, he would bring in any other cause for them than that it was best they should be as they are. So I thought that, when he had given the cause for each and for all together, that which is best for each, he would proceed to explain the common good of all; and I would not have sold my hopes for anything, but I got his books eagerly as quick as I could, and read them, that I might learn as soon as possible the best and the worse.

"Oh, what a wonderful hope! How high I soared, how low I fell! When as I went on reading I saw the man using mind not at all; and stating no valid causes of the arrangement of all things, but giving airs and ethers and waters as causes, and many other strange things. I felt very much as I should feel if someone said, 'Socrates does by mind all he does'; and then, trying to tell the causes of each thing I do, if he should say first that the reason why I sit here now is, that my body consists of bones and sinews, and the bones are hard and have joints between them, and the sinews can be tightened and slackened, surrounding the bones along with flesh and the skin which holds them together; so when the bones are uplifted in their sockets, the sinews slackening and tightening make me able to bend my limbs now, and for this cause I have bent together and sit here; and if next he should give you other such causes of my conversing with you, alleging as causes voices and airs and hearings and a thousand others like that, and neglecting to give the real causes. These are that since the Athenians thought it was better to condemn me, for this very reason I have thought it better to sit here, and more just to remain and submit to any sentence they may give. For, by the Dog! these bones and sinews, I think, would have been somewhere near Megara or Boeotia long ago, carried there by an opinion of what is best, if I had not believed it better and more just to submit to any sentence which my city gives than

to take to my heels and run. But to call such things causes is
strange indeed. If one should say that unless I had such things,
bones and sinews and all the rest I have, I should not have
been able to do what I thought best, that would be true; but to
say that these, and not my choice of the best, are the causes of
my doing what I do (and when I act by mind, too!), would be
a very far-fetched and slovenly way of speaking. For it shows
inability to distinguish that the real cause is one thing, and
that without which the cause could not be a cause is another
thing. This is what most people seem to me to be fumbling
after in the dark, when they use a borrowed name for it and
call it cause! And so one man makes the earth remain under
the sky, if you please, by putting a rotation about the earth;
another thinks it is like the bottom of a flat kneading-trough
and puts the air underneath to support it; but they never look
for the power which has placed things so that they are in the
best possible state, nor do they think it has a divine strength,
but they believe they will some time find an Atlas [6] more
mighty and more immortal and more able than ours to hold
all together, and really they think nothing of the good which
must necessarily bind and hold all things together. How glad
I should be to be anyone's pupil in learning what such a cause
really is! But since I have missed this, since I could not find it
myself or learn it from another, would you like me to show
you, Cebes," he said, "how I managed my second voyage in
search for the cause?"

"Would I not!" said he: "more than anything else in the
world!"

"Well then," he said, "it occurred to me after all this—and
it was then I gave up contemplating the realities—that I must
be careful not to be affected like people who observe and watch
an eclipse of the sun. What happens to them is that some lose
their sight, unless they look at his reflection in water or something of that sort. This passed through my mind, and I feared
that I might wholly blind my soul by gazing at practical
things [7] with my eyes and trying to grasp them by each of the
senses. So I thought I must take refuge in reasoning, to examine the truth of the realities. There is, however, something not
like in my image; for I do not admit at all that one who
examines the realities by reasoning makes use of images, more
than one who examines them in deeds and facts. Well anyway,

[6] The Titan who upheld the heavens.
[7] Natural phenomena.

this is how I set out; and laying down in each case the reasoning which I think best fortified, I consider as true whatever seems to harmonise with that, both about causes and about everything else, and as untrue whatever does not. But I wish to make it clearer, for I think you do not understand yet."

"Indeed I do not," said Cebes, "not well."

"Well, this is what I mean," he said, "nothing new, but the same as I have been saying all this time in our conversation, and on other occasions. I am going to try to show you the nature of the cause, which I have been working out. I shall go back to the old song and begin from there, supposing that there exists a beautiful something all by itself, and a good something and great and all the rest of it; and if you grant this and admit it, I hope from these to discover and show you the cause, that the soul is something immortal."

"I grant it to you," said Cebes; "pray be quick and go on to the end."

"Then consider," he said, "what follows, and see if you agree with me. What appears to me is, that if anything else is beautiful besides beauty itself, what makes it beautiful is simply that it partakes of that beauty; and so I say with everything. Do you agree with such a cause?"

"I agree," said he.

"Very well," he said, "I can no longer recognise or understand all those clever causes we heard of; and if anyone tells me that anything is beautiful because it has a fine flowery colour or shape or anything like that, I thank him and let all that go; for I get confused in all those, but this one thing I hold to myself simply and completely, and foolishly perhaps, that what makes it beautiful is only that beauty, whether its presence or a share in it or however it may be with the thing, for I am not positive about the manner, but only that beautiful things are beautiful by that beauty. For this I think to be the safest answer to give to myself or anyone else, and clinging to this I think I shall never fall, but it is a safe answer for me and everyone else, that by that beauty all beautiful things are beautiful. Don't you think so?"

We can see how Socrates's mind has turned away from the concern with nature. But it is also clear that from the start he was looking for something that he calls very simply "the good," and that what he had hoped from the physicists was to be shown how nature exemplifies the good. If it does not do so directly, he would not insist; he would look some other way. The Pythagorean element in his thought is unmistakable, as we can see from his concern with the immortality of the soul. But from the Pythagorean complex of ideas his concern sought out what music and numbers were meant, after all, to foster, namely, the "care of the soul." The proper way to go about it should be a "science of the good," that is, a scientific foundation for the ethical life. This, beyond and above numbers, should be the true object of reason. If men do evil, it can be only through error in reasoning or misinformation, since all beings desire their own good, and it can be proved that their good is the same as the universal good, since it depends from universal definitions and hence from a universal reality. The idea of a man being able to think deliberately: "Evil, be thou my good," with the consequent concept of inherent sinfulness, as developed in the Christian world, was out of the question for his rationalistic mind.

This would seem to be as far as Socrates went with theory (for him, remarks Aristotle, definitions and universals are not separate entities); the rest was practice, that is, transforming others and shaping himself into the man whose life should be the very life of those universals. Philosophy, he maintained, should be a preparation for death, so that we should meet death with a soul partaking of immortality. So he went into freely accepted death as a "good risk," as he put it with engaging understatement; and that death, marking his thought and his being with the seal of existential achievement, brought to the mind of Plato the seeds of thoughts destined to become immortal. But with this the die had been cast; the relationship of man to nature had been changed in an irreversible way.

Towards the end of that same dialogue, the *Phaedo,* Socrates goes back to discoursing of the earth, which he states to be spherical "as has been found," of the air and of the waters below. He is addressing himself specifically to the two Pythagoreans present, Simmias and Cebes, who come from Thebes and have been disciples of Philolaus. He has been discussing with them in technical terms the Pythagorean idea of the soul as a harmony. Now he, who has avoided physics for so long, comes back to the cosmos, after his own fashion. He talks of the air as of a deep sea, at the bottom of which we live, unsuspecting of the pure aether above, to which the righteous ascend after death; he talks in singular detail of the rivers and the seas which spring from vast subterranean rivers and go back to them, and in the end flow down to the fiery sea of Tartarus, on whose shores is the judgment of souls which have transgressed in this life. It began as a cosmology, almost in the vein of the physicist, but it soon shows itself as an allegory, an existential landscape of the soul, in the same sense as the physical setting of Dante's three realms is an existential landscape:

"No sensible man would think it proper to rely on things of this kind being just as I have described; but that, since the soul is clearly immortal, this or something like this at any rate is what happens in regard to our souls and their habitations—that this is so seems to me proper and worthy of the risk of believing; for the risk is noble. Such things he must sing like a healing incantation to himself, and that is why I have lingered so long over the story. But these are the reasons for a man to be confident about his own soul, when in his life he has bidden farewell to all other pleasures, the pleasures and adornments of the body, thinking them alien and such as do more harm than good, and has been earnest only for the pleasure of learning; and having adorned the soul with no alien ornaments, but with her own—with temperance and justice and courage and freedom and truth, thus he awaits the journey to the house of Hades, ready to travel when the doom ordained shall call. You indeed," he said, "Simmias and Cebes and all, hereafter at some certain time shall each travel on that journey: but me—'Fate calls me now,' as a man might say in a tragedy, and it is almost time for me to travel towards the bath; for I am sure you think it better to have a bath before drinking the potion, and to save the women the trouble of washing a corpse." *

* W. H. D. Rouse, *op. cit.* p. 518.

12

Flight to the T’rans-Uranian

SOCRATIC THOUGHT, such as we have tried to characterize, is the foundation on which Plato (428–348 B.C.)
raises his vast cathedral of the Theory of Ideas. As Socrates had seen it, the real assemblage of the world, whatever it may be, is of little relevance, compared to its "true"
constitution, which must show the mark of the good which
rules over all being. This is also the way in which Plato
sees physical reality, which he describes in a famous simile as the impenetrable dark wall of the Cave in which
souls are imprisoned until they break the shackles and turn
toward the contemplation of truth. Plato is far too profound a philosopher and far too great a writer for us to
want to analyze his "contributions to science," that is, cut
out from the context of his opus the fragments of physical
theory and the flashes of half-understood archaic knowledge that he deals out "not quite seriously," as he is willing to admit, in the guise of myth or "plausible story"
(Socrates's previously given description of the earth is a
case in point) intended as a help to the imagination where
reason cannot give a true account. For indeed, as Plato
insists to the end of his life, there cannot be a "true physics." There is one whole dialogue of his, the *Timaeus,*
which gives us a detailed cosmology in the Pythagorean
manner, and is usually quoted as his physical theory. Yet
the *Timaeus* is nothing but one myth or allegory meant to
adumbrate the workings of the World Soul, and its physics
is a shadow play.

The center of gravity of Plato's thought lies entirely
elsewhere, in the realm of Ideas which are supposed to
exist somehow beyond the world, to be contemplated only
by the eye of the mind. In the *Theaetetus,* a dialogue
which tackles the problem of knowledge, Socrates helps
Theaetetus, the great young mathematician, to discard the

current definition of knowledge as "true opinion." He examines the possible sources of knowledge. It cannot come from sensation because sensation is change and movement, both outside and in us. Or is it in thought? But we should consider the process of thought. It is "the discourse that the soul holds with itself," until it has formed an "opinion." The opinion may be true. But then how do we happen to form often puzzlingly wrong opinions? How do we know when they are true? This does not give true science (*epistēme*). Theaetetus suggests shyly that we might have "true opinion accompanied by a rational account of itself." But this, too, is found insufficient, for on what are we to found that rational account? The argument has come to a dead end. But, meanwhile, the possibility of what *we* would call the scientific approach to reality has been written off. Along that way, we meet only the "likely."

The very inconclusiveness of the dialogue—which starts out in search of a theory of true knowledge and admittedly fails in its quest—shows up the intellectual predicament. There is a gulf between abstraction and reality, between theory and things, which can be overflown upward, creatively, by Eros, downward, imaginatively, by the myth, but remains impassable to any effort at bringing them together. It is this gulf, this gap (*chorismos*) which makes nature insoluble, not through any fault of our intellect, but because she *is* essentially darkness and inchoate approximation. We cannot hope to find in matter any precise consequences of the logical connections of the world above, but only reminders, fumbling attempts to "imitate" it, doomed to remain halfway between being and nonbeing; it is, in fact, the World of Becoming. It would be even better to say that it is "trying to become." How? Why? What is it that causes it even to try, lost in the darkness below? Plato suggests it does so by some kind of "participation"—a notion still wrapped in the mists of magic. As Aristotle will remark rather acidly, it is saying no more than the Pythagoreans meant already when they spoke of things "imitating" numbers. But Plato is prevented from finding a better answer by the very width of the gap that he places between reality and Ideas. The separation is far more drastic than between Parmenides's

"Truth" and "Opinion," for the substrate of Becoming is for Parmenides the diamond-like firmness of Being, which is geometrical space; whereas in Plato space itself seems to lose all geometrical properties; it is the "receptacle" or "matrix" of the inchoate effort of matter to become. Situated even below matter, it is close to the absolute zero of "nonbeing." The way in which the Matrix of Becoming, as the cosmogonic story is told us in the *Timaeus,* "was filled with powers not alike nor evenly balanced, and was swayed unevenly and shaken like the winnower's basket," and thus brought forth the diversity of things, may prompt a modern to think of Schrödinger's atom, seen as a system of standing waves in *psi*-space, a space surely not geometrical. But even if it reveals some strange kinship of minds, the analogy is unwarranted. Plato is, like Timaeus himself, a Pythagorean in cosmology—but then he makes it clear that the physics of it is only a metaphor. His atoms are stereometric formations in empty space, brought forth by "participation." The mixing together of ingredients by the Demiurge or Manufacturing God, the subsequent distribution of the product in accord with the intervals of a musical scale to form different substances, this is again the Pythagorean idea of Empedocles, but presented this time not as science, only as "plausible myth" inside a vaster metaphysical theory.

As a matter of historic fact, this lofty point of view was reactionary; it deflected Pythagorean thought from the patient endeavor at finding numeric data inside the actual phenomena, that is, at discovering inductively where it is that number rules matter exactly. Even astronomy, the divine science, cannot be said to retain its previous status. Plato does not think that astronomy "lifts one's eyes upward" in any other way than if one were to look up at the ceiling.

Looking up with your mouth open, or down with your mouth closed, is about the same so long as we investigate any kind of sensible object. . . . The only true way of looking "up" is to investigate pure Being, which cannot be seen at all.

This is an important passage, in that it shows vividly how Plato's conception of science has nothing to do with anything happening in time and space.

Truth may come down, however, from the world of Ideas where it lives, to make some sense of reality, to "save" it or to "guide" it. So it may come down by way of the mind to "guide" the city, or to "save" the appearances in Heaven, that is, invest them with the ideal structures that they try stumblingly and half senselessly to imitate. So we may have astronomy after all, but down from the Ideas, not up from the facts. And it surely *is* a mathematical physics as Plato understood it, but that is because the stars, in their close-to-divine nature, know how to respond exactly to the Idea which informs their motion, viz., the circle. This has to be spelled out in order to give the proper meaning to the enterprise of Eudoxus, the great mathematician, in his theory of homocentric spheres. As he formalized astronomy and detached it from the physical imaginations of the Pythagoreans, he accepted Plato's program of "saving the phenomena." The theory was intended to give a strictly mathematical model on this level. Put in Platonic terms, it intended to establish the relation between the actual planetary shifts and an abstract *Eidos* or Form—uniform circular motion compounded. The appearances ("phenomena") were "saved"—but not in any physically translatable way. This was the mathematizing ideal which allowed science to be reborn later; for indeed Platonism remains for twenty centuries the framework in which mathematics is seen to be important; it not only hallows with its "golden eloquence" and preserves for the future all the Pythagorean speculations, it also establishes the ideal of a thoroughgoing rationality, the will to "follow the argument wherever it will lead us," as Socrates says. It would indeed have led quite naturally to a science of the modern type—if it had not been for the gap.

Plato stands out also as the founder of the Academy, which was the first institution for higher learning. A knowledge of mathematics was presupposed for admission. Fellowship could be for life, since the attainment of true knowledge was supposed to be derived from searching discussion and never-ending dialectical clarification of concepts held in common. The Academy lasted through various changes until A.D. 529, when it was closed by order of the Christian Emperor Justinian as a "pagan" school. It lasted thus 900 years—a longevity that no university of our times has yet attained. The charter of Bologna, its nearest competitor, will have its ninth centenary in A.D. 2020.

It is said that Plato agreed once, on insistent request, to deliver a public lecture on the Good. The lecturer, remarks Whitehead, was competent; the lecture was a failure. The Athenians, who must have come expecting some clever Sophistic teaching, were dismayed when Plato proceeded to draw geometrical diagrams and to build up propositions. Most of them left unceremoniously. The text of that lecture is lost. We have, however, what was probably the first part of it, decked in shining literary form, in the *Republic* (end of Book VI and beginning of Book VII). In this section, Plato reveals what seems to have been his ideas of the central role of mathematics in the Science of the Good. The Pythagorean Harmonic proportion which also expresses itself in the cube appears as the key to the structure of knowledge as well as to that of the cosmos itself. The argument moves on three successive levels: dialectical, systematic, and allegorical. The famous myth of the Cave turns out to be not a mere literary analogy, but a true allegoric parable, a synthesis of the doctrine. From there the lecture's conclusion may have been described by way of the dialectics of the *Philebus*. Socrates is speaking in the first person; his two interlocutors at this point are Adeimantus and Glaucon, Plato's half-brothers.*

"When a man turns his eyes," I said, "no longer to those things whose colours are pervaded by the light of day, but on those pervaded by the luminaries of night, the eyes grow dim and appear to be nearly blind, as if pure sight were not in them."
"Yes, they do," he said.
"But whenever he turns them to what the sunlight illumines, they see clearly, and sight appears to be in these same eyes."
"Certainly."
"Understand then, that it is the same with the soul, thus:

* W. H. D. Rouse, *op. cit.,* pp. 307–13, pp. 315–16.

when it settles itself firmly in that region in which truth and real being brightly shine, it understands and knows it and appears to have reason; but when it has nothing to rest on but that which is mingled with darkness—that which becomes and perishes, it opines, it grows dim-sighted, changing opinions up and down, and is like something without reason."

"So it is."

"Then that which provides their truth to the things known, and gives the power of knowing to the knower, you must say is the idea or principle of the good, and you must conceive it as being the cause of understanding and of truth in so far as known; and thus while knowledge and truth as we know them are both beautiful, you will be right in thinking that it is something different, something still more beautiful than these. As for knowledge and truth, just as we said before that it was right to consider light and sight to be sunlike, but wrong to think them to be sun; so here, it is right to consider both these to be goodlike, but wrong to think either of them to be the good—the eternal nature of the good must be allowed a yet higher value."

"What infinite beauty you speak of!" he said, "if it provides knowledge and truth, and is above them itself in beauty! You surely don't mean that it is pleasure!"

"Hush!" I said. "But here is something more to consider about its likeness."

"What?"

"The sun provides not only the power of being seen for things seen, but, as I think you will agree, also their generation and growth and nurture, although it is not itself generation."

"Of course not."

"Similarly with things known, you will agree that the good is not only the cause of their becoming known, but the cause that knowledge exists and of the state of knowledge, although the good is not itself a state of knowledge but something transcending far beyond it in dignity and power."

Glaucon said very comically, "O Lord, what a devil of a hyperbole!"

"All your fault," said I, "for compelling me to say what I think about it."

"Oh, please don't stop!" he said. "At least do finish the comparison with the sun, if you are leaving anything out."

"Oh yes," I said, "I am leaving a lot out."

"Not one little bit, please!" he said.

"I'm afraid I must leave out a good deal," said I; "but I won't willingly leave out anything now if I can help it."

"Please do not," he said.

"Conceive then," I said, "that there are these two, as we say; and one reigns over the region and things of the mind, the other over those of the eye. Now then, you have these two ideas distinct—'seen' and 'thought.'"

"I have."

"Suppose you take a line [*AE*],[1] cut into two unequal parts [at *C*] to represent in proportion [2] the worlds of things seen and things thought, and then cut each part in the same proportion [3] [at *B* and *D*]. Your two parts [*AB* and *BC*] in the world of things seen will differ in degree of clearness and dimness, and one part [*AB*] will contain images; by images I mean first

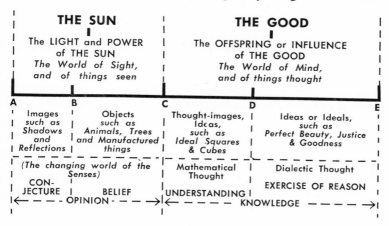

LENGTH REPRESENTS DEGREE OF CLEARNESS, NOT SIZE OF CLASS.

Note:—since $\dfrac{CE}{AC} = \dfrac{DE}{CD} = \dfrac{BC}{AB}$, it follows that $BC = CD$.

THE DIVIDED LINE

of all shadows, then reflections in water and in surfaces which

---

[1] See diagram; the diagram (and lettering) is of course not in the Greek text.

[2] and [3] A numerical value for this proportion can only be assumed. Socrates refers again to this proportion later, and there proposes to Glaucon to "leave aside" the value of the proportion, as involving too much discussion.

are of close texture, smooth and shiny, and everything of that kind, if you understand."

"Yes, I understand."

"Take the second part of this [BC] for the things which the images resemble, the animals about us and all trees and plants and all kinds of manufactured articles."

"Very good," said he.

"Would you be willing to admit," said I, "that in respect of truth and untruth there is the same distinction between the opinable and the knowable as there is between the image and its model?"

"Oh yes, certainly," he answered.

"Now then, consider how the section for 'things thought' should be divided."

"How?"

"This way. In the first part [CD] the soul in its search is compelled to use as images the things imitated—the realities of the former part [BC]—and from things taken for granted passes not to a new beginning, a first principle, but to an end, a conclusion; in the second part [DE] it passes from an assumption to a first principle free from assumption, without the help of images which the other part [CD] uses, and makes its path of enquiry amongst ideals themselves by means of them alone."

He answered, "I don't quite understand that."

"Let us try again," I said; "you will understand easier when I have said some more first. I suppose you know that students of geometry and arithmetic and so forth begin by taking for granted odd and even, and the usual figures, and the three kinds of angles, and things akin to these, in every branch of study; they take them as granted and make them assumptions[4] or postulates, and they think it unnecessary to give any further account of them to themselves or to others, as being clear to everybody. Then, starting from these, they go on through the rest by logical steps until they end at the object which they set out to consider."

"Certainly I know that," he said.

"Then you know also that they use the visible figures and give lectures about them, while they are not thinking of these they can see but the ideas which these are like; a square *in itself* is what they speak of, and a diameter[5] *in itself,* not the

---

[4] ὑποθέσεις [Hypotheseis].

[5] The Greeks spoke of a diameter of a square; we say "diagonal."

one they are drawing. It is always so; the very things which they model or draw, which have shadows of their own and images in water, they use now as images; but what they seek is to see those ideals which can be seen only by the mind."

"True," he said.

"This ideal, then, that I have been describing belongs to the first part [CD] of things thought, but the soul, as I said, is compelled to use assumptions in its search for this; it does not pass to a first principle because of being unable to get out clear above the assumptions, but uses as images the very things [in BC] which are represented by those below [in AB] and were esteemed and honoured as bright compared with those." [6]

"I understand," he said, "that you speak of what belongs to geometry and its kindred arts."

"Now, then, understand," I said, "that by the other part [DE] of things thought I mean what the arguing process itself grasps by power of dialectic, treating assumptions not as beginnings, but as literally hypotheses,[7] that is to say steps and springboards for assault, from which it may push its way up to the region free of assumptions and reach the beginning of all, and grasp it, clinging again and again to whatever clings to this; and so may come down to a conclusion without using the help of anything at all that belongs to the senses, but only ideals themselves, and, passing through ideals, it may end in ideals."

"I understand," said he, "though not sufficiently, for you seem to me to describe a heavy task; but I see that you wish to lay down that a clearer perception of real being and the world of mind is given by knowledge of dialectic, than by the so-called 'arts' which start from pure assumptions. It is true that those who view them through these are compelled to view them with the understanding and not the senses, but because they do not go back to the beginning in their study, but start from assumptions, they do not seem to you to apply a reasoning mind about these matters, although with a first principle added they belong to the world of mind. The mental state of geometricians and suchlike you seem to call understanding,

---

[6] I.e., compared with the images in *AB*.

[7] ὑποθέσεις [Hypotheseis]; root meaning is "a placing-under." The words which follow seem to suggest an assault on a fortress wall, using steps and clinging to ropes or the backs of other men, reaching the top, and dropping down on the other side to finish the fight.

not reason, taking understanding as something between opinion and reason."

"You have taken my meaning quite sufficiently," I said. "Now then, accept these four affections of the soul for my four divisions of the line: Exercise of Reason for the highest, Understanding for the second; put Belief for the third and Conjecture for the last. Then arrange the divisions in proportion, believing they partake of clearness just as the affections which they represent partake of truth."

"I understand," said he, "and I agree, and I arrange them as you tell me."

(Book VII) "Next, then," I said, "take the following parable of education and ignorance as a picture of the condition of our nature. Imagine mankind as dwelling in an underground cave with a long entrance open to the light across the whole width of the cave; in this they have been from childhood, with necks and legs fettered, so they have to stay where they are. They cannot move their heads round because of the fetters, and they can only look forward, but light comes to them from fire burning behind them higher up at a distance. Between the fire and the prisoners is a road above their level, and along it imagine a low wall has been built, as puppet showmen have screens in front of their people over which they work their puppets."

"I see," he said.

"See, then, bearers carrying along this wall all sorts of articles which they hold projecting above the wall, statues of men and other living things,[8] made of stone or wood and all kinds of stuff, some of the bearers speaking and some silent, as you might expect."

"What a remarkable image," he said, "and what remarkable prisoners!"

"Just like ourselves," I said. "For, first of all, tell me this: What do you think such people would have seen of themselves and each other except their shadows, which the fire cast on the opposite wall of the cave?"

"I don't see how they could see anything else," said he, "if they were compelled to keep their heads unmoving all their lives!"

"Very well, what of the things being carried along? Would not this be the same?"

[8] Including models of trees, etc.

"Of course it would."

"Suppose the prisoners were able to talk together, don't you think that when they named the shadows which they saw passing they would believe they were naming things?"[9]

"Necessarily."

"Then if their prison had an echo from the opposite wall, whenever one of the passing bearers uttered a sound, would they not suppose that the passing shadow must be making the sound? Don't you think so?"

"Indeed I do," he said.

"If so," said I, "such persons would certainly believe that there were no realities except those shadows of handmade things."[10]

"So it must be," said he.

"Now consider," said I, "what their release would be like, and their cure from these fetters and their folly; let us imagine whether it might naturally be something like this. One might be released, and compelled suddenly to stand up and turn his neck round, and to walk and look towards the firelight; all this would hurt him, and he would be too much dazzled to see distinctly those things whose shadows he had seen before. What do you think he would say, if someone told him that what he saw before was foolery, but now he saw more rightly, being a bit nearer reality and turned towards what was a little more real? What if he were shown each of the passing things, and compelled by questions to answer what each one was? Don't you think he would be puzzled, and believe what he saw before was more true than what was shown to him now?"

"Far more," he said.

"Then suppose he were compelled to look towards the real light, it would hurt his eyes, and he would escape by turning them away to the things which he was able to look at, and these he would believe to be clearer than what was being shown to him."

"Just so," said he.

"Suppose, now," said I, "that someone should drag him thence by force, up the rough ascent, the steep way up, and never stop until he could drag him out into the light of the sun, would he not be distressed and furious at being dragged;

---

[9] Which they had never seen. They would say "tree" when it was only a shadow of the model of a tree.

[10] Shadows of artificial things, not even the shadow of a growing tree: another stage from reality.

and when he came into the light, the brilliance would fill his eyes and he would not be able to see even one of the things now called real?"[11]

"That he would not," said he, "all of a sudden."

"He would have to get used to it, surely, I think, if he is to see the things above. First he would most easily look at shadows, after that images of mankind and the rest in water, lastly the things themselves. After this he would find it easier to survey by night the heavens themselves and all that is in them, gazing at the light of the stars and moon, rather than by day the sun and the sun's light."

"Of course."

"Last of all, I suppose, the sun; he could look on the sun itself by itself in its own place, and see what it is like, not reflections of it in water or as it appears in some alien setting."

"Necessarily," said he.

"And only after all this he might reason about it, how this is he who provides seasons and years, and is set over all there is in the visible region, and he is in a manner the cause of all things which they saw."

"Yes, it is clear," said he, "that after all that, he would come to this last.". . .

"Then again," I said, "just consider; if such a one should go down again and sit on his old seat, would he not get his eyes full of darkness coming in suddenly out of the sun?"

"Very much so," said he.

"And if he should have to compete with those who had been always prisoners, by laying down the law about those shadows while he was blinking before his eyes were settled down—and it would take a good long time to get used to things—wouldn't they all laugh at him and say he had spoiled his eyesight by going up there, and it was not worth-while so much as to try to go up? And would they not kill anyone who tried to release them and take them up, if they could somehow lay hands on him and kill him?"

"That they would!" said he.

"Then we must apply this image, my dear Glaucon," said I, "to all we have been saying. The world of our sight is like the habitation in prison, the firelight there to the sunlight here, the ascent and the view of the upper world is the rising of the soul into the world of mind; put it so and you will not be far

[11] To the next stage of knowledge: the real thing, not the artificial puppet.

from my own surmise, since that is what you want to hear; but God knows if it is really true. At least, what appears to me is, that in the world of the known, last of all,[12] is the idea of the good, and with what toil to be seen! And seen, this must be inferred to be the cause of all right and beautiful things for all, which gives birth to light and the king of light in the world of sight, and, in the world of mind, herself the queen produces truth and reason; and she must be seen by one who is to act with reason publicly or privately."

[12] The end of our search.

13

A Tidiness of Words

ARISTOTLE (384–323 B.C.), "the Master of those who know" as Dante calls him reverently, was the son of a doctor from the Ionian colony of Stagira in Thrace. He came to Athens at the age of eighteen, proceeded, says a tradition, to waste most of his fortune on dancing girls, then entered Plato's Academy, where he remained until his master's death. Being then about thirty-five, he moved to the city of Atarneus in Asia Minor, whose self-made ruler, Hermias, was his friend. When Hermias was captured and crucified by the Persians, Aristotle sailed to Mytilene, taking with him Hermias's orphaned daughter, whom he married. He settled with his little princess on the island of Lesbos, where he seems to have done much of his work on natural history during the two years that followed. In 342, Philip of Macedon invited him to his court as the tutor of his son, who was to become Alexander the Great and to bring to an end all that Aristotle knew and taught in his *Politics*.

When Alexander came to the throne, Aristotle settled in Athens and founded a university of his own, the Lyceum (which also became known as the "Peripatos" or "promenade" because discussion took place in its shaded walks). Alexander, it is said, put emissaries at his disposal to collect material on natural history from all over his empire. Thus was born the first great scientific project. After Alexander's death, the Athenians with Demosthenes rose against Macedonian rule. Aristotle left "lest they be tempted to commit another crime against philosophy," and withdrew to the island of Euboea, where he died at the age of sixty-three.

Aristotle's enterprise started from Plato's research into

the classification of Ideas. It was aimed at encompassing all the knowledge of his times, and at organizing it philosophically into one coherent whole. He had first, therefore, to forge the "Instrument" (*Organon*) of Formal Logic. As the Master of the Syllogism, he provided the foundations of liberal education for the next two thousand years. But this for him was only the premise to a system which moved from the First Philosophy (later called Metaphysics) to his Treatise on the Soul and then to Physics, i.e., cosmology, and on to Natural History, which concluded the theoretical part, while the "productive" and "practical" part embraced Poetics, Ethics, Economics, and Politics.

Aristotle, like the Presocratics, again focuses his attention on nature. But he has a way of making all his predecessors look archaic, and himself as the first representative of the full maturity of thought. Those who come before stand there, as we said earlier, like prophets in the wilderness, each voicing his lone unsupported revelation. It is his patient concern to show how each of them discovered some one aspect of the truth, in his own singular way, and how good "method" (the word is his) will fit these facets together in the true construction. Aristotle turns out thus to be the earliest historian of thought, even if, in order to fit the various thinkers in their proper place, he has to distort their ideas at times most unfairly. But it is revealing of the man who has so often been accused of haughtiness that he has turned the Socratic inquiry into an open-minded procedure almost similar to that of a modern anthropologist exploring a new culture. Let us see, he suggests, what people can mean when they use certain terms; then let us clean it up and put it all together with good method. There is no denying the scientific aspect of this exploration; but it yields essentially a verbal machinery, a "science" of coherent discourse about all that is already known. In this way Aristotle stabilized knowledge. Greece had after him many thinkers more appealing, more profound, or more effective, but none greater than he for amplitude of scope and organizing power: he remains the Teacher over the centuries. With him, in fact, is born a figure which, for better or worse, will have an important role in the Western world, that of the Professor.

THE CHOICES INVOLVED

"There is no science except of the general." Such is Aristotle's firm principle. But instead of beginning from Ideas, he takes his start from things. This shows that excellent trait called curiosity, which is often lacking in philosophers. The actual starting point of philosophical attention is, in his own engagingly simple language, *to de ti,* literally "this thing here," and the basic question about it is *to ti en einai,* "the what it is to be."

Right here, without further ado, a modern scientist might challenge the question as pointless and ask instead: What is it made of and how does it work? That is, he would focus on certain properties of the thing, mathematical, chemical, or what not, and try to tie those up into a system of universal relations. He would have reached thus another science of the general, and one which yields high results, but he would have by-passed the question of what that particular thing *is.* This is what was done even by Aristotle's elder contemporary, Democritus. To the question: What is this cat here? Democritus would have answered: "In reality nothing but atoms and the void." A penetrating answer, no doubt, but it would have taken a whole, and as yet nonexistent, body of science to give the quantitative composition of the cat; and this would have left us still immeasurably far from the cat itself. It must be admitted that the founders of modern science left the question of the cat beyond the horizon, and decided to find what quantitative cosmic laws could be deduced from the fall of stones, the orbiting of planets, or the oxidation of mercury.

Greek thought may then be excused for trying to make sense of the universe in a more direct way than ours, and one which should do justice to its manifold diversity. It might be called the search for a nondeforming perspective. And this is exactly what Aristotle stands for. There were two ways open: artistic intuition, which does not lead to the general, and coherent discourse, which does. He had therefore to choose the latter, and with it he chose inevitably the logico-verbal approach. A cat is a being in its own right, its catness part of the scheme of universals.

It is in the name of things as they are that Aristotle builds up his distinctions and categorizations, ever more subtly and elaborately knit to do justice to the innumerable "modes" of being, in the manner of a jurist seeing things from many angles. From this, in time, and with the help of Christianity, will come our concept of the uniqueness of the individual. Without question, it is the truly civilized attitude, for is not the richness of civilization tantamount to knowing how to see and name distinctions, shades of meaning, varieties of situations? What is definition but difference clearly determined? The intuitive and the formal mind will meet in this desire to enrich our capacity to discern the varieties of being, instead of throwing them back into the caldron of reduction.

But this is just what causes Aristotle to swerve away from mathematics. The tendency to reduce, to simplify, the same which has given the modern physicist his power over nature, renders that physicist helpless when it comes to complex living reality. Aristotle feels that he has to make a choice of instruments. He, too, if algebra had been invented in his time, would have described it as some type of "low cunning." There is, he suggests, a more natural and sensible way than mathematics to build up understanding of organic and "architectonic" cosmos of which there is a *gnōsis,* in which man has a true and significant place.

But since science has to be universal, he takes to legislating over mathematics itself, and bringing in, there too, the proper distinctions. It is wrong to say, he teaches for instance, that curved and straight lines are in any way commensurable, or even comparable. They are different species and must be kept distinct. And so, too, must earthly and heavenly motions be utterly distinct and noncomparable. He goes even further; he eschews geometric words for real situations. We say, he remarks, of a nose that it is "snub," of a hoop that it is "bent"; we do not use the word "curved," which is abstract and inappropriate. In this way mathematics is relegated to pure and inoperant abstraction.

It is an utterly different road from that of Plato which Aristotle has taken. But when it comes to organizing, the Platonism which has become to him a second nature reasserts itself.

THE PRIMACY OF THE MIND

This second nature is a tendency to explain in terms of the mind. It is absolutely obvious to Aristotle that the mind, comprehender of essences, comes first, and that nothing can be explained if we do not begin with that beginning. He remarks somewhere that by introducing the mind as an active factor throughout the universe, Anaxagoras looked like the only sane man among the early thinkers. This is not a good historical point of view but it is revealing.

To the fact-minded modern, this primacy of the mind may seem stranger than it is. Galileo, when he said that the book of nature is written in mathematical characters, was stating, too, one kind of idealism, the objective kind. He approached reality by one of its ideal properties, and tried to see where it would lead. Aristotle logicalizes reality from all possible aspects, which is what makes him the master of the *distinguo* and the fountainhead of much quibbling (he is able to do this methodically, in that he is sure of where he is going, for he has the Platonic model of a universal science, whereas our time is still trying to discover a particular one). But whichever way it is handled, idealism is a necessary component of all science; it *is* the search for a central perspective; hence we should make an effort to understand. Any evidence of orderly process is, for Aristotle, evidence of some kind of analogous relationship between the observer's mind and what he is looking at. The components of reality appear to fit together as the components of a thought would do. Supposing that conscious thought were to devise an apparatus for seeing, it would come up with something very similar to the eye. This, for the true idealist and transcendental philosopher, may mean that we recognize a conscious super-mind behind the universe, who thought it all out to the least detail. But even at the other pole, that supreme skeptic Mr. Hume concluded that we have evidence of something analogous to a mind—a vague footprint in the sands of time, too little to go on, as far as he was concerned, so he suggested we let it go at that. Taken in 1750, such an attitude was the essence of good sense.

Now, for Aristotle the analogy does hold; the footprint must be followed up. But he is no absolute idealist. He decides that the categories of mind are a conscious version of what takes place in nature in the first place. The form of each thing is a kind of pre-mental component (moderns would call it an "intentionality") inherent in the very process of reality, and it comes to being in the actual thing by realizing its "potency." It is through this analogy between thought and its object that we can understand.

If we do not try to *understand,* then of course we need not try any such scheme. For us inside modern physics, who want only to *explain,* the direction of thought is another. But it is far from being the natural one. We mentioned the eye as a prime example of what can be possibly understood, but hardly "explained," as we stand now. If we show a man a watch, he will not tend to explain it in terms of its machinery, unless he is a watchmaker or a very curious person. He will simply understand it as a timepiece. A watch is defined by its purpose, which is telling time, and that is also the "good" of a watch. Our understanding tends thus to be formulated in terms of the "good."

And so back to the Good, which is a dangerously simple idea. Everyone thinks he knows about his own good—at least until he finds a Socrates to paralyze him like an electric eel. But here we are beyond Socrates and man's motives. What is a flower good for, or a cockroach for that matter, or, as Franklin said, what good is a baby? Faced with the world as a whole, once we have outgrown the simple desire to say it is good for our convenience (and before we have reached the mechanistic phase), there is only one way of speaking about it and that is in terms at once rational and esthetic. For, whatever reconciliation we achieve, the thinking being can come to terms with it only on the esthetic level. A flower or a baby is simply meant to become what it is, its own "what it is to be." Its complete achievement is its own "good." And what is the total "good"? The universe makes sense as something eternal and diverse and eternally well-ordered. On this Aristotle claims to find himself in complete agreement both with Plato and with the Pythagoreans. It is in "the best tradition." Notice how careful he always is of putting back of him consensus and the best results of the thinking of all ages.

If we try to define the curve that goes from, say, Parmenides to Aristotle, a way to describe it would be this: science rejoins again the needs of society. The Eleatic and atomistic attempt was grandiose enough, but it must be admitted that it looked both stern and inconclusive. Modern science has made itself acceptable by delivering results. That science only set problems: ever new problems more and more difficult and profound, which lead ever farther away from our social and worldly perspectives. Socrates had come to discard natural philosophy. Aristotle tries to bring it back, but it has to be in another garb. Instead of the universe of rigor and necessity, of symmetry and sufficient reason, we have a universe of variety, neatness, distinction, of aptness and of plausible reason; the universe of the biologist and the jurist.

A BIOLOGICAL PHYSICS

Aristotle is averse to reduction. As for material principles, they explain, in his eyes, nothing of what is essential. Parmenides was surely right, he says, in seeing that the kind of principle we need has properties of eternity and perfection which cannot belong to matter itself. That is why, in fact, Heraclitus had brought in the *logos,* why the Pythagoreans had believed in Numbers, why Parmenides has become the "inventor of metaphysics." But we must go farther. Parmenides had been tied to a curious presentation of primal substance, or rather substrate, which he had in some way tried to intellectualize into Being. But if, as he said, the only truth is that which is obtained by legitimate thinking itself, we must take the full consequences of his statement and say that truth about Being can be had only through the mind.

It is through the mind and its creative and esthetic motives that we are in most immediate contact with the reality of process in the universe. But in what sense can one think of mind as reflecting the scheme of eternity? It can, forever, project the consistency and the variety, and the delight in the union of both. To understand a tree from the point of view of Nature is to understand that apparently Nature wants that type of tree to be there forever, and to be there beside all other types that she has been pleased to bring forth. The pleasure that we find in naming and in distinguishing the variety of things in the world will be in some way creatively, if only intellectually, akin to the pleasure that Nature herself has had in bringing them forth. Nature clearly does not care much for the individual; nor does Science. Science is of the universal, that is, of what is meaningful to nature. We can make a wooden bed and be pleased with it, but Nature does not register its existence. If we bury the bed in the earth, "it is not beds that shall spring forth from it, but wood." Where does this lead us?

To true substances. The cat, like the wood, is not made of plain atoms. It is one, continuous, specific substance called "cat," unique in the scheme; the knowable aspect of its essence is "catness," which applies to all cats. We can distinguish between "attributes" which are inherent to it (such as its shape and behavior) and "accidents" (such as its color and size). It is related to other substances in many different ways, in which the universals become evident. We have been led again to description, distinction, organization, generality, as the proper goal of science. It is natural history leading to a system of ideas, thanks to the power of classification which can rise in less than ten steps without confusion from a million individual species to a general concept. To contemplate an eternal well-organized order is to partake in some way of the mind of Nature herself. There is no possibility of evolution here, only the unchanging firmness of Design.

To know, it has been said, is to know by causes. How can we figure out a cause in this system if not by analogy with ours? Let us define a cause in the most ample and general sense as answering the question "Why?": that antecedent without which something would not be. Then let us consider, "for instance," says Aristotle, the house which is our own creation. A house would not be without (a) the material to build it, (b) a builder, (c) plans, and (d) the decision to build a house. Clearly the decision comes first, not only in time but in significance, because the decision contains implicitly in it all that the house will really be, since it is taken with a definite intention related to definite circumstances. As we go down in the order of causes, the definiteness decreases. The plan must be such as to correspond to the intention; but a certain measure of invention is allowed. The builder has only one requirement: that he be expert in building. As for the material, it is absolutely a matter of circumstances and local choices. Any material will do that corresponds to the general requirements. Now these four levels are what Aristotle calls the four types of cause: in ascending order, they are (a) the material, (b) the efficient, (c) the formal, and (d) the final. Here we have Aristotle's own kind of sufficient reason.

If we take now, instead of the analogy of the house, the analogy of the statue, the parallel comes closer. For the artist is at the same time the efficient, formal, and final cause of his work. He has conceived it out of his own esthetic decision and he carries it through with esthetic choice in complete freedom. The only thing still outside him is the material. Then we see that Nature herself is nothing but an unconscious artist who has in addition to all the other causes the material cause in herself, that is, who gets the material of her work out of herself. In this case the form that she impresses on the material goes throughout the material. Quite naturally, we have reached an important definition of life: Form actualizing itself. It has remained inside our culture to this day.

The definition is no doubt striking and ample, but that is just the trouble: it is, so to say, complete in itself. We need not search further for the nature of life, because we have already expressed it. It is Form intrinsic to the living substance. The idea works because each being in the course of its life acts exactly *as if* it were realizing a complete form of itself out of an amorphous beginning. It is the change of the seed into the bud, of the bud into the flower. It is as if an unconscious will and a projected pattern were urging the Form to manifest itself by commanding the growth of the being. The will is directed to an end —the completion of the being is full Form. This is what Aristotle called *change* and *motion*. Beings attain their full Form and at the same time begin to decay. The process of things on earth is held between these two terms: generation and corruption, coming-into-being and passing-away. It is as it were the heartbeat of life; everything that exists will go to completion and death, but also it will have generated another thing which in turn undergoes the same cycle.

The same creativeness which is the secret of God's Active Intellect in the universe is also the secret of nature; it manifests itself forever again in the pulse of individual life coming into being. No mechanical doctrine could have achieved this. We hope this has been made clear already. The mechanical world models produced under the Newtonian aegis through the eighteenth century do look childish in the face of the full problem. Aristotle had to go his own way. Since he agreed that nature is motion, he had to work out an entirely different conception of that key term itself.

Here we are at the heart of what he calls *physics*.

What we call "motion" is only one type of motion for Aristotle, who calls it "local motion" as distinct from quantitative and qualitative. This must be understood in terms of what Aristotle was trying to do, viz., organize a "science of nature" (the *Physics*) which should comprehend what we call today cosmology, physics, chemistry, and biology into a single frame of explanation, and starting from the most familiar characteristics and regularities. Nature is change. All change between "contraries" is what Aristotle calls motion. Change has to take place inside an order, or chaos would supervene. Moreover, in that order there seem to be "natures" which go on notwithstanding change, e.g., the living species, and they are a clue to the principle of order whereby things are kept or restored to their function in the order of Nature. Since there is, clearly, such an order, we can think only of two sorts of change or movement: that whereby something becomes what it really is (growth); and that whereby it becomes the material for the growth of something else (decay). Hence the famous definition that Descartes rather unfairly said made no sense in any language: movement is the act of being in potency in so far as it has not reached its full actualization or unfolding. The fulfillment must be there as a goal, potentially and directively, before it is realized; it may be a place (up, down) or a form (the grown animal); in any case it implies a *real* change, in no way relativistic. The existence of an order implies a direction and a goal. And in fact we see fire striving toward heaven, stones towards the center of the earth, as the seed strives towards the full-grown form. This leads to the idea of a place or "natural locus" as the goal of "natural movement." Any "violent movement" which would tend to break the balance is soon checked, and order restored. As to rest, it means the thing has reached its locus or has been temporarily checked on its way there. It must needs be, then, that each singular movement on earth is transitory, as it disturbs or restores the balance; but, as it needs another movement for its cause, the chain of causes is eternal. It is clear at this point that Aristotle is thinking all along of what we call *process* in general. If we translate him thus, the argument falls into place. Thus, "movement" takes place always against a resistance (here, again, the appeal is to familiar things) and comes to an end by the re-establishment of equilibrium; it is a passage between contraries; it needs an exterior cause, removing which it comes to a stop. It will be seen also why to Aristotle inertial motion—that is, motion undirected, unprompted, in a nonpatterned space—must appear as an unreal and perverse abstraction. The void cannot exist, for things would not know which way to go in it. The conflict with the strictly mechanical conception is unreconcilable. In the realm of astronomy it will lead to a system again unreconcilable with mechanics.

What is cause in all this? It is certainly not the "material" cause which is pure amorphous possibility; it is Reason in action in the other three causes—a *logos* that goes from thought to action, or, more generally still, from plan to realization. It is never, at any point, the Principle of Sufficient Reason of the scientists, which we have also called the Principle of Uniformly Distributed Ignorance— a principle which operates in terms of openness, symmetry, and continuity, not to mention discovery. Understanding is teleological. It always involves a principle of Specific Reason: "This item should be thus, and unique, because such is its place in the pattern." It leads to variety and formal discontinuity. It leads also to saying more than we know about things.

Therefore the search for invariants, which is the definition of science, takes on a very special aspect. Aristotle, true to his antimathematical bias, has no quantitative conservation principles like ours. But the Act, that is, the actualized Form, is there forever, dominating change. It is the Form in Act that is conserved, as appears to be affirmed impressively by Nature herself: "How careful of the type she seems." It may be relevant to note that our word "act" in Aristotle's Greek is *energeia*. There was a possibility of reinterpretation there that did not escape the subtle mind of Leibniz. In Aristotle himself, it comes straight from Plato. But what kind of Platonism is it?

Plato had made it very clear that true knowledge is divorced, "cut off" as he insists, from sensible reality, whose symbol is the dark wall of the Cave. Between the two worlds there is only geometry to join them, myth, and the wings of the Socratic Eros, of which we are told in the *Symposium*. For Aristotle, the Ideas are inherent in the individual substances; they are nowhere else to be found or known, except in the Active Intellect of God who thinks them forever and thus causes the world to function. But if there is nothing but physical substance, it must extend all the way to the upper limit of heaven, and be such as to account for the geometrical behavior of the stars. There will be rigid spheres, hard, transparent, crystalline, to carry the celestial bodies. The abstract mathematical models of the astronomers (of which hereafter) are transformed by Aristotle into an absurd machinery of crystal spheres turning and counterturning so as to cancel out all except the one driving 24-hour motion, that of the outer heaven or Primum Mobile, which in turn is moved by the Unmoved Mover "as a thing beloved."

That outer sphere encloses and concludes the universe. Beyond it there is only God, who is totally actualized thought, immaterial, enfolding the whole. There is no space out there, for space is "place," and place has ceased. There is no void, because the void does not exist. The universe is an achieved Form, which excludes any reality beyond it. Inside, all is Form again, in a hierarchy of causes which goes down to the individual beings. Plato's concept of Design has been de-mathematized, Ionian fashion.

We can see how Aristotle has solved the original problem of the One and the Many. The Ionians had imagined a primeval matter, a single *physis,* underlying everything. Aristotle shows that it was merely a symbol to be worked out. Matter itself can have only amorphous oneness; it is the raw material, the Possible. Above it there are the efficient causes which ultimately become one cause, the rotation of the Outer Sphere. This is supposed to bring about the motion of the sun in its yearly cycle, which in turn controls the motions of the four elements. "The cause of change lies in the obliquity of the ecliptic." The formal cause of nature is again, at the summit, one; it is the total Design; and above it is the final cause, which is also the First Cause, God himself. "It is good that there should be only one ruler." Unity is throughout. It works articulated into four levels.

In conclusion, a hierarchy—with no two-way interaction (as from the Platonic Ideas down to reality)—as indeed there must be if everything is to stay in place and shape. The upper causes rain down, so to speak, constant action and order (e.g., the sun's heat and position) without being affected by anything below or by their own output. No longer is there a struggle and balance of opposites; contrarieties are settled through the proper channels. Newton's First Law is utterly absent. The underlying image seems to be patriarchal power generating life, type, and order without losing anything of its dominant force.

With all that, Aristotle is what Plato never was—a scientist. He is the type of scientist who remains always closely bound to sensible, experienced reality. For him velocity is proportional to effort, as anyone knows who has to quicken his pace or to push a wheelbarrow; space is the collection of "places" of things, in a way which would remind us of the shipping room in a department store. By contrast, the *physicist's* way as we mean it, from Anaximander to Niels Bohr, is to project, in terms of something else than the experienced, a model, a mechanism, an abstraction, which can afford a clear and coherent representation. When he sees a ball rolling, he thinks in terms of what he has never seen, frictionless motion. When he watches water rising in a pump, he does not see Nature urging it to avoid a vacuum, he visualizes a balancing system of pressures. There is no reconciling these two ways.

As Aristotelian physics remains in the realm of the plausible and refuses to yield to the unexpected, it cannot lead to discoveries. "Final causes," said Francis Bacon bitingly, "are like Vestal virgins, dedicated to God and sterile." Worse still, they restrict the universe to a system of reasons and purposes which, however lofty, are in the image of our own concerns. But one has only to contrast the verbal jugglings of the *Physics* with the excellent compact sense of Aristotle's *Natural History* to realize that form and purpose remain durable tools of analysis in biology. Hence they could not but be a sort of center of gravity for all premodern thought. What held attention in an agrarian society were living things. We, today, are used to existing among devices of our own making, among forces and resources which have been extracted and shaped and modulated by man to his need from inert materials. Ours is a technomorphic society. It was not so even two centuries ago. It was biomorphic. Aristotle took the central perspective by assuming life and its forms as the simple reality, what is directly given and firmly maintained in nature. Such a thought need not aim at discovery: it will aim at "understanding" what we already know. Hence, although it takes its departure from things, its true profundity can be reached only in its search for what effective understanding can mean. It is in this search that Aristotle remains the unchallenged leader up to the time of Kant. We are still engaged in that original search for "what it is to be." Paraphrasing Pascal, one might say: there is a richness to be expressed by words not reducible to any physical scheme however abstract; there is a power of coherent physical representation which has to renounce that wealth of meaning. These are the two poles of philosophy and science. Aristotle thought he had achieved a total conciliation. After the end of Antiquity, his formal schemes dominated a thousand years of culture. That is why we had to take them into careful account, unscientific as they may seem to a modern.

One aspect of them, as we said, remains scientific beyond challenge, and that is the biological. The sections we give below are enough to show it. This is where the investigator of reality has achieved his "entelechy," the full potentialities of his nature. Aristotelian thought dominates Galen's textbook (A.D. 190), the final medical opus of antiquity, and hence all medicine up to Harvey and beyond; it provides the model for the great classifications of life which start in the eighteenth century with Linné, and for the comparative anatomy of Cuvier in the nineteenth century. It can be said to maintain rationality in a field forever beset with romantic vitalism: unclear imaginations, creative forces, fluid forms which lead to such resplendent failures as Lamarck and Bergson. Its undeviating firmness of design is to be found even where Aristotle would have refused to enter, namely, in modern evolutionary theory; Darwinism can be seen as another Rip van Winkle myth—an awesome game of Time with Aristotelian Forms, with blind Necessity casting the dice.

Nature Defined
(Book V, Chapter 4, of *Metaphysics*) *

"Nature" means (1) the genesis of growing things—the meaning which would be suggested if one were to pronounce the υ in φύσις, the ȳ in *Phýsis* long. (2) That immanent part of a growing thing, from which its growth first proceeds. (3) The source from which the primary movement in each natural object is present in it in virtue of its own essence. Those things are said to grow which derive increase from something else by contact and either by organic unity, or by organic adhesion as in the case of embryos. Organic unity differs from contact; for in the latter case there need not be anything besides the contact, but in organic unities there is something identical in both parts, which makes them grow together instead of merely touching, and be one in respect of continuity and quantity, though not of quality.—(4) "Nature" means the primary material of which any natural object consists or out of which it is made, which is relatively unshaped and cannot be changed from its own potency, as, e.g., bronze is said to be the nature of a statue and of bronze utensils, and wood the nature of wooden things; and so in all other cases; for when a product is made out of these materials, the first matter is preserved throughout. For it is in this way that people call the elements of natural objects also their nature, some naming fire, others earth, others air, others water, others something else of the sort, and some naming more than one of these, and others all of them.—(5) "Nature" means the *essence* of natural objects, as with those who say the nature is the primary mode of composition, or as Empedocles says:—

* W. D. Ross, *op. cit.*

Nothing that is has a nature,
But only mixing and parting of the mixed,
And nature is but a name given them by men.

Hence as regards the things that are or come to be by nature, though that *from which* they naturally come to be or are is already present, we say they have not their nature yet, unless they have their form or shape. That which comprises both of these (matter and form) exists *by* nature, e.g., the animals and their parts; and not only is the first matter nature (and this in two senses, either the first, counting from the thing, or the first in general; e.g., in the case of works in bronze, bronze is first with reference to them, but in general perhaps water is first, if all things that can be melted are water), but also the form or essence, which is the end of the process of becoming.—(6) By an extension of meaning from this sense of "nature" every essence in general has come to be called a "nature," because the nature of a thing is one kind of essence.

From what has been said, then, it is plain that nature in the primary and strict sense is the essence of things which have in themselves, as such, a source of movement; for the matter is called the nature because it is qualified to receive this, and processes of becoming and growing are called nature because they are movements proceeding from this. And nature in this sense is the source of the movement of natural objects, being present in them somehow, either potentially or in complete reality.

Is Nature an Order or Is It by Chance and Necessity?
(Book II of *Physics*) *

Now the principles which cause motion in a physical way are two, of which one is not physical, as it has no principle of motion in itself. Of this kind is whatever causes movement, not being itself moved, such as (1) that which is completely unchangeable, the primary reality, and (2) the essence of that which is coming to be, i.e., the form; for this is the end or "that for the sake of which." Hence since nature is for the sake of something, we must know this cause also. We must explain the "why" in all the senses of the term, namely, (1) that from this that will necessarily result ("from this" either with-

* W. D. Ross, *op. cit.,* translated by R. P. Hardie and R. K. Gage, Vol. 2.

out qualification or in most cases); (2) that "this must be so if that is to be so" (as the conclusion presupposes the premisses); (3) that this was the essence of the thing; and (4) because it is better thus (not without qualification, but with reference to the essential nature in each case).

We must explain then (1) that Nature belongs to the class of causes which act for the sake of something; (2) about the necessary and its place in physical problems, for all writers ascribe things to this cause, arguing that since the hot and the cold, etc., are of such and such a kind, therefore certain things *necessarily* are and come to be—and if they mention any other cause (one his "friendship and strife," another his "mind"), it is only to touch on it, and then good-bye to it.

A difficulty presents itself: why should not Nature work, not for the sake of something, nor because it is better so, but just as the sky rains, not in order to make the corn grow, but of necessity? What is drawn up must cool, and is for the sake of an end; therefore the nature of things also is so. Thus if a house, e.g., had been a thing made by Nature, it would have been made in the same way as it is now by art; and if things made by Nature were made also by art, they would come to be in the same way as by nature. Each step then in the series is for the sake of the next; and generally art partly completes what Nature cannot bring to a finish, and partly imitates her. If, therefore, artificial products are for the sake of an end, so clearly also are natural products. The relation of the later to the earlier terms of the series is the same in both.

This is most obvious in the animals other than man: they make things neither by art nor after inquiry or deliberation. Wherefore people discuss whether it is by intelligence or by some other faculty that these creatures work—spiders, ants, and the like. By gradual advance in this direction we come to see clearly that in plants too that is produced which is conducive to the end—leaves, e.g., grow to provide shade for the fruit. If then it is both by nature and for an end that the swallow makes its nest and the spider its web, and plants grow leaves for the sake of the fruit and send their roots down (not up) for the sake of nourishment, it is plain that this kind of cause is operative in things which come to be and are by nature. And since "nature" means two things, the matter and the form, of which the latter is the end, and since all the rest is for the sake of the end, the form must be the cause in the sense of "that for the sake of which."

Space and the Void: Theory of Motion
(Book IV of *Physics*) *

Let us explain again that there is no void existing separately, as some maintain. If each of the simple bodies has
a natural locomotion, e.g., fire upward and earth downward
and towards the middle of the universe, it is clear that it cannot be the void that is the condition of locomotion. What,
then, *will* the void be the condition of? It is thought to be the
condition of movement in respect of place, and it is not the
condition of this.

Again, if void is a sort of place deprived of body, when
there is a void where will a body placed in it move to? It certainly cannot move into the whole of the void. The same argument applies as against those who think that place is something separate, into which things are carried; viz., how will
what is placed in it move, or rest? Much the same argument
will apply to the void as to the "up" and "down" in place, as
is natural enough since those who maintain the existence of
the void make it a place.

And in what way will things be present either in place or
in the void? For the expected result does not take place when
a body is placed as a whole in a place conceived of as separate and permanent; for a part of it, unless it be placed apart,
will not be in a place but in the whole. Further, if separate
place does not exist, neither will void.

If people say that the void must exist, as being necessary
if there is to be movement, what rather turns out to be the
case, if one studies the matter, is the opposite, that not a
single thing can be moved if there *is* a void; for as with those
who for a like reason say the earth is at rest, so, too, in the
void things must be at rest; for there is no place to which
things can move more or less than to another; since the void
in so far as it is void admits no difference.

The second reason is this: all movement is either compulsory or according to nature, and if there is compulsory movement there must also be natural (for compulsory movement
is contrary to nature, and movement contrary to nature is
posterior to that according to nature, so that if each of the
natural bodies has not a natural movement, none of the other
movements can exist); but how can there be natural movement if there is no difference throughout the void or the in-

* *Ibid.*

finite? For in so far as it is infinite, there will be no up or down or middle, and in so far as it is a void, up differs no whit from down; for as there is no difference in what is nothing, there is none in the void (for the void seems to be a nonexistent and a privation of being), but natural locomotion seems to be differentiated, so that the things that exist by nature must be differentiated. Either, then, nothing has a natural locomotion, or else there is no void.

Further, in point of fact things that are thrown move though that which gave them their impulse is not touching them, either by reason of mutual replacement, as some maintain, or because the air that has been pushed pushes them with a movement quicker than the natural locomotion of the projectile wherewith it moves to its proper place. But in a void none of these things can take place, nor can anything be moved save as that which is carried is moved.

Further, no one could say why a thing once set in motion should stop anywhere; for why should it stop *here* rather than *here?* So that a thing will either be at rest or must be moved *ad infinitum,* unless something more powerful get in its way.*

Further, things are now thought to move into the void because it yields; but in a void this quality is present equally everywhere, so that things should move in all directions.

Further, the truth of what we assert is plain from the following considerations. We see the same weight or body moving faster than another for two reasons, either because there is a difference in what it moves through, as between water, air, and earth, or because, other things being equal, the moving body differs from the other owing to excess of weight or of lightness.

Now the medium causes a difference because it impedes the moving thing, most of all if it is moving in the opposite direction, but in a secondary degree even if it is at rest; and especially a medium that is not easily divided, i.e., a medium that is somewhat dense.

A, then, will move through B in time C; and through D, which is thinner, in time E (if the length of B is equal to D), in proportion to the density of the hindering body. For let B be water and D air; then by so much as air is thinner and more incorporeal than water, A will move through D faster than through B. Let the speed have the same ratio to the

* Here Democritus's argument from Sufficient Reason appears only to be rejected. And with it goes the inertial principle.

speed, then, that air has to water. Then if air is twice as thin, the body will traverse B in twice the time that it does D, and the time C will be twice the time E. And always, by so much as the medium is more incorporeal and less resistant and more easily divided, the faster will be the movement.

Now there is no ratio in which the void is exceeded by body, as there is no ratio of 0 to a number. For if 4 exceeds 3 by 1, and 2 by more than 1, and 1 by still more than it exceeds 2, still there is no ratio by which it exceeds 0; for that which exceeds must be divisible into the excess + that which is exceeded, so that 4 will be what it exceeds 0 by + 0. For this reason, too, a line does not exceed a point—unless it is composed of points! Similarly the void can bear no ratio to the full, and therefore neither can movement through the one to movement through the other, but if a thing moves through the thickest medium such and such a distance in such and such a time, it moves through the void with a speed beyond any ratio. For let F be void, equal in magnitude to B and to D. Then if A is to traverse and move through it in a certain line, G, a time less than E, however, the void will bear this ratio to the full. But in a time equal to G, A will traverse the part H of D. And it will surely also traverse in that time any substance F which exceeds air in thickness in the ratio which the time E bears to the time G. For if the body F be as much thinner than D as E exceeds G, A, if it moves through F, will traverse it in a time inverse to the speed of the movement, i.e., in a time equal to G. If, then, there is *no* body in F, A will traverse F still more quickly. But we supposed that its traverse of F when F was void occupied the time G. So that it will traverse F in an equal time whether F be full or void. But this is impossible. It is plain, then, that if there is a time in which it will move through any part of the void, this impossible result will follow: it will be found to traverse a certain distance, whether this be full or void, in an equal time; for there will be some *body* which is in the same ratio to the other body as the time is to the time.

To sum the matter up, the cause of this result is obvious, viz., that between any two movements there is a ratio (for they occupy time, and there is a ratio between any two times, so long as both are finite), but there is no ratio of void to full.

These are the consequences that result from a difference in the media; the following depend upon an excess of one moving body over another. We see that bodies which have a greater impulse either of weight or of lightness, if they are alike in other respects, move faster over an equal space, and in the ratio which their magnitudes bear to each other. Therefore they will also move through the void with this ratio of speed. But that is impossible; for why should one move faster? (In moving through *plena* it must be so; for the greater divides them faster by its force. For a moving thing cleaves the medium either by its shape, or by the impulse which the body that is carried along or is projected possesses.) Therefore all will possess equal velocity. But this is impossible.

It is evident from what has been said, then, that, if there is a void, a result follows which is the very opposite of the reason for which those who believe in a void set it up. They think that if movement in respect to place is to exist, the void cannot exist, separated all by itself; but this is the same as to say that place is a separate cavity; and this has already been stated to be impossible.

Situation and Motion of the Earth
(Book II of *On Heaven*) *

Let us first decide the question whether the earth moves or is at rest. For, as we said, there are some who make it one of the stars, and others who, setting it at the centre, suppose it to be "rolled" and in motion about the pole as axis. That both views are untenable will be clear if we take as our starting-point the fact that the earth's motion, whether the earth be at the centre or away from it, must needs be a constrained motion. It cannot be the movement of the earth itself. If it were, any portion of it would have this movement; but in fact every part moves in a straight line to the centre. Being, then, constrained and unnatural, the movement could not be eternal. But the order of the universe is eternal. Again, everything that moves with the circular movement, except the first sphere, is observed to be passed, and to move with more than one motion. The earth, then, also, whether it move about the centre or as stationary at it, must necessarily move with two motions. But if this were so, there would have to be passings and turnings of the fixed stars. Yet no such thing is observed. The same stars always rise and set in the same parts of the earth.

Further, the natural movement of the earth, part and whole

* W. D. Ross, *op. cit.*, translated by J. L. Stocks, Vol. 2.

alike, is to the centre of the whole—whence the fact that it is now actually situated at the centre—but it might be questioned, since both centres are the same, which centre it is that portions of earth and other heavy things move to. Is this their goal because it is the centre of the earth or because it is the centre of the whole? The goal, surely, must be the centre of the whole. For fire and other light things move to the extremity of the area which contains the centre. It happens, however, that the centre of the earth and of the whole is the same. Thus they do move to the centre of the earth, but accidentally, in virtue of the fact that the earth's centre lies at the centre of the whole. That the centre of the earth is the goal of their movement is indicated by the fact that heavy bodies moving towards the earth do not move parallel but so as to make equal angles, and thus to a single centre, that of the earth. It is clear, then, that the earth must be at the centre and immovable, not only for the reasons already given, but also because heavy bodies forcibly thrown quite straight upward return to the point from which they started, even if they are thrown to an infinite distance. From these considerations then it is clear that the earth does not move and does not lie elsewhere than at the centre. . . .

[There follow proofs that the earth is spherical.] The evidence of the senses further corroborates this. How else would eclipses of the moon show segments shaped as we see them? As it is, the shapes which the moon itself each month shows are of every kind—straight, gibbous, and concave—but in eclipses the outline is always curved: and, since it is the interposition of the earth that makes the eclipse, the form of this line will be caused by the form of the earth's surface, which is therefore spherical. Again, our observations of the stars make it evident, not only that the earth is circular, but also that it is a circle of no great size. For quite a small change of position to south or north causes a manifest alteration of the horizon. There is much change, I mean, in the stars which are overhead, and the stars seen are different, as one moves northward or southward. Indeed there are some stars seen in Egypt and in the neighbourhood of Cyprus which are not seen in the northerly regions; and stars, which in the north are never beyond the range of observation, in those regions rise and set. All of which goes to show not only that the earth is circular in shape, but also that it is a sphere of no great size: for otherwise the effect of so slight a change of place would not be so quickly apparent. Hence one should not be too sure of the incredibility of the view of those who conceive that there is continuity between the parts about the Pillars of Hercules and the parts about India, and that in this way the ocean is one. As further evidence in favour of this they quote the case of elephants, a species occurring in each of these extreme regions, suggesting that the common characteristic of these extremes is explained by their continuity. Also, those mathematicians who try to calculate the size of the earth's circumference arrive at the figure 400,000 stades.* This indicates not only that the earth's mass is spherical in shape, but also that as compared with the stars it is not of great size.

The Study of Biology, Its Reason and Method
(Book I of *On the Parts of Animals*) *

Of things constituted by nature some are ungenerated, imperishable, and eternal, while others are subject to generation and decay. The former are excellent beyond compare and divine, but less accessible to knowledge. The evidence that might throw light on them, and on the problems which we long to solve respecting them, is furnished but scantily by sensation; whereas respecting perishable plants and animals we have abundant information, living as we do in their midst, and ample data may be collected concerning all their various kinds, if only we are willing to take sufficient pains. Both departments, however, have their special charm. The scanty conceptions to which we can attain of celestial things give us, from their excellence, more pleasure than all our knowledge of the world in which we live; just as a half glimpse of persons that we love is more delightful than a leisurely view of other things, whatever their number and dimensions. On the other hand, in certitude and in completeness our knowledge of terrestrial things has the advantage. Moreover, their greater nearness and affinity to us balance somewhat the loftier in-

---

* We do not know the source of this evaluation, which would seem to be considerably in excess of the truth; but then the unit of the stade varied considerably through time. Later, Eratosthenes gave a figure correct within 150 miles, but it does not seem original with him. It is based on distances measured in Egypt, and on the information that the sun was mirrored in deep wells in Aswan on the day of the solstice, i.e. that Aswan was on the tropic. The figure must be old Egyptian, for already in the Middle Kingdom geodesic benchmarks had been set up which were true to latitude within 1' of arc.

† W. D. Ross, *op. cit.*, translated by W. Ogle, Vol. 5.

terest of the heavenly things that are the objects of the higher philosophy. Having already treated of the celestial world, as far as our conjectures could reach, we proceed to treat of animals, without omitting, to the best of our ability, any member of the kingdom, however ignoble. For if some have no graces to charm the sense, yet even these, by disclosing to intellectual perception the artistic spirit that designed them, give immense pleasure to all who can trace links of causation, and are inclined to philosophy. Indeed, it would be strange if mimic representations of them were attractive, because they disclose the mimetic skill of the painter or sculptor, and the original realities themselves were not more interesting, to all at any rate who have eyes to discern the reasons that determined their formation. We therefore must not recoil with childish aversion from the examination of the humbler animals. Every realm of nature is marvellous: and as Heraclitus, when the strangers who came to visit him found him warming himself at the furnace in the kitchen and hesitated to go in, is reported to have bidden them not to be afraid to enter, as even in that kitchen divinities were present, so we should venture on the study of every kind of animal without distaste; for each and all will reveal to us something natural and something beautiful. Absence of haphazard and conduciveness of everything to an end are to be found in Nature's works in the highest degree, and the resultant end of her generations and combinations is a form of the beautiful.

Of Birds and Their Eggs
(Book VI from *The History of Animals*) *

Generation from the egg proceeds in an identical manner with all birds, but the full periods from conception to birth differ, as has been said. With the common hen after three days and three nights there is the first indication of the embryo; with larger birds the interval being longer, with smaller birds shorter. Meanwhile the yolk comes into being, rising towards the sharp end, where the primal element of the egg is situated, and where the egg gets hatched; and the heart appears, like a speck of blood, in the white of the egg. This point beats and moves as though endowed with life, and from it two vein-ducts with blood in them trend in a convoluted course, and a membrane carrying bloody fibres now envelops the yolk,

* W. D. Ross, *op. cit.*, translated by D'A. W. Thompson, Vol. 4.

leading off from the vein-ducts. A little afterwards the body is differentiated, at first very small and white. The head is clearly distinguished, and in it the eyes, swollen out to a great extent. This condition of the eyes lasts on for a good while, as it is only by degrees that they diminish in size and collapse. At the outset the under portion of the body appears insignificant in comparison with the upper portion. Of the two ducts that lead from the heart, the one proceeds towards the circumjacent integument, and the other, like a navel-string, towards the yolk. The life-element of the chick is in the white of the egg, and the nutriment comes through the navel-string out of the yolk.

When the egg is now ten days old the chick and all its parts are distinctly visible. The head is still larger than the rest of its body, and the eyes larger than the head, but still devoid of vision. The eyes, if removed about this time, are found to be larger than beans, and black; if the cuticle be peeled off them there is a white and cold liquid inside, quite glittering in the sunlight, but there is no hard substance whatsoever. Such is the condition of the head and eyes. At this time also the larger internal organs are visible, as also the stomach and the arrangement of the viscera; and the veins that seem to proceed from the heart are now close to the navel. From the navel there stretch a pair of veins; one [1] towards the membrane that envelops the yolk (and, by the way, the yolk is now liquid, or more so than is normal), and the other [2] towards that membrane which envelops collectively the membrane wherein the chick lies, the membrane of the yolk, and the intervening liquid. On the tenth day the white is at the extreme outer surface, reduced in amount, glutinous, firm in substance, and sallow in colour.

The disposition of the several constituent parts is as follows. First and outermost comes the membrane of the egg, not that of the shell, but underneath it. Inside this membrane [3] is a white liquid; then comes the chick, and a membrane round about it,[4] separating it off so as to keep the chick free from the liquid; next after the chick comes the yolk, into which one of the two veins was described as leading, the other one leading into the enveloping white substance. [A membrane [3] with a liquid resembling serum envelops the entire structure. Then

[1] The vitelline vein and artery.
[2] The allantoic vein and artery.
[3] The allantois.
[4] The amnion.

comes another membrane [4] right round the embryo, as has been described, separating it off against the liquid. Underneath this comes the yolk, enveloped in another membrane (into which yolk proceeds the navel-string that leads from the heart and the big vein), so as to keep the embryo free of both liquids.]

About the twentieth day, if you open the egg and touch the chick, it moves inside and chirps; and it is already coming to be covered with down, when, after the twentieth day is past, the chick begins to break the shell. The head is situated over the right leg close to the flank, and the wing is placed over the head; and about this time is plain to be seen the membrane resembling an after-birth that comes next after the outermost membrane of the shell, into which membrane the one of the navel-strings was described as leading (and, by the way, the chick in its entirety is now within it), and so also is the other membrane resembling an after-birth, namely that surrounding the yolk, into which the second navel-string was described as leading; and both of them were described as being connected with the heart and the big vein. At this conjuncture the navel-string that leads to the outer after-birth collapses and becomes detached from the chick, and the membrane that leads into the yolk is fastened on to the thin gut of the creature, and by this time a considerable amount of the yolk is inside the chick and a yellow sediment is in its stomach. About this time it discharges residuum [5] in the direction of the outer after-birth, and has residuum inside its stomach; and the outer residuum is white. By and by the yolk, diminishing gradually in size, at length becomes entirely used up and comprehended within the chick (so that, ten days after hatching, if you cut open the chick, a small remnant of the yolk is still left in connexion with the gut), but it is detached from the navel, and there is nothing in the interval between, but it has been used up entirely. During the period above referred to the chick sleeps, wakes up, makes a move and looks up and chirps; and the heart and the navel together palpitate as though the creature were respiring. So much as to generation from the egg in the case of birds.

[5] The urates of the allantoic fluid.

14

Mathematics

A LADY POET of our own time once wrote that "Euclid alone has looked on Beauty bare." This is unfair to organized Greek mathematics. Its ranking names are Eudoxus, Archimedes, and Apollonius.

Eudoxus (390–337 B.C.)* was a pupil of Archytas and a friend of Plato. His works are lost, and have had to be reconstructed out of his successors'. We know that he traveled to Egypt and then set up a school in Athens, where he achieved considerable glory both as a mathematician and as a philosopher. With his work on geometric curves and on astronomy we shall have to deal hereafter. Greek mathematics owes to him its greatest single achievement, the creation of *infinitesimal analysis*. It remained wrapped in a cloud for ages, to the desperation of the men of the seventeenth century, who had to rediscover it all over again; but at least they knew what they were looking for.

More amply said, Eudoxus is the inventor of rigorous procedures, of which his "method of exhaustion" is only the more important aspect. We cannot come to grips here with such a technical subject, but we can at least outline its significance. And we can use modern language, since the idea starts from what is called today the "Dedekind cut." Eudoxus' definition of the equality of ratios is word for word the same as was given by Dedekind in 1872. It starts from the notion of an "ordered domain" D of elements of any kind, such as are points on a line segment, ordered by increasing distance from one end; or, more generally, the domain of rational numbers. Then one may define a "cut"

---

* These are not the standard dates, as a study of the sources has led us to shift them by 18 years. See Giorgio de Santillana, "Eudoxus and Plato," in *Isis,* No. 86 (Vol. 32, 2), June, 1949.

as a division of the domain D into two sections *a* and *b*, having no members in common, with every member of *b* greater than any member of *a*, every member of D less than any member of *a* also belonging to *a*, every member of D greater than a member of *b*, also belonging to *b*. Such a cut defines a "number," which may happen to be a member of D, as in the case where *a* has a maximum or *b* a minimum. But in other cases, such as the case where *a* consists of all rational numbers with squares less than 2, *b* of all those with squares greater than 2, *a* will have no (rational) maximum, and *b* no rational minimum: there will be a "gap," and in that case we can regard the cut *a*, *b*, as itself defining a new sort of number not rational, namely the square root of 2. This would be the modern procedure. But for the geometer, numbers are points on a line, not pairs of classes of them; and we require a special axiom to secure that an irrational "number" in this sense always corresponds to some point on a line, and only one point. That axiom can be stated in Greek paraphrase as follows: "To what there exist things (of the domain D) less (constituting *b*) and things greater (constituting *a*) there also exists an equal" (the determining element of *a*, *b*). Now we have seen that there are rational numbers with squares less, and with squares greater, than 2, but none whose square is equal.

Eudoxus had to start from this knowledge when he set out to determine the surface of curvilinear figures. The series of squares ordered in the sense of increasing magnitude is a continuous domain in the Dedekind sense. Hence, there must be one square which has exactly the surface of the given curvilinear figure. How to determine it rigorously was the aim of the method of "exhaustion." After setting upper and lower limits to the quantity searched for through successive decomposition (e.g., in the case of the circle, by polygons closing in from within and without) one compares with the expression suggested for that quantity. The comparison is brought in with the ritual words: "otherwise, indeed, it would be greater (or smaller). Let us suppose it to be greater (or smaller)": there follows *reductio ad absurdum* which ends by establishing the equivalence.

It is thus, we know, that Eudoxus established the volumes of the cone and pyramid.

This is the first form of integral calculus. Lacking a kinematics, the Greeks had little inducement to develop a corresponding differential calculus. Exhaustion remained a method for proving rigorously what had usually been found by other ways. When calculus was rediscovered in the seventeenth century, it started by being loose and limber, not to say fanciful, and became rigorous only after two centuries. The Greeks started from the other end, and this is probably what hamstrung their progress. It we let a gap grow between discovery and proof, it does not go with impunity. A mathematician may have to choose between semicorrect methods which allow his thoughts to develop and rigorous methods which check them. Neither way is without danger, but it may be worth while taking risks. The productiveness of men like Euler is a case in point. Fermat and Huygens have fully grasped the exhaustion procedure, but they skip it and go ahead. Newton and Leibniz stress rigor much less than fecundity and consistency of results. By setting themselves rigorous standards for acceptance and publication of results, it would appear that the Greeks also set limits to the span of discovery to which their prodigious mastery entitled them. Starting from Eudoxus, it becomes increasingly difficult to go beyond Archimedes.

Of the great mathematicians of antiquity, Archimedes (287–212 B.C.) stands out as first among his peers. "His treatises," writes Sir Thomas Heath,

are, without exception, monuments of mathematical exposition; the gradual revelation of the plan of attack, the masterly ordering of the propositions, the stern elimination of everything not immediately relevant to the purpose, the finish of the whole, are so impressive in their perfection as to create a feeling akin to awe.

In the achievement of classic style Archimedes was by no means alone. Some such praise might be given also to the *Conic Sections* of Apollonius (b. 262 B.C.). It is to his fame as a prodigious engineer that Archimedes owes the

halo of legend. We see this legend taking shape in Plutarch's account * of the last defense of Syracuse against the
Romans, in which Archimedes was to meet his death:

. . . These machines he had designed and contrived, not as
matters of any importance, but as mere amusements in geometry; in compliance with King Hiero's desire and request,
some little time before, that he should reduce to practice some
part of his admirable speculation in science, and by accom-
modating the theoretic truth to sensation and ordinary use,
bring it more within the appreciation of the people in general.
Eudoxus and Archytas had been the first originators of this
far-famed and highly-prized art of mechanics, which they
employed as an elegant illustration of geometrical truths, and
as means of sustaining experimentally, to the satisfaction of
the senses, conclusions too intricate for proof by words and
diagrams. As, for example, to solve the problem, so often required in constructing geometrical figures, given the two extremes, to find the two mean lines of a proportion, both these
mathematicians had recourse to the aid of instruments, adapting to their purpose certain curves and sections of lines. But
what with Plato's indignation at it, and his invectives against it
as the mere corruption and annihilation of the one good of
geometry, which was thus shamefully turning its back upon
the unembodied objects of pure intelligence to recur to sensation, and to ask help (not to be obtained without base super-
visions and depravation) from matter; so it was that mechanics
came to be separated from geometry, and, repudiated and
neglected by philosophers, took its place as a military art. . . .
When . . . the Romans assaulted the walls in two places
at once, fear and consternation stupefied the Syracusans, believing that nothing was able to resist that violence and those
forces. But when Archimedes began to ply his engines, he at
once shot against the land forces all sorts of missile weapons,
and immense masses of stone that came down with incredible
noise and violence; against which no man could stand; for
they knocked down those upon whom they fell in heaps,
breaking all their ranks and files. In the meantime huge poles
thrust out from the walls over the ships sunk some by the
great weights which they let down from on high upon them;
others they lifted up into the air by an iron hand or beak like

* Plutarch's *Lives* (the Dryden translation). New York: The
Modern Library, G5.

a crane's beak, and, when they had drawn them up by the prow, and set them on end upon the poop, they plunged them to the bottom of the sea; or else the ships, drawn by engines within, and whirled about, were dashed against steep rocks that stood jutting out under the walls, with great destruction of the soldiers that were aboard them. A ship was frequently lifted up to a great height in the air (a dreadful thing to behold), and was rolled to and fro, and kept swinging, until the mariners were all thrown out, when at length it was dashed against rocks, or let fall. At the engine that Marcellus brought upon the bridge of ships, which was called *Sambuca,* from some resemblance it had to an instrument of music, while it was as yet approaching the wall, there was discharged a piece of rock of ten talents weight, then a second and a third, which, striking upon it with immense force and a noise like thunder, broke all its foundation to pieces, shook out all its fastenings, and completely dislodged it from the bridge. . . . Whence the Romans, seeing that indefinite mischief overwhelmed them from no visible means, began to think they were fighting with the gods.

Yet Marcellus escaped unhurt, and deriding his own artificers and engineers, "What," said he, "'must we give up fighting with this geometrical Briareus, who plays pitch-and-toss with our ships, and, with the multitude of darts which he showers at a single moment upon us, really outdoes the hundred-handed giants of mythology?" And, doubtless, the rest of the Syracusans were but the body of Archimedes' designs, one soul moving and governing all; for, laying aside all other arms, with this alone they infested the Romans and protected themselves. In fine, when such terror had seized upon the Romans, that, if they did but see a little rope or a piece of wood from the wall, instantly crying out, that there it was again, Archimedes was about to let fly some engine at them, they turned their backs and fled, Marcellus desisted from conflicts and assaults, putting all his hope in a long siege.

Yet Archimedes possessed so high a spirit, so profound a soul, and such treasures of scientific knowledge, that though these inventions had now obtained him the renown of more than human sagacity, he yet would not deign to leave behind him any commentary or writing on such subjects; but, repudiating as sordid and ignoble the whole trade of engineering, and every sort of art that lends itself to mere use and profit, he placed his whole affection and ambition in those purer speculations where there can be no reference to the

vulgar needs of life; studies, the superiority of which to all
others is unquestioned, and in which the only doubt can be
whether the beauty and grandeur of the subjects examined, or
the precision and cogency of the methods and means of proof,
most deserve our admiration. It is not possible to find in all
geometry more difficult and intricate questions, or more simple
and lucid explanations. . . . No amount of investigation of
yours would succeed in attaining the proof, and yet, once seen,
you immediately believe you would have discovered it; by so
smooth and so rapid a path he leads you to the conclusion
required. And thus it ceases to be incredible that (as is commonly told of him) the charm of his familiar and domestic
Siren made him forget his food and neglect his person, to that
degree that when he was occasionally carried by absolute violence to bathe or have his body anointed, he used to trace
geometrical figures in the ashes of the fire, and diagrams in
the oil on his body, being in a state of entire preoccupation,
and, in the truest sense, divine possession with his love and
delight in science. His discoveries were numerous and admirable; but he is said to have requested his friends and relations
that, when he was dead, they would place over his tomb a
cylinder containing a sphere, inscribing it with the ratio [3/2]
which the containing solid bears to the contained.

Plutarch's pious Platonism drives him to apologize for
Archimedes' mechanical interest in a way that would not
have been endorsed by Archimedes himself (nor, indeed,
as he has to admit, by his predecessors either). His statics,
his hydrostatics, carry the same seal of perfection as the
rest of his work, and it is clear he felt no guilt when he determined centers of gravity and gave a most complete investigation of the positions of rest and stability of a right
segment of a paraboloid of revolution floating in a fluid;
even if this involved endowing geometric figures with the
attributes of matter.

In fact, we have since 1906 Archimedes' own philosophy in his little book on *Method,* discovered by Heiberg in
a palimpsest in Constantinople. In it he shows himself quite
indifferent to the Platonic anathema, and pays a fitting
tribute to his Ionian predecessors:

Certain things first became clear to me by a mechanical
method, although they had to be demonstrated by geometry

afterwards because their investigation by the said method did not furnish an actual demonstration. But it is of course easier, when we have previously acquired, by the method, some knowledge of the questions, to supply the proof than it is to find it without any previous knowledge. This is a reason why, in the case of the theorems that the volumes of a cone and a pyramid are one-third of the volumes of the cylinder and prism respectively having the same base and equal height, the proofs of which Eudoxus was the first to discover, no small share of the credit should be given to Democritus who was the first to state the fact, though without proof.

With all this, the *Method* of Archimedes does not tell us the whole story. There is, undeniably, at times a certain mystery veiling the way in which he arrived at his results, and even his use of the rigorous method of exhaustion to clinch his proofs does not reveal all the secrets of this geometrical form of calculus; so that Wallis was to write in the seventeenth century:

not only Archimedes but nearly all the ancients so hid from posterity their Method of Analysis (though it is clear that they had one) that more modern mathematicians found it easier to invent a new Analysis than to seek out the old.

One imagines that Archimedes would not have been displeased with this remark, he who had said in the introduction to his book *On Spirals* that he would not begrudge mathematicians the pleasure of finding out for themselves.

Archimedes is the founder of mathematical physics as we mean it today. Notwithstanding many efforts in the intervening centuries, mathematical physics did not start again until his books were translated and published in the sixteenth century. It is to him that Galileo and Stevinus owe their techniques and their frame of thought. In fact, Galileo explicitly acknowledges that he is doing for dynamics what Archimedes had done for statics. He adds:

I write about motion *ex suppositione,* as defined thus and so. Hence if the consequences did not correspond to fact, I would not be overly concerned, just as it detracts nothing from Archimedes' demonstration that there should be no body in nature which moves along spiral lines. I have simply been fortunate in that the motion of heavy bodies corresponds exactly to the curve I defined.

15

The Main Issue in Astronomy

ASTRONOMY HAS NEVER been a simple science. Were it not that the heavens have commanded awesome respect and concentrated attention for many millennia before our era, mankind would not have set its best minds to unravel their elusive periods and motions. But as Babylonian and then Greek science reach their maturity, astronomy seems to harden into technical complication unrelieved by any great theoretical break-through. It has often been said that the failure of the ancients was in not having found their way to the great Copernican "simplification." This is largely an error of perspective. The new ideas did appear in due course. Why they did not break through is a very intricate historical problem, to which we have only partial answers, as we shall see. It may have been a matter of unfortunate timing. It is surely not because Greek astronomy was too complicated. The Greeks, whose tool was geometry, had to lay bare for all to see the painful complication of their sphere, "with centric and eccentric scribbled o'er —cycle and epicycle, orb in orb." But modern computations of orbits are no less complicated, in fact more, even if circles in vast numbers are inconspicuously tucked away in one line of print as convergent analytical series.

The fact is that technical growth and philosophical decisions are bound up together inextricably. The Pythagoreans, who brought astronomy to Greece, had some Babylonian data, but they did not have the arithmetical methods of the Babylonians, which were the equivalent of modern Fourier series. Nor could they have accepted them in the raw empirical state in which they came. But they had what the Babylonians did not have—a theoretical outlook, and a vision of heavenly circles. On these they had to found things anew. Being mathematical physicists from the outset, they insisted on the mathematizing ideation which showed them the invariants of reality in the image of celestial points of fire arranged in some kind of cosmic stereostructure, and they searched for the laws of periodicity in vibrating strings as well as among the stars. We have seen how the daring imagination of Philolaus even displaced the earth from the central place in the cosmos. But after the generation of Archytas it would seem as if the inductive effort, the direct contact with reality, proved too difficult, the equipment too scanty, for their hopes. There was an increasing stress on the "wondrous" and the spiritual. On the other hand, mathematics had progressed with such ease and power that it was felt to provide the proper terrain for the scientific endeavor. Geometry and number theory grew, so to speak, by themselves. The lifting power of number removed the mind to the region of higher abstraction, where reality could not follow.

The return to astronomy with Eudoxus takes place indeed under auspices vastly different from the earlier ones. Eudoxus, the creator of the method of "exhaustion," was befriended by Plato, who was then at the height of his career, but he seems to have gone mostly his own way and to have taught a philosophy of a very different kind. As none of his writings have survived, and references are scarce, we are left to guess about the relationship of the two men. It is generally accepted that the program for astronomical research that Plato formulated as "accounting for appearances" or "saving the phenomena" by abstract explanation was taken up by Eudoxus, but it may have been the other way around. It simply corresponded to what was then the state of the art. It was the Pythagorean endeavor brought to its logical conclusion by means of precise observation (we know that Eudoxus built himself a kind of armillary sphere that he called *arachnē* or "spider"). Philolaus himself, with all his geometric imagination, had never offered a theory of the planets beyond saying that they go in circles, each with a velocity of its own. But why those changes in velocity, why those loops, those "stations" and "retrogradations" in their orbits which complicate their motion to a "dance," as it had been called?

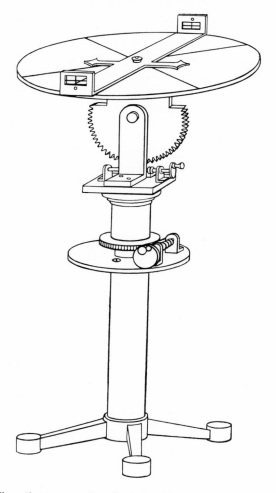

Fig. 12. The dioptra as described by Heron and reconstituted by Schöne. It is the equivalent of a modern transit instrument. An early version of it was certainly used by Eudoxus.

The canon of uniform circular motion could not be abandoned. It provided the most reliable theoretical tool. With the rich and sophisticated geometry at his disposal, Eudoxus invented curves which would fit the planetary displacements, and could be constructed out of several ideal circular motions with different axes and angular velocities. Thus each planet would need several component "spheres";

one of them giving the over-all 24-hour rotation of the heavens around the North Pole, the other ones for the planet's proper motion. The first one of this group had its axis on the poles of the ecliptic, and it turned, for the outer planets, in the planet's zodiacal period, for the inner planets, in one year. But then there were still the stations and retrogradations to be accounted for, as well as the up-and-down displacements in latitude, which correspond in reality to the inclination of *our* orbit. So a third sphere was brought in, with an axis perpendicular to that of the second, that is, placed on the ecliptic; it rotated in the synodic period of the planet, which is the interval between two successive oppositions to the sun. On the surface of the third sphere the poles of the fourth were fixed, its axis with an inclination different for each planet, rotating in an opposite direction to the third. That fourth sphere carried the planet. The motions of 3 and 4 combined in a curve called a lemniscate, or figure-of-eight, along which the planet moved, while the whole figure was carried around by the second sphere in a zodiacal revolution.

The idea of the lemniscate was found particularly good, because, it was said, the figure could be generated by intersecting a sphere with a cone or a cylinder, the three perfect solids of revolution. It should be clear that the scheme was a purely mathematical model. The spheres, 27 of them, including those for the sun and moon, were all homocentric, nested into one another, but each nest of spheres corresponding to one planet had to start again with the sidereal revolution as a first component. Aristotle, needing a "physical" explanation, tried to make the system into one of real substantial spheres; but of course, then, he had to bring in other contrary spheres in equal number to cancel out the specific individual motion transmitted from one planet to the next lower one, since for him the original motion came from the *primum mobile* outside. It made no sense mechanically: it was, in fact, preposterous; but it was not what Eudoxus had meant.

We are here at a fateful parting of the ways. Aristotle's physics is an assembly of Ionian components held together by verbal and logical devices from which mathematics has been banned. Mathematics, on the other hand, has reached its own freedom and self-sufficiency divorced from its original semimagical projection on physics. Aristotle's position is that since the heavens are a real thing, they must be made of a real substance whose properties and genus we can only describe from what we see (e.g., crystalline, frictionless, unalterable), reconciling them into a whole with *ad hoc* suppositions. Eudoxus instead makes no physical suppositions but tries a purely abstract model, and sees how far it will take him. The limits are clearly set; we can add spheres for correction as Callippus did, but the model is designed to account for the angular displacements of the planets as observed and for nothing else. The system may appear complicated, but as Schiaparelli remarked when he reconstructed it, the theory made use of three elements only, the epoch of superior conjunction, the period of sidereal revolution (of which the synodic period is a function), and the inclination of the axis of the third sphere on that of the fourth. For the same purpose modern astronomers require six elements. It was, then, a marvel of economy.

The system was and remained a provisional working model. Eudoxus could not but know that Mars and Venus, at least, show startling variations in brightness (as much as 1 to 60 in the case of Mars) appearing at their maximum in the middle of the retrograde movement. He must have known, too, the change in apparent diameter of the sun and moon through their cycle, which was noted very early. All this implied variations in distance from the earth which made it very awkward to speak of homocentric spheres. Some other model must supply the missing elements.

This provides the starting point for the Pythagorean counteroffensive: it must have been still in Eudoxus' time, or just after it. The simple way to explain variations both in speed and in distance, while still preserving uniform circular motion, was to make those circles eccentric to the earth. It was known that Mars is always brightest when it culminates at midnight and therefore is in opposition to the sun, while it becomes fainter and fainter as it approaches the sun in the zodiac. This seemed to show an eccentric circle, and since Mars looked nearer to the earth when opposite the sun, the center of that circle ought to be somewhere on the straight line joining the earth and the sun. That straight line based on the sun moved all around with it in one year, and hence the center of the eccentric must move around too in the same period year; this explained why the oppositions of Mars do not take place in one particular point of the zodiac, but may occur at any point of it.

The system would comprise two types of eccentrics: those smaller than the sun's circle, and those larger. The first (Mercury and Venus) would seem to oscillate within a limited angular distance right and left of the sun; the latter (Mars, Jupiter, Saturn) would throw their loop around the earth, and make these planets night stars. A sketchy outline it remained, no doubt, probably a mere drawing on sand, for it seemed unreasonable that those circles should move around a center of nothingness, a mere geometrical point. But a vivid and imaginative mind took hold of it, Heracleides of Pontus, who was a disciple of Plato with strong Pythagorean leanings, and a "writer of paradoxical things" that one wishes had been preserved for us. Heracleides suggested that the center of revolution for the two lower planets ought to be the sun itself; and as for the 24-hour revolution of the sky, he brought it back, reviving Philolaus's precedent, to a revolution of the earth itself. One perceives here the pursuit of some reasonably physical solution, and unmistakably in the Pythagorean vein, for it pointed the way to the sun's being the real Central Fire.

From the first, the Pythagoreans had imagined a cosmos whose life came from the center outwards. At the center was the Monad or Decad of intelligent fire, generator and ruler which held them all together; beyond, the Olympus of stars, the dark outer void. Aristotle, dismissing this fancifulness, as he called it, had placed the motive power and the intelligence of the universe at its last circumference, beyond the fixed stars, and restored the immobile earth to the center. We have quoted his reasons for doing so. For him the 24-hour revolution of the sky was natural, as corresponding to the fastest motion, that of the *primum mobile* itself. To the Pythagoreans, instead, the order of the planets from the moon up indicated decreasing velocities, ending in immobility in the starry heaven. The two images were not reconcilable. But as those of the Pythagorean tradition had to face the consolidated authority of Aristotle combined with Eudoxus, they were led in their counterattack to place the center of force in the sun.

The merit for having gone all the way belongs to Aristarchus of Samos, a great astronomer of the following generation (c. 280 B.C.). Like Heracleides and his own master Strato, he seems to have inclined to a corpuscular theory of reality, which remains the hallmark of the "physicalists," both Democritan and late Pythagorean. He probably started by generalizing Heracleides' construction and placing the center of all planetary orbits in the sun, with the sun still circling around the earth, according to what we call now the Tychonian system, because Tycho Brahe proposed it in 1577. But he must have realized that this was only a way station towards a system making physical sense, for he came to the conclusion, as Archimedes reports, "that the fixed stars and the sun are immovable, but that the earth is carried in a circle round the sun which is in the middle of the course." The break-through had been achieved. This is what we call the Copernican system, and it was invented within fifty years of Aristotle's death.

Aristarchus was aware of the difficulties his system entailed, chief of which is the lack of an observable annual parallax of the fixed stars. Philolaus had already had to cope with that, but at least his own orbit of the earth was minuscule, and might not show up against the stars if they were kept at a reasonable distance. But now Aristarchus had placed the earth "in the third heaven," going the Great Orb in a year in the place of the sun. Could such a circle, too, be as nothing seen from the stars? It must be. We have for this, again, the reference of Archimedes himself in the *Sand-Reckoner:*

He supposes . . . that the sphere of the fixed stars is of such a size that the circle, in which he supposes the earth to move, has the same ratio to the distance of the fixed stars as the center of the sphere has to the surface. But this is evidently impossible, for as the center of the sphere has no magnitude, it has no ratio to the surface.

The great Archimedes might have accepted this as only an image, instead of deploring his colleague's lack of precision. As an image, it can stand. It corresponds to saying there will be no parallax.

One wonders all the more, since such a passing slap at his colleague is really quite irrelevant to the subject Archimedes has undertaken to discuss, namely, is there a way to express numbers beyond the range of the ordinary Greek notation, e.g., the number of grains of sand that would be contained in the sphere of the cosmos. In fact, he has brought in Aristarchus only to have the support of his authority in supposing the cosmos much larger than commonly thought.* He might have considered, too, that the reasons for this poetic audacity on the part of Aristarchus did not lie only in geometrical relativism. They were mainly physical, and very novel at that. The only work of Aristarchus which has reached us is a little treatise *On the Dimensions and Distances of the Sun and Moon,* in which the first serious attempt is made at determining these quantities of observation. He observed the angle B between the sun and moon at a time when the latter is half illuminated, that is, when the angle A is a right angle (see Fig. 13): a method ingenious but perforce miserably imprecise. He found 3° at most for the angle in the sun (it is actually 10'). From this he deduced that the distance of the sun must be at least eighteen times as great as the distance of the moon, and hence also the sun at least three hundred times bigger than the earth. A body of this size ought to be the center of gravity for the cosmos. It was all very well to say—as was being said—that celestial bodies move naturally and without effort in a circle, and that we should not apply our terrestrial standards of weight and lightness to matters celestial, impassible, and uncorruptible. Philolaus had applied them, when he "made of

---

* Actually, Archimedes insists on some kind of proportion, no matter how big, rather than Aristarchus's incommensurability (exhaustion is based on commensurable quantities). To get a meaning out of the latter's words, he suggests that, if we conceive a sphere with radius equal to the distance between the sun and the earth, then

(diam. of earth) : (diam. of said sphere)
:: diam. of said sphere) : (diam. of sphere of fixed stars)

By arbitrarily setting the diameter of the sun's orbit at 10,000 earth diameters (far more than Aristarchus) he obtains for the diameter of the cosmos or sphere of fixed stars $10,000^3$ times the sphere of the sun's orbit. The grains of sand to fill it are then reckoned at less than 10^{63}. It all remains an intellectual play.

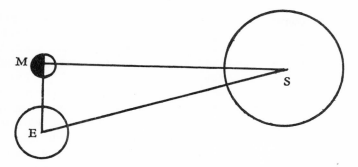

Fig. 13. Aristarchus's method for measuring the distance of the sun.

the earth a star," which implied conversely that the stars
are not without some earthiness either. Aristarchus had
now lined up a massive argument in favor of that point of
view. It would be reasonable, in fact, to assume that he
made bold to suggest his Copernican hypothesis only after
measuring the distance of the sun. He probably did no
more than sketch it out (Archimedes says he "outlined
certain hypotheses"); and Archimedes may have thought
that this was not a serious way of dealing with a well-
worked-out problem, where masses of quantitative data
had to be accounted for. Still, it reveals on the part of the
greatest mathematical physicist of antiquity, of the very
man who had given the theory of centers of gravity, a
strange insensibility to dynamic considerations. What Galileo was to feel intuitively, even before checking Copernicus's data, Archimedes did not feel at all. Was it the
appalling esthetic disproportion involved in a scheme which
left the solar system like a grain of sand in empty space?
The fact is that he closed his mind to the new idea. This is
almost the only clear fact which stands out in this strange
episode of miscomprehension.

As for public opinion, it reacted almost not at all. This
was too far removed from common sense to deserve
comment. The philosophers reprimanded Aristarchus for
speaking out of turn on a subject which they considered to
be their proper domain. Cleanthes, the Stoic, scolded Aristarchus for impiety; others accused him of undermining
the art of divination, which had recently been imported
into Greece from the Near East. It was about the same

general reaction which was to greet Copernicus. It was not strange. That was why the Pythagoreans had cloaked themselves in the magic and prophetic authority of the sect. A lone astronomer, speaking in physics only from scientific reasons, was alone indeed.

The astronomers themselves reacted coolly. They had by now become specialists, and had learned to mind their own business. They insisted that their business was to state the *how* and leave it at that. We know only of one who adopted the system a century later, Seleucus of Seleucia, an Oriental Greek from the Persian Gulf. For expert opinion, the system came probably too late to force a change of minds. Aristarchus had "saved the appearances"; he had outlined the proper symmetry of homocentric circles and velocities, but it was clear already that they could not be true sun-centered circles. They were again eccentrics with imaginary centers. Then to what profit upset the visible order of the skies and put the system of the world on its head? The most sensible and manageable approach remained the geocentric. Instead of eccentrics, besides, there was an equivalent solution devised by Apollonius, which looked much better: a succession of correctly earth-centered circles, carrying on their circumference secondary smaller circles, the *epicycles*. By adjusting the diameters and velocities in both epicycle and deferent (as the large circles were called), all the loops and irregularities could be accounted for. This led the minds back to the well-used geocentric coordinates of positional astronomy, for which a whole technique had been developed and enriched by trigonometry at the time of Hipparchus (150 B.C.). In conclusion, the abstract model had been enthroned, flexible in the way of more precision, needing no new ideas. The final synthesis by Ptolemy in the *Almagest* (A.D. 140) shows in fact great mathematical resourcefulness, a new use of Babylonian techniques, but no change except a yielding of principles: the uniformity of circular motion, to which so much had been sacrificed, had to be abandoned at last in favor of more complicated hypotheses. But by that time no one thought of forcing his way back. The tool controlled the men.

If we see here the story of how proper specialists went about their subject, it may appear natural enough. The

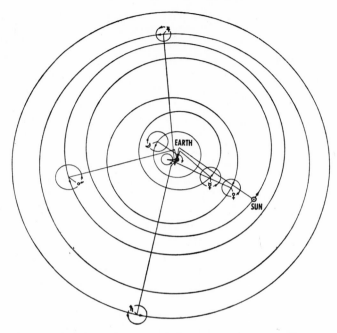

Fig. 14. The Ptolemaic System. Greek speculation concerning the celestial universe culminated in the system of astronomy named after Claudius Ptolemy (A.D. 140), the last of the great Greek astronomers. The Ptolemaic system was an ingenious answer to the problem of predicting the future positions of the heavenly bodies, and, within the limits of pretelescopic observations, was completely adequate and workable for this purpose. It became the accepted system in the Western world throughout the Middle Ages. The Moon (☽), Mercury (☿), Venus (♀), the Sun (☉), Mars (♂), Jupiter (♃), and Saturn (♄), were assumed to revolve around the central, motionless Earth in a complex system of "deferent circles" (the large circles eccentric to the Earth) and "epicycles" (the small circles mounted on the deferents). The planets were assumed to travel around on the epicycles while the epicycles revolved about the Earth on the deferent circles, and their relative senses of rotation are indicated by the arrows in this simplified drawing. No major changes were made in this system of astronomy for about fourteen hundred years until Copernicus devised his heliocentric system, published in 1543.

astronomers of antiquity had set themselves the task of accounting numerically for celestial motions, and, barring a few odd phenomena, they had done so with a precision which attained to 5′ of arc. The precession of the equinoxes had been discovered and established by Hipparchus; the distance of the moon had been given by him with an error of 0.3 per cent. This was what counted. It took no fewer than thirty-nine wheels within wheels to account for the motions, some of the wheels very abstract indeed, like Ptolemy's "equant circle" which regularized speeds not at all regular on the deferents: but after all, if it was a mathematical model, those were permissible devices.

But *was* it a mathematical model after all? Centuries of use made it familiar, and it began to be felt as something real. Here we see what arrested thought can do. Ptolemy, in his *Hypotheses on the Planets,* wonders what kind of crystalline substance the skies may be, what kind of axles they may need in their turning. But then, Ptolemy (who professes himself a Platonist) had not only taken from the Babylonians their techniques, he had accepted their astrology; he was the author of that great astrological treatise, the *Tetrabiblos.* Geocentrism had become for him a reality.

It is as if those astronomers, like the sailors of Ulysses, had put wax in their ears to resist the insistent harmony which made itself guessed just beyond reach. Here were the anomalies of the planets, always in the direction of the sun (in our language, because they correspond to the major axes of the orbits). Here was the presence of the sun everywhere, regulating the progressions and retrogradations, as Cicero and Macrobius heard from astronomers; here was this resplendent body, giver of life, "orderer and prince of the whole," which had always been understood to be bigger than the earth, indeed after Aristarchus was known to be at least 300 times bigger—was it not reasonable, as Copernicus was to suggest, to "place the luminary at the center of the temple of the universe"? The refusal to do so amounts to a denial of straight scientific intuition.

We can see, then, that the failure to break through is not a matter of sheer precisionism and intellectual restraint. It is due to a real mental block established over late antiquity. It comes from a deliberate position and from a positive refusal of scientific intuitions on the part of the ruling group of the culture, who were the philosophers. The main offenders here were not the uncompromising moralists of the Socratic succession, Cynics or others, who declined to be interested in science and did not care. It was the coalition of Stoics, Aristotelians, and later Platonists who had confiscated the term and concept of "physics" for their own cosmology, and controlled its meaning, in agreement with the great body of public opinion.

Two centuries after Aristarchus, about 100 B.C., Posidonius, who at the time ruled over Stoic philosophy, measured anew the size of the sun, by a different method. He assumed the distance of the sun to be 10,000 earth diameters—a figure, ironically enough, taken from Archimedes —and concluded to a diameter equal to 39¼ earthly diameters against Aristarchus's 6¾ (in reality it is 108.9). This showed the sun then, by his own estimate, to be several thousand times larger than the earth. Yet so firmly were his philosophical (and by then, astrological) preconceptions anchored in his mind, that his geocentrism remained unshaken.

Pappus, a ranking mathematician of the third century A.D., in defining the task of mechanics, distinguishes between natural motions toward a locus, and the science of "devising means of impelling bodies to change their positions, contrary to their natures. In this last case only, mechanics uses theorems." From mechanics as well as from astronomy, the road is blocked at both ends. We shall give two representative texts, one from Eudemus and one from Geminus, to show how solid is the roadblock.

Eudemus (fl. about 325 B.C.) was, with Theophrastus, the first historian of science. He compiled histories of arithmetic, geometry, and astronomy for the encyclopedic project of his master Aristotle. His works are now lost, with the exception of a few extracts. His writings on the history of astronomy are the most reliable of any of the ancients'. This paraphrase of part of his *On Astronomy* comes from the *Mathematical Introduction to the Study of Plato* by the Platonist Theon of Smyrna, who flourished in the time of Hadrian. (The translation, which is unpublished, is by N. Sivin.)

Eudemus of Rhodes on Astronomical Hypotheses

Just as it is impossible in geometry and music to deduce the consequences of their principles without making hypotheses, so in astronomy it is necessary, in order to speak of the motion of the planets, to establish hypotheses. Above all it is necessary, as everyone agrees, to choose principles serviceable in mathematical studies. The first is that the composition of the world is ordered and governed by a single principle, that a reality is found to underlie the things which exist or which appear to exist, and that, where the world extends beyond the limits of our vision, we should say that it has its limits rather than that it is the infinite.

The second principle is that the risings and settings of the heavenly bodies are not due to these bodies successively lighting up and going out; if their state were not eternal, there would be no order maintained in the universe. The third principle is that there are seven moving bodies, neither more nor less—a truth known from long observation. The fourth is the following: since it does not stand to reason that all the bodies are in motion or that all are at rest . . . , it is necessary to inquire as to which is necessarily at rest and which is in movement. It must be believed, he adds, that the earth, Hearth of the Gods, following Plato, is at rest, and that the planets move together with the whole of the celestial vault which envelops them. Next he energetically rejects, as contrary to the foundations of mathematics, the opinion of those who want to make those bodies which appear in motion [the stars] to be at rest, and those bodies immobile by nature or by situation [the earth], to be in motion.

He then says that the planets have a circular, regular, and uniform motion, in terms of longitude, distance, and latitude. . . . Such is his judgment, although we could be mistaken on this point. . . .

Moreover, he does not believe the eccentric circles to be the deep cause of the motion. He thinks everything which moves in the sky to be carried about a unique center of motion and of the world, so that it is only as a consequence, and not by an antecedent motion . . . , that the planets describe epicycles or eccentrics within the thickness of the concentric spheres. For each sphere has a double surface, the interior concave and the exterior convex, between which the planets move following epicycles and concentric circles, with a movement which makes them describe, as an apparent consequence, eccentrics.

He says again that, according to the appearances, the motions of the planets are irregular, but that in principle and in reality they are regular. The movement is simple and natural for all: there is only a very small number of displacements on spheres which are disposed in an orderly way. He censures those philosophers who, considering the stars inanimate, add to the spheres and their circles several additional spheres; so Aristotle [for whom each planet has four spheres] and, among the mathematical astronomers, Menaechmus and Callippus have proposed deferent spheres and spirals.

Having established all this, he thinks that the sky, with all the stars, moves about the immobile earth, with a very small number of circular, uniform, harmonious, concentric, and independent motions. He shows that, according to Plato, these hypotheses account for the appearances.

What follows is an extract preserved for us by Simplicius. Geminus, who wrote about 70 B.C., seems to have been a Stoic philosopher, but also an encyclopedist of mathematics of considerable distinction. He discussed the foundations of the science and attempted to prove the parallel postulate. We can take it, then, that his attempt at drawing the line between physics and astronomy proceeds from a sympathetic understanding of both camps. It is all the more noteworthy that he yields nothing of the prerogatives of philosophy.

Geminus on Physics and Astronomy *

(Simplicius, in *Phys.* II, 2). Alexander [of Aphrodisias] carefully quotes a certain explanation by Geminus taken from his summary of the *Meteorologica* of Posidonius; Geminus's comment, which is inspired by the views of Aristotle, is as follows:

"It is the business of physical inquiry to consider the substance of the heaven and the stars, their force and quality, their coming into being, and their destruction, nay, it is in a position even to prove the facts about their size, shape, and arrangement; astronomy, on the other hand, does not attempt to speak of anything of this kind, but proves the arrangement of the heavenly bodies by considerations based on the view that the heaven is a real Cosmos, and, further, it tells us of the shapes and sizes and distances of the earth, sun, and moon, and of eclipses and conjunctions of the stars, as well as of the quality and extent of their movements. Accordingly, as

* *Greek Astronomy,* translated and edited by Sir Thomas L. Heath. London: J. M. Dent & Sons, Ltd., 1932. Reprinted by permission of the publisher.

it is connected with the investigation of quantity, size, and quality of form or shape, it naturally stood in need, in this way, of arithmetic and geometry. The things, then, of which alone astronomy claims to give an account it is able to establish by means of arithmetic and geometry. Now in many cases the astronomer and the physicist will propose to prove the same point, e.g., that the sun is of great size, or that the earth is spherical; but they will not proceed by the same road. The physicist will prove each fact by considerations of essence or substance, of force, of its being better that things should be as they are, or of coming into being and change; the astronomer will prove them by the properties of figures or magnitudes, or by the amount of movement and the time that is appropriate to it. Again, the physicist will, in many cases, reach the cause by looking to creative force; but the astronomer, when he proves facts from external conditions, is not qualified to judge of the cause, as when, for instance, he declares the earth or the stars to be spherical; sometimes he does not even desire to ascertain the cause, as when he discourses about an eclipse; at other times he invents, by way of hypothesis, and states certain expedients by the assumption of which the phenomena will be saved. For example, why do the sun, the moon, and the planets appear to move irregularly? We may answer that, if we assume that their orbits are eccentric circles, or that the stars describe an epicycle, their apparent irregularity will be saved; and it will be necessary to go further, and examine in how many different ways it is possible for these phenomena to be brought about, so that we may bring our theory concerning the planets into agreement with that explanation of the causes which follows an admissible method. *Hence we actually find someone* [1] [*Heraclides of Pontus*] *coming forward and saying that, even on the assumption that the earth moves in a certain way, while the sun is in a certain way at rest, the apparent irregularity with reference to the sun can be saved.* For it is no part of the business of an astronomer to know what is by nature suited to a position of rest, and what sort of bodies are apt to move, but he introduces hypotheses under which some bodies remain fixed, while others move, and then considers to which hypotheses the phenomena actually observed in the heaven will corre-

---

[1] The theory in question (identical with the Copernican hypothesis), is that of Aristarchus of Samos. The original text obviously had "someone" without any name, and "Heraclides of Pontus" was wrongly interpolated.

spond. But he must go to the physicist for his first principles, namely that the movements of the stars are simple, uniform, and ordered, and by means of these principles he will then prove that the rhythmic motion of all alike is in circles, some being turned in parallel circles, others in oblique circles." Such is the account given by Geminus, or Posidonius in Geminus, of the distinction between physics and astronomy, wherein the commentator is inspired by the views of Aristotle.

16

On the Face in the Round of the Moon

HARDLY A WRITER has been more influential in history than Plutarch of Chaeronea (A.D. 50–120); that is, until the time of our grandfathers. The founders of the American as well as of the French Republic were brought up on his *Lives*. Thanks to him, the characters of the great Greek and Roman leaders were more familiar to many generations of the literate than were even the most outstanding contemporary figures. It has been said that Cicero and Plutarch were the educators of modern Europe. They were the "classics" of a liberal bringing up.

The real Plutarch is something else again. From his many preserved works he emerges as amiable, diffuse, full of erudite information and scattered lore—a somewhat journalistic temperament, and marvelously representative of his own time.

We know little of his life. He was a man of the early Empire, a contemporary of Seneca, Tacitus, and Pliny. But for all that he wrote about the Romans he remained a provincial Greek. He had a mere "reading knowledge" of Latin, was in Rome only on two occasions, and then only on business for his native city.

His "moral essays" are a mine of garrulous information: "Of Isis and Osiris," "Why the Oracles cease to give answer," "Of the late vengeance of the gods," "Of talkativeness," "Of the contradiction of the Stoics," "What brute beasts make use of reason," "Of Fortune," "Of the first principle of cold," "Roman Questions," "Whether it were rightly said, Live concealed," "How a young man ought to hear poems," "How a man may inoffensively praise himself," and so on.

Plutarch perpetually suggests Montaigne, who was the

best reader he ever found. He writes less well, but his range is greater. His genial facility, his sharp objective eye and quick crowded exposition, allow for all the moods of thought of his time: shadows, omens, and specters have a charm for him. Like his Pythagorean and Platonic masters, he likes to accept all that is wondrous; but the daylight of thought and action is his.

Emerson, speaking of Plutarch, has a striking remark: "We are always interested," he says, "in a man who treats the intellect well." He means, of course, if he be a man of the world, as Plutarch was. He adds, in a vein which may sound singularly out of tune with our times: "All his judgments were noble." This strikes home. A certain ingenuous nobility of thought that we admire in the past has its source in him. Wrote Henry IV of France to his wife, Marie de Medicis, who had taken up Plutarch in Amyot's translation: "To love him is to love me. . . . This book has been my conscience."

We are going to give about one third of a celebrated discursion of his: "On the Face in the Round of the Moon." It provides a good sample of educated opinion in late Hellenism on cosmology. If we compare Plutarch with the essayists of our own time, say with Emerson or Aldous Huxley, a considerable difference becomes apparent. We are caught in progress: he is not. While he can be quite crisp and matter-of-fact on history, his discussion of a scientific issue, as here, may seem vague and diffuse, lacking the definiteness that modern science has built into our language; his intellectual points of reference roam over a vast span of time, and he cites as authorities men who lived three, four, and five centuries before him. Clearly, although he is conversant with the achievements of his own epoch, there is for him, living under the Empire, no such thing as a steady intellectual advance. It is as if we had to quote Leonardo as an authority on science. Parmenides and Empedocles he holds to be on the whole better authorities than the Stoics and Atomists who are his contemporaries; and he shows good judgment in preferring the older wisdom to the constructions of his own time. When he affirms, e.g., the inanity of all the theorizing about a center of the cosmos, we see how his Pythagorean formation allows him to disregard quietly what, since

Aristotle and the Stoics, had become a commonplace.

As the argument weaves hither and thither, the contrast between Platonic and Stoic physics, between Design and Begetting, is gradually solved in the direction of Design; and with it, characteristically, comes a reasonable conclusion about the physical nature of the moon. But it is as if no one could make it "stick." Fifteen centuries later, Galileo will have to restate the case, and this time with the help of the telescope, against exactly the same type of opponents. It is as if time had not moved. With science thus unable to speak with assurance, it is no wonder that the dialogue should shift for a conclusion, as it does, to the realm of the allegorical. When Sylla, towards the end, recalls strange incomprehensible myths from protohistoric astronomy (cf. p. 13), and then suggests on high authority that a good explanation of the moon is its function as a staging area for departed souls before they move out into the cosmos, there is no challenge to the story, it is respectfully accepted by all as an intimation of higher things. The escape from physics is accomplished. But we notice that Plutarch has not foreclosed any domain of speculation. He acts as if the whole of thought were contemporary, all issues still open. Something like that occurs with us too, when we write about art or religion; but however intemporal our treatment, it will be sicklied o'er with the shadow of historical thought: we cannot hope for Plutarch's naive directness. For him there is no past. This, too, is what makes a classic.

The dialogue *On the Face in the Round of the Moon* * has had the extraordinary honor of inspiring both Copernicus and Newton. It is here that Copernicus found the mention of Aristarchus's system that he acknowledges in his book. It is here that Newton (who had read the dialogue in his adolescence) found an intimation of a gravitational force between the earth and the moon, which caused him to write later that there must have been an esoteric knowledge of universal attraction among the ancients, as evidenced in Plutarch.

The characters in the dialogue belong, as befits the era,

* Plutarch's *Morals,* corrected and revised by William W. Goodwin. Boston: Little, Brown and Company, 1870.

to cosmopolitan Hellenism. Five of them have Greek names, one Oriental, and two Roman, which are, curiously enough, Lucius and Sylla.

. . . Nay rather, answered Lucius—lest we should seem too injurious to Pharnaces, in thus passing by the opinion of the Stoics,* without opposing any thing against it—let us make some reply to this man, who supposes the moon to be wholly a mixture of air and mild fire, and then says that, as in a calm there sometimes arises on a sudden a breeze of wind which curls and ruffles the superficies of the sea, so, the air being darkened and rendered black, there is an appearance and form of a face.

You do courteously, Lucius, said I, thus to veil and cover with specious expressions so absurd and false an opinion. But so did not our friend; but he said, as the truth is, that the Stoics disfigured and mortified the moon's face, filling it with stains and black spots, one while invoking her by the name of Diana and Minerva, and another while making her a lump and mixture of dark air and charcoal-fire, not kindling of itself or having any light of its own, but a body hard to be judged and known, always smoking and ever burning, like to those thunders which by the poets are styled lightless and sooty. Now that a fire of coals, such as they would have that of the moon to be, cannot have any continuance nor yet so much as the least subsistence, unless it meets with some solid matter fit to maintain it, keep it in, and feed it, has, I think, far better than it is by these philosophers, been understood by those poets who in merriment affirm that Vulcan was therefore said to be lame because fire can no more go forward without wood or fuel than a cripple without a crutch. If then the moon is fire, whence has it so much air? For that region above, which is with a continual motion carried round, consists not of air, but some more excellent substance, whose nature it is to subtilize and set on fire all other things. And if it has been since engendered there, how comes it that it does not perish, being changed and transmuted by the fire into an ethereal and heavenly substance? And how can it maintain and preserve itself, cohabiting so long with the fire, as a nail always fixed and fastened in one and the same place? For being rare and diffused, as by Nature it is, it is not fitted for permanency

* For Stoic physics, see below, p. 296 f.

and continuance, but for change and dissipation. Neither is it possible that it should condense and grow compact, being mixed with fire, and utterly void of water and earth, the only two elements by which the nature of the air suffers itself to be brought to a consistency and thickness. And since the swiftness and violence of motion is wont to inflame the air which is in stones, and even in lead itself, as cold as it is; much more will it that which, being in fire, is with so great an impetuosity whirled about. For they are displeased with Empedocles for making the moon a mass of air congealed after the manner of hail, included within a sphere of fire. And yet they themselves say, that the moon, being a globe of fire, contains in it much air dispersed here and there—and this, though it has neither ruptures, concavities, nor depths (which they who affirm it to be earthly admit), but the air lies superficially on its convexity. Now this is both against the nature of permanency, and impossible to be accorded with what we see in full moons; for it should not appear separately black and dark, but either be wholly obscured and concealed or else co-illuminated, when the moon is overspread by the sun. For with us the air which is in the pits and hollows of the earth, whither the rays of the sun cannot penetrate, remains dark and lightless; but that which is spread over its exterior parts has clearness and a lightsome color. For it is by reason of its rarity easily transformed into every quality and faculty, but principally that of light and brightness, by which, being never so little touched, it incontinently changes and is illuminated. This reason, therefore, as it seems greatly to help and maintain the opinion of those who thrust the air into certain deep valleys and caves in the moon, so confutes you, who mix and compose her sphere, I know not how, of air and fire. For it is not possible that there should remain any shadow or darkness in the superficies of the moon, when the sun with his brightness clears and enlightens whatsoever we can discern of her and ken with our sight.

Whilst I was yet speaking, Pharnaces interrupting my discourse said: See here again the usual stratagem of the Academy brought into play against us, which is to busy themselves at every turn in speaking against others, but never to afford an opportunity for reproving what they say themselves; so that those with whom they confer and dispute must always be respondents and defendants, and never plaintiffs or opponents. You shall not therefore bring me this day to give you an account of those things you charge upon the Stoics, till you have first rendered me a reason for your turning the world upside down.

Then Lucius smiling said: This, good sir, I am well contented to do, provided only that you will not accuse us of impiety, as Cleanthes thought that the Greeks ought to have called Aristarchus the Samian into question and condemned him of blasphemy against the Gods, as shaking the very foundations of the world, because this man, endeavoring to save the appearances, supposed that the heavens remained immovable, and that the earth moved through an oblique circle, at the same time turning about its own axis.* As for us therefore, we say nothing that we take from them. But how do they, my good friend, who suppose the moon to be earth, turn the world upside down more than you, who say that the earth remains here hanging in the air, being much greater than the moon, as the mathematicians measure their magnitude by the accidents of eclipses, and by the passages of the moon through the shadow of the earth, gathering thence how great a space it takes up? For the shadow of the earth is less than itself, by reason it is cast by a greater light. And that the end of this shadow upwards is slender and pointed, they say that Homer himself was not ignorant, but plainly expressed it when he called the night *acute* from the sharp-pointedness of the earth's shadow. And yet the moon in her eclipses, being caught within this point of the shadow, can scarce get out of it by going forward thrice her own bigness in length. Consider then, how many times the earth must needs be greater than the moon, if it casts a shadow, the narrowest point of which is thrice as broad as the moon. But you are perhaps afraid lest the moon should fall, if it were acknowledged to be earth; but as for the earth, Aeschylus has secured you, when he says that Atlas

Stands shouldering the pillar of the heaven and earth,
A burden onerous.

If then there runs under the moon only a light air, not firm enough to bear a solid burthen, whereas under the earth there are, as Pindar says, columns and pillars of adamant for its support, therefore Pharnaces himself is out of all dread of the earth's falling, but he pities the Ethiopians and those of Ta-

* This passage is the sole source from which Copernicus learned of the existence of a "Copernican" system in antiquity. It gave him courage, as he writes, to try again.

probane [Ceylon], who lie directly under the course of the moon, fearing lest so ponderous a mass should tumble upon their heads. And yet the moon has, for an help to preserve her from falling, her motion and the impetuosity of her revolution; as stones, pebbles, and other weights, put into slings, are kept from dropping out, whilst they are swung round, by the swiftness of their motion. For every body is carried according to its natural motion, unless it be diverted by some other intervening cause. Wherefore the moon does not move according to the motion of her weight, her inclination being stopped and hindered by the violence of a circular revolution.* And perhaps there would be more reason to wonder, if the moon continued always immovable in the same place, as does the earth. But now the moon has a great cause to keep herself from tending hither downwards; but for the earth, which has no other motion, it is probable that it has also no other cause of its settlement but its own weight. . . .

Yes surely, said Pharnaces, being in its proper and natural place, the very middle and centre of the universe. For this it is to which all heavy and ponderous things do from every side naturally tend, incline, and aspire, and about which they cling and are counterpoised. But every superior region, though it may perhaps receive some earthly and weighty thing sent by violence up into it, immediately repels and casts it down again by force, or (to speak better) lets it follow its own proper inclination, by which it naturally tends downwards.

For the refutation of which, being willing to give Lucius time for the calling to mind his arguments, I addressed myself to Theon, and asked him which of the tragic poets it was who said that physicians

With bitter med'cines bitter choler purge.

And Theon having answered me that it was Sophocles; this, said I to him, we must of necessity permit them to do; but we are not to give ear to those philosophers who would overthrow paradoxes by assertions no less strange and paradoxical, and for the oppugning strange and extravagant opinions, devise others yet more wonderful and absurd; as these men do, who broach and introduce this doctrine of a motion tending towards the middle, in which what sort of absurdity is there not to be found? Does it not thence follow, that the earth is

---

* This is the passage where Newton in his adolescence found the idea of gravitation. It is probably the core of the legendary apple.

spherical, though we nevertheless see it to have so many lofty hills, so many deep valleys, and so great a number of inequalities? Does it not follow that there are antipodes dwelling opposite to another, sticking on every side to the earth, with their heads downwards and their heels upwards, as if they were woodworms or lizards? That we ourselves go not on the earth straight upright, but obliquely and bending aside like drunken men? That if bars and weights of a thousand talents apiece should be let fall into the hollow of the earth, they would, when they were come to the centre, stop and rest there, though nothing came against them or sustained them; and that, if peradventure they should by force pass the middle, they would of themselves return and rebound back thither again? . . . Some of which positions are so absurd, that none can so much as force his imagination, though falsely, to conceive them possible. . . . For this is indeed to make that which is above to be below; and to turn all things upside down, by making all that is as far as the middle to be *downwards,* and all that is beyond the middle to be *upwards.* . . .

Bearing then upon their shoulders, and drawing after them, I do not say a little bag or box, but a whole pack of juggler's boxes, full of so many absurdities, with which they play the hocus-pocus in philosophy, they nevertheless accuse others of error for placing the moon, which they hold to be earth, on high, and not in the middle or centre of the world. And yet, if every heavy body inclines towards the same place, and does from all sides and with every one of its parts tend to its own centre, the earth certainly will appropriate and challenge to itself these ponderous masses—which are its parts—not because it is the centre of the universe, but rather because it is the whole; and this gathering together of heavy bodies round about it will not be a sign showing it to be the middle of the world, but an argument to prove and testify that these bodies which had been plucked from it and again return to it have a communication and conformity of nature with the earth. For as the sun draws into himself the parts of which he is composed, so the earth receives a stone as a part belonging to it, in such manner that every one of such things is in time united and incorporated with it. And if peradventure there is some other body which was not from the beginning allotted to the earth nor has been separated from it, but had its own proper and peculiar consistence and nature apart, as these men may say of the moon, what hinders but it may continue separated by itself, being kept close, compacted, and bound together by its own parts? For they do not demonstrate that the earth is the middle of the universe; and this conglomeration of heavy bodies which are here, and their coalition with the earth, show us the manner how it is probable that the parts which are assembled in the body of the moon continue also there. But as for him who drives and ranges together in one place all earthly and ponderous things, making them parts of one and the same body, I wonder that he does not attribute also the same necessity and constraint to light substances, but leaves so many conglomerations of fire separated one from another; nor can I see why he should not amass together all the stars, and think that there ought to be but one body of all those substances which fly upwards.

But you mathematicians, friend Apollonides, say that the sun is distant from our upper sphere infinite thousands of miles, and after him the day-star or Venus, Mercury, and other planets, which being situated under the fixed stars, and separated from one another by great intervals, make their revolutions; and in the meantime you think that the world affords not to heavy and terrestrial bodies any great and large place or distance one from another. You plainly see, it would be ridiculous, if we should deny the moon to be earth because it is not seated in the lowest region of the world, and yet affirm it to be a star, though so many thousands of miles remote from the upper firmament, as if it were plunged into some deep gulf. For she is so low before all other stars, that the measure of the distances cannot be expressed, and you mathematicians want numbers to compute and reckon it; but she in a manner touches the earth, making her revolution so near the tops of the mountains, that she seems, as Empedocles has it, to leave even the very tracks of her chariot-wheels behind her. . . .

But leaving the stars, as well erring as fixed, see what Aristarchus proves and demonstrates in his treatise of magnitudes and distances; that the distance of the sun is above eighteen times and under twenty times greater than that of the moon from us. And yet they who place the moon lowest say that her distance from us contains fifty-six of the earth's semidiameters, that is, that she is six and fifty times as far from us as we are from the centre of the earth; which is forty thousand stadia, according to those that make their computation moderately. Therefore the sun is above forty millions and three hundred thousand stadia distant from the moon; so far is she from the sun by reason of her gravity, and so near does she approach to the earth. So that if substances are to be distinguished by places, the portion and region of the earth challenges to itself the moon, which, by reason of neighborhood and proximity, has a right to be reputed and reckoned amongst the terrestrial natures and bodies. . . . Now against him who holds that whatever is above the earth is immediately high and sublime, there is presently another opposition to encounter and contradict it, that whatever is beneath the sphere of the fixed stars ought to be called low and inferior.

In a word, how is the earth said to be the middle, and of what is it the middle? For the universe is infinite; and infiniteness having neither beginning nor end, it is convenient also that it should not have any middle; for the middle is a certain end or limit, but infiniteness is a privation of all sorts of limits. Now he that affirms the earth to be the middle, not of the universe but of the world, is certainly a pleasant man, if he does not think that the world itself is subject to the same doubts and difficulties. For the universe has not left a middle even to the very world, but this being without any certain seat or foundation, it is carried in an infinite voidness to no proper end; or if perhaps it has stopped, it has met with some other cause or stay, not according to the nature of the place. As much may be conjectured of the moon, that by the means of another soul and another Nature, or (to say better) of another difference, the earth continues firm here below, and the moon moves. . . .

Nevertheless, supposing, if you please, that it is against Nature for earthly bodies to have any motions in heaven, let us consider leisurely and mildly—and not violently, as is done in tragedies—that this is no proof of the moon's not being earth, but only that earth is in a place where by nature it should not be; for the fire of Mount Aetna is indeed against nature under ground, nevertheless it ceases not to be fire. And the wind contained within bottles is indeed of its own nature light and inclined to ascend, but is yet by force constrained to be there where naturally it should not be. . . . And even your Zeus, such as you Stoics imagine him and depaint him to be, is he not of his own nature a great and perpetual fire? Yet now he submits, is pliable, and transformed into all things by several mutations. Take heed therefore, good sir, lest, by transferring and reducing every thing to the place assigned it by Nature, you so philosophize as to bring in a dissolution of the whole world, and put all things again into that state of

enmity mentioned by Empedocles, or (to speak more properly) lest you raise up again those ancient Titans and Giants
to put on arms against Nature, and endeavor to introduce again
that fabulous disorder and confusion, where all that is heavy
goes one way apart, and all that is light another;

> Where neither sun's bright face is seen,
> Nor earth beheld, spread o'er with green,
> Nor the salt sea,

as Empedocles has it. Then the earth felt no heat, nor the sea
any wind; no heavy thing moved upwards, nor any light thing
downwards; but the principles of all things were solitary, without any mutual love or dilection one to another, not admitting
any society or mixture together; but shunning and avoiding
all communication, moving separately by particular motions,
as being disdainful, proud, and altogether carrying themselves
in such manner as every thing does from which (as Plato says)
God is absent; that is, as those bodies do in which there is
neither soul nor understanding; till such time as, by Divine
Providence, desire coming into Nature engendered mutual
amity, Venus and Love—as Empedocles, Parmenides, and
Hesiod have it—to the end that changing their natural places,
and reciprocally communicating their faculties, some being by
necessity bound to motion, others to quiet and rest, and all
tending to the better, every thing remitting a little of its power
and yielding a little from its place, . . . they might make at
length a harmony, accord, and society together.

For if there had not been any other part of the world
against Nature, but every thing had been in the same place and
quality it naturally ought to be, without standing in need of
any change or transposition or having had any occasion for
it from the beginning, I know not what the work of Divine
Providence is or in what it consists, or of what Zeus has been
the father, creator, or worker. . . .

Indeed, good sir, went on Lucius, if you should suppose the
other stars, and the whole heaven apart, to be of a pure and
sincere nature, free from all change and alteration of passion,
and should bring in also a circle, in which they make their
motion by a perpetual revolution, you would not perhaps find
any one now to contradict you, though there are in this infinite doubts and difficulties. But when the discourse descends so
far as to touch the moon, it cannot maintain in her that perfection of being exempt from all passion and alteration, nor
that heavenly beauty of her body. But to let pass all other

inequalities and differences, the very face which appears in the body of the moon necessarily proceeds from some passion of her own substance or the mixture of another; for what is mixed suffers, because it loses its first purity, being filled by force with that which is worse. . . . In brief, my friend Aristotle,* if the moon is earth, she is a most fair and admirable thing, and excellently well adorned; but if you regard her as a star or light or a certain divine and heavenly body, I am afraid she will prove deformed and foul, and disgrace that beautiful appellation, if of all bodies, which are in heaven so numerous, she alone stands in need of light borrowed of another, and, as Parmenides has it,

Looks always backwards on the sun's bright rays.

Our friend therefore indeed, having in a lecture of his demonstrated this proposition of Anaxagoras, that the sun communicates to the moon what brightness she has, was well esteemed for it. As for me, I will not say what I have learned of you or with you, but having taken it for granted, will pass on to the rest. It is then probable that the moon is illuminated, not like a glass or crystal, by the brightness of the sun's rays shining through her, nor yet again, by a certain collustration and conjunction of light and brightness, as when many torches set together augment the light of one another. For so she would be no less full in her conjunction or first quarter than in her opposition, if she did not obstruct or repel the rays of the sun, but let them pass through her by reason of her rarity, or if he did by a contemperature shine upon her and kindle the light within her. For we cannot allege her declinations and aversions in the conjunction or new moon, as when it is halfmoon or when she appears crescent or in the wane; but being then perpendicularly (as Democritus says) under him that illuminates her, she receives and admits the sun; so that then it is probable she should appear, and he shine through her. But this she is so far from doing, that she is not only then unseen, but also often hides the sun, as Empedocles has it:

The sun's bright beams from us she turns aside,
And of the earth itself as much doth hide,
As her orb's breadth can cover;

* This is of course not Aristotle the philosopher, but a character in the dialogue. Aristoteles was rather a common name. The beginning of the dialogue, in which the characters were introduced, is lost.

as if the light of the sun fell not upon another star, but upon night and darkness. . . .

It remains then that, according to the opinion of Empedocles, the light of the moon which appears to us comes from the repercussion and reflection of the sun's beams. And for this reason it comes not to us hot and bright, as in all probability it would, if her shining proceeded either from inflammation or the commixtion of two lights. . . .

Sylla then, taking up the discourse, said: There is indeed a great deal of probability in all that you have spoken. But as to the strongest objection that is brought against it, has it, think you, been any way weakened by this discourse? Or has our friend quite passed it over in silence?

What opposition do you mean? said Lucius. Is it the difficulty about the moon, when one half of her appears enlightened?

The very same, answered Sylla. For there is some reason, seeing that all reflection is made by equal angles, that when the half-moon is in the midst of heaven, the light proceeding from her should not be carried upon the earth, but glance and fall beyond and on one side of it. For the sun, being placed in the horizon, touches the moon with its beams; which, being equally reflected, will therefore necessarily fall on the other bound of the horizon, and not send their light down hither; or else there will be a great distortion and difference of the angle, which is impossible.

And yet, by Jupiter, replied Lucius, this has not been forgotten or overpassed, but already spoken to. And casting his eye, as he was discoursing, upon the mathematician Menelaus; I am ashamed, said he, in your presence, dear Menelaus, to attempt the subverting and overthrowing of a mathematical position, which is supposed as a basis and foundation to the doctrine of catoptrics concerning the causes and reasons of mirrors. And yet of necessity I must. For it neither appears of itself nor is confessed as true, that all reflections are at equal angles; but this position is first checked and contradicted in concave mirrors, when they represent the images of things, appearing at one point of sight, greater than the things themselves. And it is also disproved by double mirrors, which being inclined or turned one towards the other, so that an angle is made within, each of the glasses or plain superficies yields a double resemblance; so that there are four images from the same face, two answerable to the object without on the left side, and two others obscure and not so evident on the right side in the bottom of the mirror. . . .

If we must, of necessity, yield thus much to our dearly beloved geometry, first, this should in all likelihood befall those mirrors which are perfectly smooth and exquisitely polished; whereas the moon has many inequalities and roughnesses. . . . It is not probable that the moon has but one superficies all plain and even, as the sea; rather that of its nature it principally resembles the earth, of which old Socrates in Plato seemed to mythologize at his pleasure; whether it were, that under covert and enigmatical speeches he meant it of the moon, or whether he spake it of some other. For it is neither incredible nor wonderful, if the moon, having in herself nothing corrupt or muddy, but enjoying a pure and clear light from heaven, and being full of heat, not of a burning and furious fire, but of such as is mild and harmless, has in her places admirably fair and pleasant, resplendent mountains and purple-colored cinctures or zones. . . .

And if the sight of all these things comes to us through a shadow, sometimes in one manner and sometimes in another, by reason of the diversity and different change of the ambient air, the moon does not therefore lose the venerable persuasion that is had of her, or the reputation of divinity; being esteemed by men a heavenly earth, or rather (as the Stoics say) a troubled, thick, and dreggish fire. For even the fire itself is honored with barbarian honors among the Assyrians and Medes, who through fear serve and adore such things as are hurtful, hallowing them even above such things as are of themselves indeed holy and honorable. But the very name of the earth is truly dear and venerable to every Greek, and there is through all Greece a custom received of adoring and revering it, as much as any of the Gods. And we are very far from thinking that the moon, which we hold to be a heavenly earth, is a body without soul and spirit, exempt and deprived of all that is to be offered to the Gods.

17

Geography

CLAUDIUS PTOLEMY (c. A.D. 140) is not only the greatest astronomer of antiquity and the author of its best textbook on *Optics,* he is also its most comprehensive mathematical geographer. In his *Geography,* he assembles and evaluates an immense number of data from many sources to present a coherent picture of the inhabited earth as it was then known. Some of the data were astronomically checked, others were rough estimates of travelers and navigators. Ptolemy carries on the tradition of Eudoxus, Dicaearchus, Eratosthenes, Hipparchus, and Marinus of Tyre, and in his turn influences all geographical thought for the next fifteen hundred years. The *Geography* begins with a discussion of the principles of the sciences and of the methods of cartography, in particular the projections of a spherical surface on a plane. The rest of the work is almost entirely taken up with cataloguing the longitude and latitude of some 8,000 different places—cities, islands, mountains, river mouths, etc.—throughout the known earth. We do not have the maps he constructed out of those, but there are modern reconstructions.

Concerning the extent of the known world, Ptolemy is still wide of the mark in excess, but he effects a substantial reduction of Marinus's findings. Unfortunately, his conclusions about the relation of earth to ocean depend on his adoption of 180,000 stades for the circumference of the earth. There is a difficult question here. Eratosthenes had given a correct evaluation of 252,000 stades. Is it a matter of different units? The figure of 180,000 stades, ascribed to Posidonius by Strabo, has been held by some to be based on alternative measurement of the distance from Rhodes to Alexandria (3,750 instead of 5,000 stades), and by others to be based on a stade four thirds as long as that mentioned above (i.e., two fifteenths of a Roman mile) and thus to be exactly equivalent to the first estimate of 240,000 stades. Whether the figure of 180,000 stades adopted by Ptolemy (see p. 274) was understood by him to be equivalent to 240,000 stades on the basis of the smaller stade is a matter of debate. Strabo certainly did not so interpret it. The value of the stade (600 feet) varied with the various measurements of the foot. It has been maintained that Strabo's low estimate was a factor in Columbus's decision to "reach the East by way of the West." One wonders. The maps that Columbus would have used (the Catalan map of 1375, the Genoese map of 1457, that of Fra Mauro of Venice) do give the circuit of the globe with an error of less than 10 per cent. People seem again to have known more than is to be found in the books.

We give here a general description of the earth from Book VII of Ptolemy.*

The portion of the earth that we inhabit is bounded on the east by an unknown land that adjoins the eastern peoples of Asia Major, the Sinae [Chinese] and the inhabitants of Serica; on the south too by unknown lands, which enclose the Indian Sea and bound the country in the south of Libya called Ethiopia Agisymba; on the west by the unknown land that embraces the Ethiopian gulf of Libya, and thereafter by the western Ocean which lies along the westernmost parts of Libya and Europe; and on the north by the Ocean continuous [with the western Ocean] which surrounds the Britannic Islands and the northernmost parts of Europe and is called the Duecaledonian and the Sarmatic Seas, and also by the unknown land that borders on the northernmost countries as Asia Major, Sarmatia, Scythia, and Serica [China].

Of the seas contained within the inhabited portion of the earth, our sea, together with the smaller seas that are a part of it—the Adriatic, the Aegean, the Propontis [Marmara] and the Pontus [Black Sea], and the Sea of Maeotis [Azov]—opens into the Ocean only at the straits of Heracles [Gibraltar], like a peninsula having as its isthmus, as it were, these straits

* Morris R. Cohen and Israel E. Drabkin, *A Source Book in Greek Science.* Cambridge: Harvard University Press, 1959. Reprinted by permission of the publisher.

of Heracles. But the Hyrcanian or Caspian Sea is surrounded on all sides by land, like an island with land and sea reversed.

Similarly, the whole Indian Sea, along with the gulfs that are connected with it, the Arabian, Persian, Gangetic, and the one that is properly called the Great Gulf, is entirely surrounded by land.

And so, of the three continents Asia is joined to Libya by the isthmus of Arabia, which also separates our sea from the Arabian Gulf, and also by the unknown land that surrounds the Indian Sea. Again Asia is joined to Europe at the passage of the Tanais [Don] River. Libya is separated from Europe only by the strait, and while not directly joined to Europe, is yet indirectly connected with it through Asia. For Asia is continuous with both Europe and Libya, being contiguous with them in the east.

Now the largest of the three continents is Asia, second largest Libya, and third Europe. Of the seas that were said to be entirely surrounded by land, the largest is the Indian Sea, second largest our own, third the Hyrcanian or Caspian. Again, the more important gulfs, in order of size, are as follows: first the Gangetic, second the Persian, third the Great Gulf, fourth the Arabian, fifth the Ethiopian, sixth Pontus, seventh the Aegean, eighth the Sea of Maeotis, ninth the Adriatic, and tenth the Propontis.

Of the more important islands or peninsulas the largest is Taprobane [Ceylon], second largest Albion of the Britannic Islands, third the Golden Chersonese [Malaya?], fourth Hibernia of the Britannic Islands, fifth the Peloponnesus, sixth Sicily, seventh Sardinia, eighth Cyrnus [Corsica], ninth Crete, tenth Cyprus.

On the assumption that a great circle contains 360°, the southern limit of the known portion of the earth is indicated by the parallel of latitude 16° 25' south of the equator, the parallel through Meroe in Egypt being the same distance north of the equator. The northern limit is indicated by the parallel 63° north of the equator, drawn through the island of Thule [Iceland]. Thus the entire latitude of the known earth is 79° 25', or, approximately, 80°, and in stades approximately 40,000. That is, one degree contains 500 stades, as has been ascertained by the more exact measurements. The circumference of the whole earth is 180,000 stades.

Again, the eastern limit of the known portion of the earth is indicated by the meridian drawn through the chief city of the Sinae, 119° 30' east of the meridian through Alexandria as measured on the equator, i.e., approximately eight equinoctial hours. And the western limit is indicated by the meridian drawn through the Fortunate Isles [the Canaries], 60° 30′, or four equinoctial hours, west of the meridian through Alexandria. The westernmost meridian is 180°, i.e., a semicircle, or twelve equinoctial hours, distant from the easternmost.

Thus the entire longitude of the known portion of the earth, measured along the equator, contains 90,000 stades; measured along its southernmost parallel approximately 86,330⅓; measured along the northernmost parallel 40,000 stades; measured along the parallel through Rhodes, 36° distant from the equator, the parallel on which measurements have generally been made, approximately 72,000; measured along the parallel through Syene [Aswan], 23° 50′ distant from the equator and approximately bisecting the entire breadth, 82,336. This corresponds to the ratio between the aforesaid parallels and the equator.

Thus the longitude of the known portion of the earth is greater than its latitude, in the climata [1] furthest north, by approximately 1/50 of the latitude; in those near the parallel through Rhodes by approximately 5/6; in those near the parallel through Syene by the amount of the latitude plus approximately 1/18 thereof; in the southernmost parts by the amount of the latitude plus approximately 1/6 thereof; in the climata near the equator by the amount of the latitude plus 1/4 thereof.

And the length of the longest day or night on the southernmost of the aforesaid parallels is 13 equinoctial hours (just as on the parallel through Meroe), on the equator 12 hours, on the parallel through Syene 13½ hours, on that through Rhodes 14½, on the northernmost parallel, that through Thule, 20. The difference over the whole latitude is nine equinoctial hours.

[1] The word *climata* corresponds to an archaic division of the heavenly latitudes into seven zones.

18

Machines and Computers

IN THE HELLENISTIC and Roman empires the need for large-scale engineering made itself felt for the first time. The Eudoxian-Euclidean-Archimedean approach of abtraction and pure logic lost interest, and in its place came approximation and measured imperfection. The Forms were replaced by formulae, the mathematicians by technicians. The latter may be represented by Heron of Alexandria, who probably flourished about the year A.D. 60.

To Alexandria, the melting pot of antiquity, came the practical knowledge of the "barbarians," to be combined with the Hellenic heritage by now willing Greeks. Such was the role of Heron, a distinguished engineer and the last of a line with brilliant predecessors, among whom the name of Ctesibios stands out. Heron was the founder of the first organized school of engineering. He built the first jet-reaction steam engine, a little twirling boiler with two angled outlets which squirted water and steam until it ran out. His *Pneumatics* is full of such gadgets and devices. He also built rudimentary steam- and water-action turbines with paddle wheels to drive foundry bellows, and improved the compressed air gun devised by his predecessor Philo, the military engineer. Unfortunately, most of his inventiveness is spent on automata for display: "We shall dispose several figures of birds near a fountain; and near them the figure of an owl. When it turns its head away, the birds sing; when it turns it towards them, they are silent." And so on.

His outlook, as we can guess it from a few remarks, was that which is proper to a hard-headed engineer. "Philosophers," he says, "have searched long for the means to be at peace, yet only the mechanician is able to supply that means, by way of applied ballistics." The crack is not without its modicum of truth. Yet the great defenses of the

Roman Empire built along the frontiers by Heron's pupils were not to prove an adequate defense against the barbarians, although provided with the latest heavy equipment in applied ballistics. By then it was the home front that had caved in.

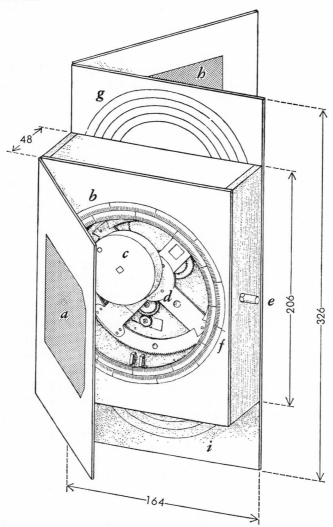

Fig. 15. The Antikythera Machine Reconstructed. The measures are in millimeters.

Heron has left us a voluminous technical encyclopedia or "cookbook," replete with numberless mathematical short cuts, some accurate, some yielding the equivalent of slide-rule answers. There is, for example, the so-called "'Heron's formula," by the use of which one can find the area of any given triangle, given its three sides, without knowing its altitude. He claimed very little if any originality (there is reason to believe that "Heron's formula" is not even due to him), and he often quotes authorities (including Plato, Aristotle, Eudoxus, and Archimedes). Where a quicker or easier method was found, Heron recorded it. It is almost as though he sensed the sand running from the Greek clock.

Heron's work gave us, until a few years ago, the most we know about ancient technology, and we could not form a very high idea of it. A chance discovery helped us recently to a better view. Among the remains of a sunken Greek ship near the island of Antikythera were found the corroded fragments of a mechanism, which were assembled and interpreted in 1959 by Dr. D. J. de S. Price.* They were shown to belong to an astronomical computer of a very advanced type, which could be dated from internal evidence to 82 B.C., and makes Heron's devices look like "a thousand-and-one things a boy can do."

We know that the Greeks built planetariums. The description of the spindle of Necessity in Plato's *Republic* might indicate one such machine. They were geometrical models, and they must have involved orreries of which we have no description. The Antikythera mechanism seems to have been an arithmetical counterpart of these devices. It is like an astronomical clock without an escapement, or like a modern analogue computer which uses mechanical parts to save tedious calculations.

The Greeks had given great importance to the already age-old study of cycles. The lunisolar cycle of Callippus was 76 years, four times the Metonic cycle of 19 years, or 235 synodic lunar months. These figures engraved on a fragment of the plate indicate that the purpose of the de-

---

* Figure 15 is from "Ancient Greek Computer; with Biographical Sketch," by Derek John de Solla Price, in *Scientific American,* June, 1959. Reprinted by permission of the author and *Scientific American.*

vice was to mechanize such cycles. One could design, says Dr. Price, gearing that would operate from one dial having a wheel that revolved annually, and turn by this gearing other wheels which would move pointers indicating the sidereal, synodic, and draconitic month. Similar cycles were known for the planets, and were studied especially in connection with astrology; in fact, this type of arithmetical theory is the central theme of Seleucid Babylonian astronomy, which was introduced in the last few centuries B.C. Such arithmetical schemes are quite distinct from the geometrical theory of cycles and epicycles in astronomy, which was essentially Greek. The two types of theory were unified and brought to a peak in the second century A.D. by Ptolemy.

Dr. Price's tentative reconstruction, which we reproduce here (Fig. 15), may give an idea of the complication of the mechanism. An input was provided by an axle (perhaps connected with a clockwork) that came through the side of the casing and turned a crown-gear wheel. This moved a big, four-spoked driving wheel that was connected with two trains of gears that led respectively up and down the plate and were connected by axles to gears on the other side of the plate. On that side the gear trains continued, leading through an epicyclic turntable and coming eventually to a set of shafts that turned the dial pointers. When the input axle was turned, the pointers all moved at various speeds around their dials. While the front dial showed the annual motion of the sun in the zodiac, the back dials gave not only the moon phenomena, but the risings and settings, stations and retrogradations, of the planets. The Antikythera machine is the direct predecessor of the considerably simpler Arab mechanisms which we know; and since those mechanisms are the foundation for the whole range of subsequent European invention in the field of clockwork, the Greek machine is also the ancestor of our own devices. With its scientific graduation and its precision work, it points to a large body of technology that has since been lost to us.

19

Decline and Fall

IT IS A COMMON experience of our time that enough change takes place in one generation to more than fill a century for our grandfathers. Things seem to go the other way in antiquity after about 200 B.C.—a divide which is marked not only by the death of Archimedes but by the consolidation of Roman dominion over the Hellenistic empires. Intellectually, what had been decades become centuries. Aristotle had spoken of the men who had preceded him by a hundred years as "the ancients" (*palaioi*). But writers of three and four hundred years later refer to him and his likes as we would to thinkers of a generation ago. Great changes have taken place, social, political, and philosophical. Maturity has undeniably come in, and the world is witnessing the rise of the imposing intellectual structure of Roman Law. Yet—by our standards—it is as if nothing essential had happened.

As an extreme case let us take two men who are surely independent thinkers in their own right: Simplicius and Philoponus. They not only have all the learning of the right kind, they are vigorous minds and comprehensive intellects. They think originally. Their elaborations on Plato and Aristotle have provided us with invaluable material. But they are not their successors. They live after A.D. 500, a full eight centuries later. Eight hundred years —twice the time that went from Anaximander to Archimedes. Christianity is already ruling the world—in fact, one of the two, Philoponus, is a Christian. It hardly comes to mind on reading them. Stretching a point, one might say that the next scholarly step is Eduard Zeller's great *Outlines of the History of Greek Philosophy,* published in 1860. They are not so much the last "commentators" as they are currently labeled, as early professors in the modern sense, experts in what is there no longer.

The reasons for this change of pace may concern us, too. We can discern several:

A. The Hellenistic states which came after the conquests of Alexander (and Rome is only the last of them) had not only become a very mixed civilization, they had become uniformly "big-time," with huge and fearsome structures of power. State cults of divine rulers, state-encouraged superstitions, the worship of blind Fortune, had replaced the old city gods. In their wake had come new mystery cults from the East, exotic gospels of salvation, magic doctrines and practices and novelties for big-city dwellers—very much as these things have come in our time to southern California. Science was represented no longer by free men and respected elders of the community, but by subsidized intellectuals who were told to go and perform and quote one another in ample institutions like the library of Alexandria, and also (this was an order) to provide moral uplift and entertainment for the arts-loving ruling class. The insistence, which to us seems excessive, on virtue and character-building is not all escape literature, witness Tacitus and Marcus Aurelius. But there is a ring of frustration in it.

B. Economic decline has set in. There seems to be a failure of imagination at the root of it all. A great and stable and ever more complicated administration needs economic growth to keep pace with it, and the Roman Empire seems to have been strangely incapable of economic and political growth; even more so than the Chinese. Urban luxury, bread-and-games, world-wide services, the unending attrition of border wars, the subsidizing of intractable tribes, are forms of conspicuous waste which cannot rest on merely agrarian economies and growing masses of plantation slave labor. The Romans never developed, as the Middle Ages did, a system of credit banking. The medium remained coin, and the deficit and the needs for an increased circulation were met by usury and debasing of the coinage. The burden of taxes became so crushing that farmers fled from their land, had to be brought back in chains as "tied to the sod." Growing regulations meant increasing avoidance, growing expenditure, harsher enforcement, in a never-ending circle. Workers trying to flee over the border were sentenced to death by fire. Dullness, conformity, and gloom spread like a pall of smog over the last centuries. Science became manuals and encyclopedias, literature became stale rhetoric on "classic" models, or tales of the wondrous.

C. The failure of imagination explains, among other things, why men became so reactionary-minded, even when they thought they were entertaining the most lofty and liberal ideals. Something like that was to occur again in the American South. When Aristotle, the great master of ethics, said that slavery is a fact of nature, and that we shall need slaves so long as the shuttle will not run in the loom by itself, he had registered one of those great mental blocks which foretell the end of a cycle. And this leads us to what is obviously crucial, the lack of an applied science.

Pure science is always a hazardous and unfinished affair, stretching out its structures in perilous balance over the unknown. It does not suit men's whims or comfort their fears. In order to be accepted by a tough-minded society, it must produce unquestionable and stunning results, as happened with Newton's laws. Otherwise, it will be told to lay off and not disturb people's minds unnecessarily. Men like Galileo, when they dare to speak openly, will be reproved. It happened at the freest moment of Greek thought with Anaxagoras; it happened again in a different context with Aristarchus and his Copernican suggestion. Much has been said of a "loss of nerve" in Greek speculation after 300 B.C. The expression may not be accurate, but it circumscribes something that certainly took place: an inflection away from certain lines of research, a lack of aggressiveness, a kind of settling down.

The decisive point lies in the use of mathematics. After the early efforts of the Pythagoreans to set up a mathematical physics, it is as if the enterprise were abandoned as unfruitful. The turning point lies within the career of Eudoxus, who was Archytas's pupil. It is, as we said earlier, as if the lifting power of pure number had been finally released to rise into the realm of abstraction, providing henceforth nothing but transposed mathematical models for reality. It "saved" the phenomena instead of explaining them. The spheres of Eudoxus, Plato's *Timaeus* as a whole, are such models. The relation of number to reality has been transformed irretrievably, for even Archimedes is unable to reverse the trend. The higher qualitative virtues of number, so to speak, have been saved at the expense of actual application.

Attention was drawn some years ago by Werner Jaeger to the fact that, beginning with Isocrates the orator, one of Aristotle's teachers, there are thinkers deliberately opposed to *akribeia,* precision in measurement and precision in general. Aristotle's philosophy is in itself, as we have seen, a turning away from mathematics to other metaphysically more "relevant" forms of accuracy. This did not preclude measurement as such, witness Dicaiarchos's (Aristotle's own pupil's) enterprise in measuring the height of mountains, but demoted it, in a way, to philosophical irrelevance. The issue verged substantially on the existence of physical truths not susceptible of measurement, and hence, whenever other reasons so suggested, on the possibility of ignoring quantitative data. A disturbing example comes to us from mathematical geography. The name of Ptolemy is synonymous for us with the greatest effort of antiquity at astronomical exactitude. Ptolemy's respect for precision in heavenly movements even led him into painful and unesthetic complications, which Copernicus was later to hold against him. Yet the same Ptolemy, when it came to establishing a mathematical geography on the available data, was willing to "adjust," if not the data, at least the inferences. The size of the Western Ocean appeared on the spherical map as disproportionately large, extending as it did unbrokenly from the Canaries to China. Ptolemy tried to compromise by extending all the dimensions of land (part dimly known) from east to west and taking the Stoic position that China must be just half the globe away from the Canaries.

The publication of Ptolemy's *Geography* in the Renaissance was to cause no small surprise among Italian scholars, and the problem of the size of the earth and of the exact value of ancient measures became an issue; the debates were a stimulus to Columbus's enterprise. Thus we find, even in this most practical of fields, an overriding concern, that we may call theoretical only if we give the word *theōria* its original meaning.

The relationship of Greek thought to nature remains fundamentally different from ours: it is not a search for the point of attack from which to attempt a break-through, but a quest for harmony, proportion, an over-all order to which to adjust. Man sees himself as living *with* nature, not opposite to nature, a member of the great republic of gods, men, and all that is. From the very start we feel the persistent effort to justify the cosmos, to rid its powers of their dark and dreadful ambiguity. Order, fitness, justice, reconciliation, reassurance, are the themes which occur at times in the moral key, but always showing reason, the clarity of truth, *alētheia,* as the saving power against terrified animal subjection. In Democritus, the resolute physicist, we find again "a mind devoid of fear" as the highest good. The very word for science is *epistēmē,* derived from a verb which means "standing up to." This meaning may be more helpful than many economic theories to explain why science in Greece was not as subject to the pressure for practical results as it was from the Renaissance to our days. In the Anaximandrian equation the central symbol is "fittingness"; in the Pythagorean *mathēsis* or "doctrine," the spiritual tensions are reconciled in a scheme of intellectual salvation. We base our thinking on nature as necessity. For the Greek, necessity is not quite of nature, it is seen as part of the purifying vision: the logic of a theorem, the rigorous timing of the celestial orbs, will be felt as analogous to the determination of holy ritual. The Logos determines, rules, makes clear; it does not by itself necessitate. Galileo will insist that the universe is ruled by the necessity of mathematical law, but the Pythagoreans would have mentioned Reason alone, and even Democritus, we remember, said it is ruled by Reason *and* Necessity, as if they were two different entities. Necessity and Reason are closely coupled since Anaximander, but they remain formally distinct even with the Stoics, complementary as it were. The dark mythical figure of Necessity, *Anankē,* is imagined as a kind of inchoate heavy passiveness, which precedes the order of *physis* and reason; when Thucydides uses the word he means the massive inertia whereby events keep going in a certain direction once they have been set in motion. Behaviors and determinations come from the inherent reason: "Nature," says Aristotle in a revealing phrase, "refuses to be badly administered." Wonderfully said, but it implies that it is administered from a higher order, and then we cannot expect the objects of nature to behave according to inherent laws; we can hardly think of questioning them by way of experiment.

The later subjection of the astronomical profession to the dictates of the philosophers is, so to speak, inscribed in the very origins; it expresses a hierarchical concept which exists originally inside the single creative mind. In Hellenistic times it became an organizational split which was to be healed only by Galileo and Kepler, who created the figure of the "astronomer phylosophicall." It is some such reason, apparently, which precluded the application of mathematics to terrestrial motion and change. Archimedes' statics, based on symmetry and proportion, remains inside the classic frame; it does not point the way to the entirely new complex of ideas still to be born. Thus the ancient world remains without a science of dynamics, and that may be not the last cause of its downfall. An accepted explanation for the failure to use steam power in antiquity (Heron's steam jet reactor remained a toy) is the lack of a craftsman class specialized in precision machining of metal. After the reconstruction of the Antikythera machine, this explanation does not look persuasive. The men who built that machine were fully the equals of Harrison and Watt. They could have built a chronometer: it is symbolic that their skill was used on computing astronomical cycles and epicycles. But there is worse. Most of the inventions displayed by Heron in applied mechanics are aimed only at catching the eye of the public. They are automata and trick mechanisms meant for parks, palaces, and temples, very much like those which were developed in our eighteenth century for the amusement of a mercantile aristocracy. What was really lacking were the inceptors of the scientific revolution, idea-men like Galileo, Huygens, Newton and Bernoulli. For the lack of such, ancient capitalism remained mercantile and usurary, and ultimately foundered on its own slave labor.

The achievements of Greek science, such as they were, did provide the starting point for our scientific rebirth in the seventeenth century. But the spirit of those achievements remained embodied, during the intervening period, in a few great scientific-philosophical doctrines which could claim a true religious content, and thus not only guided but gave shape to Western thought in the difficult time of transition. They were, one might say, the carrier waves. It is through them that the continuity was preserved, and without them further developments would remain incomprehensible. We shall conclude, therefore, with a sketch of three forms of scientific religion: Atomism, Stoicism, and Neoplatonism.

20

Three Forms of Scientific Religion

"A MIND devoid of fear, the highest good." These words would probably not come first to mind in thinking of present-day physicists. Yet it is not so very long ago that Hamlet could say:

> . . . who would fardels bear,
> To grunt and sweat under a weary life,
> But that the dread of something after death,
> The undiscover'd country from whose bourn
> No traveller returns, puzzles the will. . . .

Such thoughts seem to have haunted antiquity much more than appears on the surface. The whole effort of the tragic poets is to move their hearers to another plane, that of acceptable fate, nor is Socrates's death speech to be understood otherwise. It is the testament of the free man. Conversely, in Hellenistic times, rulers seem to have favored terrors and superstition as instruments of power over the masses. This may help us to understand the firm position of Democritus on "a mind devoid of fear." Even the worldly Cicero, who professes the proper kind of lofty idealism, and chides the atomists for not explaining enough about virtue, finds nothing to criticize in that statement:

But the security of Democritus, which is a sort of tranquillity of mind, should have been barred from this discussion [about the aims of life] because that very tranquillity of mind is itself the blessed life. . . . And even if he placed that life in knowing things, none the less from his investigations of nature he wished a good mind to result.

In fact, the direct answer to Hamlet is provided by Democritus's last great interpreter, the Roman Lucretius:

> When Man's life upon earth in base dismay,
> Crushed by the burthen of Religion, lay,
> Whose face, from all the regions of the sky,
> Hung, glaring hate upon mortality,
> First one Greek man against her dared to raise
> His eyes, against her strive through all his days;
> Him noise of Gods nor lightnings nor the roar
> Of raging heaven subdued, but pricked the more
> His spirit's valiance, till he longed the Gate
> To burst of this low prison of man's fate.
> And thus the living ardour of his mind
> Conquered, and clove its way; he passed behind
> The world's last flaming wall, and through the whole
> Of space uncharted ranged his mind and soul.
> Whence, conquering, he returned to make Man see
> At last what can, what cannot, come to be;
> By what law to each Thing its power hath been
> Assigned, and what deep boundary set between;
> Till underfoot is tamed Religion trod,
> And, by His victory, Man ascends to God.

This is the kind of language that will later be used to glorify the Saviour for the harrowing of Hell and the subduing of the powers of darkness. Yet it applies to Epicurus the prophet of atomism, an astringent physical doctrine whose message is "reason and necessity," whose bleak assurance is the mortality of the soul. It will become clearer if we consider that Lucretius was denouncing what was officially called the state religion, but what statesmen among themselves referred to as *superstitio,* literally, "left over" of old beliefs. Critias, Plato's kinsman, had spoken once of "the shrewd and wise-thoughted" man who invented gods as the best way to frighten people and keep them in their place. After the end of the city-states, in the era of world powers, the old city cults had been remelted into official religion whose rites and pontifical charges were held firmly in hand by the rulers. Julius Caesar, Cicero, and their friends of the senatorial class favored Platonistic or vaguely theistic attitudes such as were philosophically fashionable among the elite, but did not care any more for religion as they administered it than did Ben Franklin, who administered none. Scaevola, the wise Pontifex Maximus, that is, head of the state cult, is quoted by Varro as saying that the opinions of philosophers should not be broadcast among the people, for "it is expedient that states should be deceived in the matter of religion." This is the attitude that Machiavelli, like Polybius, was to admire as the foundation of Roman greatness. Later, a true philosophic mind and lofty moralist like Seneca could only groan at what he had to do: "The whole base throng of gods assembled by a superstition coeval with time we must worship, without forgetting that we do so to set an example, not because they exist." We can understand, then, the intransigence of Epicurus.

Epicurus was of Athenian stock, but born in the colony of Samos, in 341 B.C.—a few years after the death of Plato. When he was eighteen, the fortunes of war made of him a displaced person, as we say today with grisly administrative euphemism. He lived, a refugee among miserable refugees, in Colophon, became a schoolmaster, then his peculiar genius at philosophical exposition brought about a turn in his fortunes. Friends bought a little house and a garden for him in Athens, and he spent there the rest of his life, teaching the Philosophy of the Garden, as people came to call it. The Garden was not only a school: it was a sort of retreat or religious community, in which women, even slave women, took part freely. The atmosphere was one of almost romantic friendship and tenderness, such as was not to occur again for centuries until the Christian *agape*. But indeed Epicurus was treated by his disciples as the Deliverer, and every word he said as a doctrine of salvation.

Yet what he was teaching was pure and simple Democritus, as he had learned it in his early youth. It was enough for him that it should be a clear and hard doctrine, raising no difficult problem, and that it should lead to the "four-square platform" which counted: "Nothing to fear from gods; nothing to feel in death; good can be achieved; evil can be borne."

Surely this was still Democritus, but with a difference. The Abderite had been a mathematician, a man of subtle and universal curiosity; Epicurus proclaimed his contempt for the sciences and his lack of intellectual interests. "From Culture in every shape, my lad, spread sail and fly!" Such was the advice he gave to disciples. When other philosophers were working out calculations about the size of the sun and the commensurability of the sun and moon cycles, Epicurus no less contemptuously than Heraclitus remarked that the sun was probably about as big as it looked, or maybe smaller; since fires at a distance look larger than they are. As for the cycles, how did anyone know that it was not a new sun that kept popping up every day? Such an attitude may seem strange. But we should remember again that Auguste Comte, the founder of modern Positivism, displayed a very similar aversion to pure knowledge for less good reasons. We can watch our contemporary empiricists and logical positivists denouncing with fussy concern anything that would indicate outmoded beliefs, forever busy swatting "metaphysics" whenever it appears, and viewing with alarm any interest in harmless philosophical obscurities. Yet they live in an unshakably scientific civilization which has nothing to fear except from itself. Epicurus at least had more stringent reasons in his own time: he not only had a sharper experience of administrative oppression which caused him to flee from public life, he also saw the affectations of Platonic astro-theology abetting the resurgent power of divine kingship, and astrology becoming fashionable through the Stoics. His alarm caused him to reject a science of heaven altogether.

If the scientific view refuses to comprehend as much as it can, then, inevitably, it starts to shrink. Epicurus may suggest at times interesting refinements to Democritus's doctrine; but on one point—indeed the main point—he misses the idea. The inertial principle, such as Democritus had conceived it through a prodigious feat of abstraction, escapes him. If atoms move, he says, it is because they are "falling" forever through infinite space. An eternal rain to nowhere. But if their paths are all parallel, how do they collide? Here Epicurus brings in "chance," as distinct from both reason and necessity, and postulates a momentary spontaneous "swerve," wholly unmotivated, which is enough to create vortexes—and ultimately life. The image is clearly that of the great flow of the Anaximandrian Unbounded with its eddies. But what had been genius in

Anaximander is here regression. Epicurus had his reasons, which to him were sufficient. He wanted an initial element of indeterminacy, of spontaneity, at the core of the atom, so that it should work out as freedom at every point, in nature and specifically in life. He saw it developing in the higher organisms by reason of their complexity, until it became our own experience of the values of life. This attempt was in no wise more unreasonable than that of moderns who try to deduce free will from quantum indeterminacy; it was only more flagrant because here indeterminacy had been brought in on purpose. Feeling had been re-established at the expense of Necessity.

Scientifically, it was irreparable. The coupling of "reason and necessity" in Democritus's thought had been the blinding flash of mechanistic intuition which broke the unspoken taboos of Greece and set the mind free to follow a new, if harsher, path. That is why, of all the doctrines of antiquity, Democritus's atomism is the only one which re-emerges practically intact in our era. It is of another nature. Epicurus draws the curtain and re-establishes the comfort of a cosmos of sorts. We find him teaching the worship of the gods, albeit a purified philosophical worship of remote cosmic entities which can do nothing for us. This is not a concession to popular sentiment; it is genuine. The wonderful invocation to Venus, the generative power, which opens Lucretius's poem is a true prayer, certainly truer than those addressed by his contemporaries to the institutional deities. And although Lucretius is capable of describing brilliantly natural mechanisms, yet he does not speak of natural laws, but, like Empedocles whom he so much admires, of "pacts of nature," *foedera naturai*. Thus the classic vision is preserved.

Epicurus had not only taken up the counteroffensive of Sophistic enlightenment to show the delusions of Plato's Republic: he went further than the Sophists ever dared in denouncing the claims to wisdom of the ruling classes, and all the social make-believe. To him these were all instruments of oppression, and against them he founded his own version of the Society of Friends.

We can see now what he feared in Culture, spelt with a capital C. There is surely nothing uncultural in his disciple Lucretius, when he invokes the "serene temples of wisdom," far from the strife and delusions of mortals. On the other hand, Seneca's whinings are not as cultural as they seem. We might also add that the misunderstanding of reason and necessity was not wholly Epicurus's mistake. The Greeks, although addicted to playing dice and knuckle-bones since the dawn of their history, had never been moved to investigate the laws of chance. They were much more moved to seeing in the lucky throw the unexplained intervention of Tyche, Fortune. Thus, one part of Democritus's theory had been left vague, reason and chance divorced, mechanical randomness unexplored. It was left to Epicurus to fill the gap in his own way.

The message in any case is clear: freedom does not come to the soul from above, and only to the elect as Plato would have it in his *Laws;* it comes from the very core of things with life itself. Hence it is every man's inalienable inheritance. "Great numbers of people are with them," says Cicero with undisguised alarm.

STOICISM

While the Epicureans isolate themselves quietly from the world, the Stoics are ready to welcome the revolutionary changes that come with Alexander and his successors. Here is already a radical difference: Zeno of Citium (c. 308 B.C.) was the founder of the new sect; a Cypriote whom they called, from his looks, "the little Phoenician." He lectured in the Stoa Poikile, the "Frescoed Portico," in Athens; hence the name of "Stoic" given to his school.

Says Plutarch, not a Stoic himself, but a perceptive observer:

It is true indeed that the so much admired commonwealth of Zeno, first author of the Stoic sect, aims singly at this, that neither in cities nor in towns we should live under laws distinct one from another, but that we should look upon all men in general to be our fellow-countrymen and citizens, observing one manner of living and one kind of order, like a flock feeding together with equal right in one common pasture. This Zeno wrote, fancying to himself, as in a dream, a certain scheme of civil order, and the image of a philosophical commonwealth. But Alexander made good his words by his deeds; for he did not, as Aristotle advised him, rule the Grecians like a moderate prince and insult over the barbarians like an absolute tyrant; nor did he take particular care of the first as his friends and domestics, and scorn the latter as mere brutes and vegetables; which would have filled his empire with fugitive incendiaries and perfidious tumults. But believing himself sent from Heaven as the common moderator and arbiter of all nations, and subduing those by force whom he could not associate to himself by fair offers, he labored thus, that he might bring all regions, far and near, under the same dominion. And then, as in a festival goblet, mixing lives, manners, customs, wedlock, all together, he ordained that every one should take the whole habitable world for his country. . . .

In fact, Zeno taught that the whole of mankind formed one great fellowship, for which later the very word "society" was invented: one humanity in one world. He taught that men should share resources reasonably and live together as co-citizens of the world city. This doctrine could become revolutionary, as indeed King Cleomenes of Sparta understood it in his short-lived socialistic experiment; it could imply only moral solidarity and individual dignity, as it was mainly understood in later and harsher times, when Stoic discipline gave men the inner freedom to step out of life rather than face indignity. As Plutarch remarks prudently, "For lofty and passionate souls the Stoic doctrine can become dangerous and extreme, but when blended with a deep and gentle ethos it brings out what is best in it." It depended very much on how one understood that central tenet, "the law dictated by nature." You can make a physicist out of it, or a scholastic, or a philosophical jurist. Or you can get a Rousseau.

The Stoics taught that "man must live according to nature." So, for that matter, did the austere Cynics and the cheerful Hedonists, but they meant simply man's own nature, as opposed to social convention. The Stoics tried to fit man's being inside a closely reasoned view of the whole and called themselves "physicists."

For their *physis,* they went back to Heraclitus. What they needed out of this most unphysical of physicists was the dynamic vision, the Fire element which rules the universe and carries with it the *logos* of its changes. One might think that the next step out of Heraclitus would be a metaphysical interpretation of the *logos,* such as Plato had attempted. The Stoics instead went back resolutely to a physical Fire, "intelligent, ever-living." This was probably due to the great prestige of the medical school of Diocles, who had founded their physiology upon the pneuma. But what is good for doctors can become hard for philosophers. What the Stoics really needed was an understanding of the *logos* that rules the universe. Heraclitus had placed it at the core of all things, which is where they wanted it; to make it truly physical made it look very ambiguous indeed.

The system becomes vitalistic from the ground up. There is no inanimate or animate object which is not held together by the pneuma, receiving from it its form and qualities. The whole universe is held together in the same way in the infinite void that surrounds it; it is as living as each of its parts, its fiery soul suffuses the whole of it. We are here on very different ground from Plato and his successors. However "immattered" Aristotle's forms may be, however dynamic his universe may be with pulsating life, the Forms still have an explicitly stated priority in the mind. The whole scheme is essentially a *design* superimposed on matter. When there is design there are archetypes in the mind of God, and even if Aristotle dodged the issue and went another way, it is reasonable to expect those archetypes to be mathematical. It is in the irrepressible spirit of the Platonic tradition.

For the Stoics instead, who remained intransigent monists, the fact of Life is direct and primary, embodied as it is in its basic substance. Whatever Reason there is will emerge perpetually from the darkness of Begetting. The universe creates itself forever out of its own inner forces, which also hold it together. There is no distinction between above and below. It is a completely organismic view, with no outside mind required to rule the whole. This rigorous monism carries with it the advantage of strong determinism. The Stoic universe, too, is ruled by "reason and necessity," albeit of a kind, with no concessions to such notions as the Epicurean "free swerve" in atoms, nor, on the other hand, to the inadequacy of matter in responding to the perfect design, as in Platonism. The Stoic world is a "block universe," complete in itself. The vitalistic intuition carries with it an almost mystical sense of union with the travail of the forces of nature as we feel them reflected in us. It expands into a sense of vast cosmic solidarity which in turn defines the solidarity among men.

Atomism leads, quite naturally, to a theory of men as individuals, each attaining his individual adjustment to the outside forces. Its sense of community, as shown in the Garden, amounts to a huddling together. Stoicism insists on making man one with the universe. He feels himself operating on the cosmic scale, akin to the gods. Virtue and happiness are attained in the consciousness of the total bond; freedom lies in the acceptance of over-all determination. "The fates lead the willing and drag the unwilling." But this is far from being passive subjection to chance, for the ends of fate are good, as being ruled by universal Reason.

As that Reason was *in* the world and of the world, and there was nothing beyond the world, wisdom had to be a physics first and last.

Stoic rationalism had many "modern" devices to implement the sketchy Heraclitean outline. The cosmology of the Sage of Ephesus could not but look primitive after two centuries of progress in astronomy; the Stoics agreed with Plato in seeing the heavens as the highest work of Reason. But if Aristotle had seen the general cause of change in the oblique path of the sun on the ecliptic, what could be the meaning of all the other motions? Posidonius, a great and much-traveled Stoic scholar of the later generation, who was a friend of Cicero's, showed one more clue. During a stay in Cádiz, he observed the Atlantic tides and showed that they were tied up with the moon. It was natural to generalize from there; if the universe was all one organism, everything must tie up with everything else. A newfangled science brought in from the Orient, already favored by Zeno, gave the answer. It was astrology, and it taught that the planets affect events on earth in different ways, not only according to the "houses" they traverse in the zodiac, but also according to their positions with respect to the sun and moon and to one another. Here was the perfect multidialed machinery which programmed events on earth with infinitely complex cyclic regularity. Every single thing down here had its fate apportioned to it with unfailing precision. As the heavenly bodies came around to the same pattern in the cosmic Great Year, the world could be said to begin again for ever. "Fate rules the globe, all stands under changeless law."

This is the doctrine that was put into powerful verse by Manilius (A.D. 30), the other Roman poet who can compare with Lucretius. It is far from being pointless. Modern physiology has had again to search for clocking mechanisms to successive phases in organic life, and has found them in hormonal releases. In a way, the Stoics were looking for their equivalents. This "cosmorganic" vision, as one might call it, brought up the issue of the continuum in a new way. If all things influence one another at a distance, and the heavens act on all, what is the mechanism? Some kind of field theory is needed. But modern field theories can only determine a vector at each point of space: what had to be determined here were complex forms and behaviors, in fact, what makes each one thing different from another. Influences, effluences, "sympathies," correspondences, had to be invented. The Stoics made the task more difficult for themselves by insisting on "material" causes, since for them the universe was all matter, including the gods. "Nature for them," says Cicero, "is a craftsmanlike fire, proceeding methodically to the work of generation." This fire had to be everywhere at once, as life is in the animal, shaping and moving each part. That was indeed why fire had seemed to be such a natural prime element, because it can be everywhere at once in the form of heat. Not only heat as energy, but heat as active matter, "caloric" as it was still called two centuries ago. This was, in a way, a more interesting conception than Democritus's "mobile atoms of fire," which begged the question. Fire meant action: "everything of a hot fiery nature supplies its own source of motion and activity; and everything which is nourished and grows possesses a definite and uniform motion." Cicero has grasped here the essential dynamism of the idea. But it is tied up with a special matter, pneuma, which is the fire element combined with air, or shall we say, fire-in-the-air. We can see how the properties combine. Air provides elasticity and expansion; fire, action and modulation. Jointly they make up the *tonos,* the "tension," of pneuma, which is supposed to hold things together. A surviving fragment from the vast works of Chrysippus (281–208 B.C.) tells us how:

The structure of matter [apart from the passive and motionless substrate of earth and water] is simply air, for bodies are bound together by air. Likewise all that is bound together in a material structure derives its quality from the binding air which in iron is called hardness, in stone thickness, and in silver whiteness. . . . All these qualities are pneumata and aerial tensions inherent in the parts of matter and determining their form.

Here again is an attempt at explaining by way of matter what the atomist had left unsolved: the problems of form and constancy of form, which look not at all like random effects. The atom theory, based on discontinuity, could suggest difference of arrangement: a clear but labile mechanism. The Stoics go to the other extreme by postulating a continuum, and indeed one of far more complex structure than the straight geometric continuum of Parmenides. They have to invent some equivalent to functions and variables which should determine varying structures at different points in the field, and they have to do that without the help of abstractions, because they do believe only in what is "corporeal." Their pneuma is something akin to the modern electromagnetic aether, even if it remains corporeal and subject to all the ambiguities of that word. The changes in it, as matter, can be only monotone, more or less fire vs. air. Being matter, it cannot penetrate other matter, it can only diffuse in it. But it can diffuse very subtly, in accord with the nature of the continuum.

No one particular body can be simple, since it is the intersection point of universal shaping influences plus universal correspondence, all carried by pneuma, and a function of the "pneumatic tension" at that point—a true synthesis. The old word "mixture," that Empedocles had strained to the limit, was still doing service, but new meanings had to be injected into it. Aristotle had tried in his own way (see p. 149f) to establish a distinction between mixture and true compound, but that way looked all too simple here, since it had depended on Form to provide determination and structure, and even the cohesive force. Now all had to come from the matter itself, and from the pneumatic tension in it. How? The solution suggested was brilliant, and originated, it would seem, in the theory of perception. Says Cleomedes the astronomer, a Stoic of the first century B.C.: "Without one binding tension and the all-permeating pneuma we would not be able to see and hear." As all things are supposed to receive messages from one another through the continuum, the general mechanism must be akin to the taut string, or to sound waves (of which the first clear mention appears in the Stoics) or the transmitted "stress" on pneuma whereby we see through space. A very important idea is coming to the fore here, that of modulation. The Stoics are surely not the first to have thought about the expansion and interference of water waves in a confined environment—we are here clearly in the Pythagorean domain—but, as Sambursky has brought out on a number of neglected texts, they used that model creatively. Waves traveling back and forth continuously between center and circumference in a tub create by interference systems of "standing waves" which may particularize into clear figures. For the Stoics, this kind of standing vibration (of which the first example in one dimension had been given by the Pythagorean monochord) seems to have provided an image for the coexistence of motion and rest in the same single system. They called it *tonikē kinesis,* "tension motion." Expansion, contraction, elasticity, added new possibilities to those of the water model. Additional images were provided by muscular behavior. The boundaries of bodies—or rather of their basic matter—seem to have been conceived of as providing secondary resonators to the universal vibration, if we are to believe a remark of Philo:

The physical nexus is a very strong bond. It is the pneuma that returns upon itself. It begins in the center of the substance and stretches outwards to its edges . . . and returns back again to the place from which it started.

By this sophisticated use of the idea of modulation, the Stoics had managed to overcome at least in part the contradiction of their basic idea of a "corporeal" force, which must obey the laws of noninterpenetrability of matter. Their Fire had become an energetic continuum, and the solutions worked out for it bear a striking—if sketchy— resemblance with modern continuum theory. It bore them all the way from matter to Reason, since the *logos* itself can become an over-all tensional motion. It was, at the other end of the intellectual spectrum, as good an idea as the atomic. Even better. It had all been implicit in Heraclitus's original duality, which we ventured to call that of carrier wave and message (p. 47), a profoundly creative idea. But it had the disadvantage of being too complex (hence soon lost) and of explaining too much too easily.

When Newton, who was by instinct an atomist, was led by his discoveries to envisage a field theory, he had to grope his way along with Stoic reminiscences, as we can watch him doing at the end of the third part of his *Principia:*

There must be a certain most subtle spirit which pervades and lies hid in the most gross bodies; by the force and action of which the particles of bodies attract one another at near distances, and cohere, if contiguous.

In fact, he will ask himself elsewhere, what is it that makes the very individual particle hang together? Here he continues:

And electric bodies operate to greater distances as well repelling as attracting the neighbouring corpuscles; and light is emitted, reflected, refracted, inflected and heats bodies; and all sensation is excited, and the members of animal bodies move at the command of the will, namely by the vibrations of this spirit, propagated along the solid filaments of the nerves. . . .

The greater the range of phenomena to be explained, the stronger the temptation to hark back to that enticingly unclear, multipurpose, catchall concept, the pneuma with its tensile force.

The trouble with Stoicism was the composite character which overlay the original monistic impulse. We find in the system the Fire of Heraclitus and the Air of Anaximenes, the Pythagorean harmonies, if muted, the mixtures of Empedocles, and the astral theology of Plato, all transformed by deep Oriental influxes. Its physics is imaginative but eclectic, its theory of knowledge painfully circular (founded as it is on the *logos* which shows us reason); only its ethical teaching is strong and coherent, carried through with doctrinaire rigidity. It is therefore no injustice if the School of the Porch has come down in history essentially as a builder of character. Some of the teachers may have affected an uncouth and curmudgeonish behavior; others may have relied for a look of gravity on the furrowed brow, on a luxuriant growth of beard ("His beard," says Lucian of one of them, "is worth to him a thousand sesterces"), the roster of their disciples is nonetheless impressive.

The stern Stoic sense of social responsibility and moral obligation made it peculiarly acceptable to the Roman senatorial elite; it became thus a kind of philosophical religion for the ruling class of the Empire, very much as Zen Buddhism was to be in Japan, or the Kantian doctrine to nineteenth-century agnostics in Europe. It entered Rome as the most modern and "serious" form of Greek thought after the Carthaginian Wars, at a time when the "circle of the Scipios" was opening itself to the influence of culture, considering the responsibilities of world empire, and shaping the new idea of *humanitas,* or "the civilized way." Polybius, the great historian, and Panaetius, the philosophic orator, helped the Roman political leaders to think out their problems; Cicero favored their creed: it made what is called in history Greco-Roman civilization.

The Stoic cosmological outlook remained built into Western thought with singular tenacity. The phrases we have quoted show that Newton himself, the man who would "feign no hypotheses," was inclined to fall back, wherever his secure deduction could not reach, on the Stoic hypothesis of a "most subtile fluid." It was still the same generative craftsmanlike fire, the power which in Renaissance thought articulated the universe and kept it together. The advent of the new mechanical philosophy of mass and motion forced it back for a while, but the eighteenth-century revolt against mechanism, what is called the Romantic Movement, brought it back to the center of the stage. Goethe's romantic naturalism is wholly inspired by the ancient philosophy of Begetting, as against Aristotelian Design.

Lamarck's theory of evolution was the last serious attempt to make science out of the old Heraclitean idea that the world is intrinsically flux and process, and that science is to study neither the configurations of matter nor the categories of form, but the manifestations of that activity which is ontologically fundamental, as bodies in motion and species in being are not.

This helps clear up another misunderstood contrast. The real conflict over these recent centuries of ours is not between "science and religion"; it is between romantic naturalism and a philosophy of order and design. The pagan feeling of a cosmic organism may lead to a high pantheism, but its morality will remain naturalistic. Galileo and Newton, who believed in Design, were Christians, but Diderot was an atheist; Goethe was a pantheist. They were both descendants of the Stoics. With German romantic *Naturphilosophie* of the nineteenth century, the break with physical science and Design is consummated. Philosophy goes its own way, founding itself on historical becoming rather than on physical abstractions, and the same old Stoic revolutionary ferment which had inspired the attempt of Tiberius Gracchus in the second century B.C. sets in motion in our era the force of dialectical materialism.

Stoicism has had the singular fate of being best known to us through the books of Epictetus, a slave, and Marcus Aurelius, an emperor. Both are strikingly similar in tone, and it bears witness to the ethical strength of the doctrine.

Marcus Aurelius Antoninus (A.D. 121–180) came in his adolescence under the influence of Stoic masters to whom he pays touching tribute, and adopted early the "philosophic," i.e., ascetic, way of life. On the death of his adoptive father, Antoninus Pius, he became emperor in 161. The twenty years of his reign were not untroubled. He had to cope with general corruption, with revolts like the military coup of Avidius Cassius, with the incompetence of his family, with pestilence, and with the incursions of Sarmatians and other wild tribes on the Danubian frontier, where he waged successful war for years on end. His empire extended from the Euphrates to the Atlantic, from the hills of Scotland to the sands of Africa. One can guess what were the trials, the troubles, the anxiety, and the sorrows of him who had the world's business on his hands. He steadied himself by jotting down occasional reminders and meditations in his notebook: they have reached us under the simple title "To Himself." The gentleness, resignation, and ethical purity of the text, its disdain of worldly sciences, make it sound almost Christian, and indeed it has been the companion in later ages of many high Christian characters. But the resemblance is deceptive. Marcus Aurelius's devotion is essentially cosmological in character, as befits a Stoic, and the gods ("if they exist" . . .) only represent the Reason of the Cosmos. The blend of rational and spiritual, the coolness of his detachment, still show the scientific origin. As for the Christians, who were multiplying in his time, Marcus Aurelius seems to have known them little and liked them less. He considered them fanatical troublemakers and obstructionists, and at best a mixed lot. He allowed repression against them to go on, as laid down in the statute books.

Marcus is not only the last Stoic author of antiquity, he is also the last "republican" emperor, that is, the last representative on the throne of the old Roman senatorial class. After citing with admiration the names of Cato and Brutus, along with those of Helvidius and Thrasea and other heroes of the Stoical protestation against Caesarism, he holds up before himself "the idea of a polity in which there is the same law for all, a polity administered with regard to equal right and equal freedom of speech, and the idea of a kingly government which respects most of all the freedom of the governed." The demand for administrative unity might seem to be reconciled with the older ideal; but the Stoic emperor represented the departing and not the coming age.

To the Epicureans of his own time, the Emperor Marcus may have looked a pathetic counterexample. Here was a man denied their own refuge into quiet obscurity and light-hearted friendship among equals. A conscientious administrator shouldering the burden of responsibility, he could not even save his inner peace, no matter how repeatedly he adjured himself. He was worn out and killed by inches by the machine he had set himself to control.

From M. Aurelius Antoninus to Himself

Begin the morning by saying to thyself, I shall meet with the busybody, the ungrateful, arrogant, deceitful, envious, unsocial. All these things happen to them by reason of their ignorance of what is good and evil. But I who have seen the nature of the good that it is beautiful, and of the bad that it is ugly, and the nature of him who does wrong, that it is akin to me, not [only] of the same blood or seed, but that it participates in [the same] intelligence and [the same] portion of the divinity, I can neither be injured by any of them, for no one can fix on me what is ugly, nor can I be angry with my kinsman, nor hate him. For we are made for co-operation, like feet, like hands, like eyelids, like the rows of the upper and lower teeth. To act against one another, then, is contrary to nature; and it is acting against one another to be vexed and to turn away.

Every moment think steadily as a Roman and a man to do what thou hast in hand with perfect and simple dignity, and feeling of affection, and freedom, and justice, and to give thyself relief from all other thoughts. . . .

Of human life the time is a point, and the substance is in a flux, and the perception dull, and the composition of the whole body subject to putrefaction, and the soul a whirl, and fortune hard to divine, and fame a thing devoid of judgment. And, to say all in a word, everything which belongs to the body is a stream, and what belongs to the soul is a dream and vapor, and life is a warfare and a stranger's sojourn, and after-fame is oblivion. What then is that which is able to conduct a man? One thing, and only one, philosophy. But this consists in keeping the daemon within a man free from violence and unharmed, superior to pains and pleasures, doing nothing without a purpose, nor yet falsely and with hypocrisy, not feeling the need of another man's doing or not doing anything; and besides, accepting all that happens, and all that is allotted, as coming from thence, wherever it is, from whence he himself came; and, finally, waiting for death with a cheerful mind, as being nothing else than a dissolution of the elements of which every living being is compounded. But if there is no harm of the elements themselves in each continually changing into another, why should a man have any apprehension about the change and dissolution of all the elements? For it is according to nature, and nothing is evil which is according to nature.

Everything harmonizes with me, which is harmonious to thee, O Universe. Nothing for me is too early nor too late, which is in due time for thee. Everything is fruit to me which thy seasons bring, O Nature: from thee are all things, in thee are all things, to thee all things return. The poet says, Dear city of Cecrops; and wilt not thou say, Dear city of Zeus?

Observe constantly that all things take place by change, and accustom thyself to consider that the nature of the universe loves nothing so much as to change the things which are and to make new things like them. For everything that exists is in a manner the seed of that which will be. But thou art thinking only of seeds which are cast into the earth or into a womb: but this is a very vulgar notion.

Constantly regard the universe as one living being, having one substance and one soul; and observe how all things have reference to one perception, the perception of this one living being; and how all things act with one movement; and how all things are the co-operating causes of all things which exist; observe too the continuous spinning of the thread and the contexture of the web.

Always remember the saying of Heraclitus, that the death of earth is to become water, and the death of water is to become air, and the death of air is to become fire, and reversely. And think too of him who forgets whither the way leads, and that men quarrel with that with which they are most constantly in communion, the reason which governs the universe; and the things which they daily meet with seem to them strange. . . .

As thou intendest to live when thou art gone out, . . . so it is in thy power to live here. But if men do not permit thee, then get away out of life, yet so as if thou wert suffering no harm. The house is smoky, and I quit it. Why dost thou think that this is any trouble? But so long as nothing of the kind drives me out, I remain, am free, and no man shall hinder me from doing what I choose; and I choose to do what is according to the nature of the rational and social animal.

Take care that thou art not made into a Caesar, that thou art not dyed with this dye; for such things happen.

He who has seen present things has seen all, both everything which has taken place from all eternity and everything which will be for time without end; for all things are of one kin and of one form.

From Antisthenes: It is royal to do good and to be abused.

He who is discoursing about men should look also at earthly things as if he viewed them from some higher place; should look at them in their assemblies, armies, agricultural labors, marriages, treaties, births, deaths, noise of the courts of justice, desert places, various nations of barbarians, feasts, lamentations, markets, a mixture of all things and an orderly combination of contraries.

A spider is proud when it has caught a fly, and a man when he has caught a poor hare, and another when he has taken a little fish in a net, and another when he has taken wild boars, and another when he has taken bears, and another when he has taken Sarmatians. Are not these robbers, if you examine their opinions?

The periodic movements of the universe are the same, up and down from age to age. And either the universal intelligence puts itself in motion for every separate effect, and if this is so, be thou content with that which is the result of its activity; or it put itself in motion once, and everything else comes by way of sequence in a manner; or indivisible elements are the origin of all things.—In a word, if there is a god, all is well: and if chance rules, do not thou also be governed by it.

Look down from above on the countless herds of men and their countless solemnities, and the infinitely varied voyagings in storms and calms, and the differences among those who are born, who live together, and die. And consider, too, the life lived by others in olden time, and the life of those who will live after thee, and the life now lived among barbarous nations, and how many know not even thy name, and how many will soon forget it, and how they who perhaps now are praising thee will very soon blame thee, and that neither a posthumous name is of any value, nor reputation, nor anything else.

What a soul that is which is ready, if at any moment it must be separated from the body, and ready either to be extinguished or dispersed or continue to exist; but so that this readiness comes from a man's own judgment, not from mere obstinacy, as with the Christians, but considerately and with dignity and in a way to persuade another, without tragic show.*

NEOPLATONISM

The third of what we called the scientific religions, which outstrips the others in historical significance, inasmuch as it provided the foundations for Christian philosophy, is Neoplatonism. This is not simply, as its name might suggest, a revival of Platonism. In fact, the succession of trends inside the Academy founded by Plato shows bewildering shifts in three centuries, from one end of the philosophical spectrum to the other. The immediate successors of Plato, Speusippus and Xenocrates, plunge into Pythagorean numerology in a way which earns them the derision of Aristotle. After that, the swing through the Middle and the New Academy is very much towards sober criticism, in the spirit of old Democritus whom Plato had so much detested, and it ends up in total skepticism ("discrimination") and philosophical indifference with Pyrrho. Then it swings back to critical skepticism with the brilliant Carneades (c. 150 B.C.), who might be called the Hume of antiquity and the mind most akin to a modern philosopher of science. The trouble was that there was not enough of a body of successful science to carry the weight of his sharp distinctions, so that they led to a universal relativism. The medical thinkers, at least, could make some good use of his cautions. It is through a doctor, Sextus Empiricus (third century A.D.), that we know the most about his lost works. To Sextus himself we owe a remark which should be good for all time: "Those who speak unclearly are like people who, for some purpose of their own, should be shooting arrows into the night."

But if the skeptical movement revives the spirit of free and open inquiry of the Platonic dialogues, it could hardly satisfy the minds of late antiquity in search of reassurance. It is no wonder, therefore, if the pendulum swings further back to Plato the theologian, the dispenser of "golden eloquence," of sublimity and certainty beyond this world.

* *Thoughts of Marcus Aurelius,* translated and edited by George Long. New York: David McKay Co., Inc.

With Plotinus the Egyptian (A.D. 204–270) it was felt as if *that* Plato had come back to earth. True, Plotinus is no great writer, and a much more strict systematist; what he cannot find in Plato to integrate his system (for Plato always avoided having one) he borrows from the Stoics and from Aristotle. But the spirit is surely that of mystic and transcendent Platonism, such as had been outlined by the Master in his later years. While the other doctrines posit matter, in more or less subtle forms, as the ultimate constituent of reality, Plotinus brings in a thoroughgoing spiritualism. For him everything, including corporeal substance, is ultimately Intellect. Later philosophical thinking has translated this word, *nous,* with "spirit," but Plotinus, in direct line with Plato and Parmenides, means still the original Eleatic identity of Thought with Being. Only that can really be which is outside time, motionless, indivisible, simple and single, without taint of variety, multiplicity, and alteration. But Being must have a cause, and so, beyond Being and Thought, even beyond the Platonic Good, there must be the source of all, the One, the Absolute Godhead so infinitely remote from our understanding that we can speak of it only in negatives. It is a source of infinite power (infinity has thus entered theological speculation), unchanging, which irradiates from itself all that is. It can be inferred as the metaphysical unity on which all things necessarily depend, but as for apprehending it, Plotinus insists that we have to rely on an entirely different faculty from thought, namely, mystical intuition.

Let Porphyry speak, who was his immediate pupil and his biographer:

We have explained that he was good and gentle, mild and merciful; we who lived with him could feel it. We have said that he was vigilant and pure of soul, and always striving towards the Divine, which with all his soul he loved. . . . And thus it happened to this extraordinary man, constantly lifting himself up towards the first and transcendent God by thought and the ways explained by Plato in the *Symposium,* that there actually came a vision of that God who is without shape or form, established above the understanding and all the intelligible world. To whom I, Porphyry, being now in my sixty-eighth year, profess that I once drew near and was made one with him. At any rate he appeared to Plotinus "a goal close at hand." . . . And he attained that goal four times, I think, while I was living with him—not potentially but in actuality, though an actuality which surpasses speech.

This is true mysticism. The term is old (it is linked with primitive rites and a Greek root signifying "silence") but the rational part, as concluding a theory of knowledge, is new in Western thought. It may come directly from India, by way of Plotinus's teacher, Ammonius Sakkas, whose name seems to connote an Indian origin. It will take on immense importance in Christianity and in Islam. Its meaning is not the vague thing which has become today's common usage. It stands for that which, to logical thought, is an impenetrable paradox, but comes before or beyond thought. Not being properly a kind of cognition, it can become the ground of no inference. The system of knowledge itself, apart from it, remains as rational as a mathematical deduction.

The highest level or "hypostasis" (lit.: "sub-stance") below the One is that of the Intellect, which reflects from itself the world of ideas. Below that is the world of Soul, where motion has come in because of lack of fulfillment, metaphysical motion of course, consciousness and discursive thought, which reflects itself in a multiplicity of individual souls, and as it moves down further becomes physical life, and at last crystallizes into matter. What we call sensible reality is thus a realm of sheer scattering. Things become increasingly complicated, but they are not enriched by the multiplicity of their determinations, for they become thus only more relative and dependent. The more organic beings lost sufficiency of life, the more numerous and more differentiated are the organs which they need. "Everything which departs from itself grows weaker," and the true self of all things is in that center of the One which irradiates, as it were, out into farther and farther spheres. At the limit of darkness is the pure multiplicity or extension of dead matter, close to nonbeing. For no individual thing exists in nature, except through some presence of soul in it. Creative "reasons" or *logoi* descend to nature from the ideas to organize it. They are "a power which acts on matter, unconscious, only active." Nature, then, is rational, but only as an emanation, a reflection of a reflection, of the Intellect.

This idea of "emanation" is central in Plotinus's system. It replaces Plato's term of "participation." The simile from the light of Intellect to the light of the sun, that we have found in Plato, becomes true "irradiation" from the One, through the successive hypostases of Being. The "divided line" which in Plato separates utterly the real world from that of Ideas has become here rather a transparent screen through which the creative flow patterns itself into the images of reality. Life comes forever from the inaccessible One down to the depths of the great sea of Being, bringing a light of reason and design so that every possible manifestation of divine energy, each note on the infinite scale, should come to effect. Conversely, there is an ascending effort from all parts of being which tries to return to the original source, until in the soul of man it is liberated for "the flight of the alone to the alone."

A splendid vision, but all too all-comprising. Plotinus himself is terse and spare, a strict theorist, but the universe that he portrays invites all the Oriental beliefs and imageries to invade it, as they had invaded even the cosmos of the Stoics. Plotinus, too, invites this invasion, by sharing the "unitarian" bent of his Alexandrian predecessors, only too prone (like Philo Judaeus) to turn their faiths and myths into allegories of the one true philosophy. With Soul and souls at all levels, entities, daemons, angels, can multiply beyond belief, and in with them rush back all the ancient fears, horrors, hopes, and superstitions. The well-tilled garden of Greek philosophy is smothered under a growth of weeds.

The fateful choice, it must be admitted, had been made right at the time of Plato. It is there that we have the parting of the ways. Out of the Platonic complex, one way led to a thoroughgoing mathematization of the universe, open and speculative, such as the Pythagoreans had attempted: the other, which was the choice of Plato's old age, concentrated upon an enclosed and rigid world order, dominated by an astral theology. That oppressive machinery of organized religion ruled by astral divinities, as projected in Plato's *Laws,* with earthly power in the hands of an authoritarian caste of sages, looks undeniably like the beginning of a retreat into the Oriental cocoon. It claims to lead to a higher philosophical faith: in reality, it points back to Babylon. Even the mathematical element degenerated in Plato's immediate successors into numerology and myth. The late Neo-Pythagorean developments in Roman times never recaptured the scientific spirit of the early school, and went in recklessly for numerology and the "wondrous."

It is not strange, therefore, that the Plotinian school should lead directly into that elusive many-faced doctrine called Gnosticism (where *gnōsis* had come to mean "knowledge" only in a mystical and esoteric sense), a blending of myths old and new, magic practices and deep insights, which was concocted by Oriental minds undeniably subtle and powerful.

The direct successors of Plotinus, Porphyry and Iamblichus, notwithstanding their insistence on arithmology and on reviving the Pythagorean tradition, mark the turn towards a Gnostic content: philosophy becomes the shell, cults and magic become the true substance. Porphyry teaches the strange new art of "theurgy," which means "operating with gods." It consists, literally, in building up, out of the forces and elementals available to the initiate, spirits, angels, and daemons on recipe, such as will assist us on our way to purification. It is really only an extension of the art of alchemy as it was then understood, and amply practiced, but it reaches out to subvert utterly the theoretical vision of Pythagoras and Plato.

If it has come to this, it must surely mean that the relation of man to the universe has been subverted too. The Stoics had taught cosmic necessity, the Neoplatonists, escape from the world. But here the dreadful theriomorphic figures of planetary gods from Babylon, revived by innumerable cults, impel men to escape from a necessity which is terrifying. The Hermetic and Mithraic communities, and other offshoots of Gnosticism, always insist on the power of the Seven Planets, often called the seven Archontes, "Rulers," or Kosmokratores, "Lords of the Universe," those who shape our fate inexorably. They are supposed to be invoked with the seven vowels of the Greek alphabet and with all sorts of other magic Sevens, to be faced with formulas and incantations innumerable.

For they are seen as daemons who enforce a perverse necessity. Saturn, as of old, is their ruler, Lord of Melancholy. The religion of late antiquity is passionately absorbed in plans of escape from the prison of the Lords of Creation. The classic figure of the Teacher, the man who imparts a body of knowledge, is replaced by that of the Master, whose oracular sayings have to be interpreted as something absolute—a revelation. He is the Man Who Saves.

It is a strange but not unnatural outcome of Plato's astral theology. And indeed the next step is inspired again by Plato's speculative play in the *Timaeus* with the problem of creation. His fantasy of a Demiurge or divine Craftsman compounding and shaping the universe in imitation of the world of Ideas is now seized upon with eager pessimism. Maybe the world *is* the work of a fallen intelligence, separated from the upper realm of light, who has stolen the design of Ideas for his own purposes, and set up the seven lords of the planets as jailkeepers of a world designed for his own pride and self-aggrandizement, populating it further with powers and daemons we can hardly control. This surely is a radical hypothesis to explain the prevalence of evil in this world, which could hardly have been willed by the God of Light. The initial duality between spirit and matter set by Plato is pushed here to its extreme limits, the whole of the material world having become pure darkness and evil, the consequence of cosmic sinfulness.

It is really as if the world had ceased to make sense. While the worldlings and the material-minded build up the cult of the Goddess of Chance and beg the response of her "lots," the sensitive souls, the religious, the thoughtful, seek only an escape beyond the stars, where they hope to find order and meaning at last. The only "knowledge" that counts in this predicament is the operational techniques of theurgy, magic rites, atonement, and purification to allow the soul to escape the prison of the seven Rulers and move on to the Eighth Sphere, where the true harmony is supposed to begin. We can see better now why Epicurus had opposed the astronomical sciences, guessing whither they would lead. "He would have none of those things."

Conversely, this new and strange vision of reality opened the door to what in no way fitted the outlook of classic Greek philosophy: gospels of redemption old and new. Ancient Orphic motives combine with the Oriental idea of a divine Mediator coming from the God of Light to assist those who are in darkness. "It is clear," says Bousset, an eminent authority, "that the figure of the Redeemer did not wait for Christianity to force its way into the religion of Gnôsis, but was already there under various forms." He is described as descending from Heaven through the spheres of the planetary Rulers to save mankind, sometimes the world as a whole. The Rulers let him pass because he is disguised; they know him not. When his work is done he ascends to Heaven, dragging with him the defeated powers as captives in his triumph.

When Christianity brought these ideas to a focus, Gnostic theory was contained in it as a powerful component. It provided the new religion with some of its greatest thinkers, like Origen. Gradually, however, the wilder imaginations were weeded out, and the philosophy of transcendence brought back to the classical purity of Plotinus. Thus, although it is true that Christianity let the achievements of ancient science lapse into semioblivion for centuries, it was not the only, nor even the prime, responsible factor. The movement of revulsion had antedated it by centuries.

Much rather can it be said that Christianity sorted out and preserved a most essential element: the seeds not of science, but of future scientific imagination. "What do I want to know?" St. Augustine asks of himself in a famous monologue. " 'Nothing but God and the soul.' 'Nothing else?' 'Absolutely nothing else.' " This is final. But within the confines thus set, there arises the need for *a* science, the science of the soul: and thus Neoplatonism becomes the great philosophy and the chief science of the high Middle Ages; it stands under the invocation of Plato, while Aristotle comes in only later.

The central symbol of Neoplatonism is light and irradiation; its pattern is Pythagorean number, with an almost obsessive insistence on the Triad. Its "metaphysics of light" dematerializes the universe; but it also offers the physical imagination new ways for thinking in terms of abstract, all-pervading, disembodied energy; it sets geometry and number among the higher mysteries of the divine design. It is significant that Proclus, the great systematic and theologian of Neoplatonism of the fifth century A.D. (410–485), himself an unrestrained initiate to the strangest Gnostic cults and rites, should have been the author of several works on astronomy and spherical trigonometry as well as of a *Commentary on the First Book of Euclid* which is among our chief sources on Greek mathematics. Thus the highest form of spiritual speculation carries with it down the Middle Ages the dormant seed of mathematics, ready to burst into life in the Renaissance. While Aristotle's world remains to the last impervious to mathematization, the ideas of the Platonic lineage find their way back into astronomy and physics, and live on in our universe of periodicities, electromagnetism, and relativistic space-time.

The "metaphysics of Light" carries with it also the idea that truth must ultimately be intuitive, and that it is only the "true" or higher intellect which can perceive that light. Wrote Guido Guinizelli, Dante's forerunner, in 1250: "The sun doth shine upon the mud all day—vile it remains, nor doth the sun lose heat." * Only the "gentle" or true-bred mind, capable of intellectual love, he implies, can receive life from that light. This is the idea that Copernicus passionately advocates in the preface to his great work. It still remains, to use modern terms, science's rather exclusive theory of values, and its Distant Early Warning Line against the onsweep of mechanized formalism and the electronic dinosaurs.

* *Fere lo sole el fango tutto 'l giorno*
Vile riman, nè 'l sol perde calore.

SUGGESTIONS
FOR FURTHER READING

The books listed below have been chosen because they are standard or because they are readily available—in most cases, for both reasons. Listings of paperback editions are preceded by an asterisk.

Bailey, Cyril. *The Greek Atomists and Epicurus.* Oxford: Clarendon Press, 1928.

Brock, A. J. *Greek Medicine, Being Extracts Illustrative of Medical Writers from Hippocrates to Galen.* London: J. M. Dent & Sons, Ltd., 1929; New York: E. P. Dutton and Company, Inc.

*Burnet, John (tr. and ed.). *Early Greek Philosophy.* (4th ed.). London: Basil Blackwell; New York: The Macmillan Company, 1930; Meridian Books, Inc., 1957.
Standard analysis (first published 1898) of Pre-Socratic philosophy, with selected texts.

Clagett, Marshall. *Greek Science in Antiquity.* New York: Abelard-Schuman, Limited, 1956.
Particularly valuable for the exact sciences in late antiquity.

Cohen, Morris R., and Israel E. Drabkin. *A Source Book in Greek Science.* Cambridge: Harvard University Press, 1959.
A comprehensive technical anthology, with short introductions.

*Cornford, Francis. *Plato's Cosmology. The Timaeus of Plato.* Trans. with a Running Commentary. New York: Liberal Arts Press, 1957 (1937).
Cornford's translations of Plato's dialogues are uniformly excellent and readable.

Diels, Hermann. *Die Fragmente der Vorsokratiker.* Ed. by Walther Kranz. (7th ed.). 3 vols. Berlin: Weidmann, 1954.
The fount from which all springs: the most comprehensive collection of what the Pre-Socratics said (in Greek, with German

translations) and what the ancients said about them (in Greek or Latin only).

*Farrington, Benjamin. *Greek Science*. London: Penguin Books Limited (Pelican A142), 1953.
Concentrates on "the connections of Greek science with practical life, with techniques, with the economic basis and productive activity of Greek society." A vindication of Atomism against Plato.

*Frankfort, Henri, et al. *Before Philosophy*. London: Penguin Books Limited (Pelican A198), 1959 (1946).
An authoritative study of the "mythical world-view" in Egypt and Mesopotamia.

Freeman, Kathleen. *Ancilla to the Pre-Socratic Philosophers. A Complete Translation of the Fragments in Diels, Die Fragmente der Vorsokratiker*. Oxford: Basil Blackwell & Mott, Ltd., 1948. Cambridge: Harvard University Press.
English translation of the fragments in the 5th edition of Diels.

————. *The Pre-Socratic Philosophers;* a Companion to Diels, *Die Fragmente der Vorsokratiker*. Oxford: Basil Blackwell, 1946; Cambridge: Harvard University Press, 1947.
A systematic treatment, with summaries of what ancient writers said about the Pre-Socratics.

Heath, Thomas L. *Aristarchus of Samos. The Ancient Copernicus. A History of Greek Astronomy to Aristarchus Together with Aristarchus's Treatise on the Sizes and Distances of the Sun and Moon, a New Greek Text with Translation and Notes*. Oxford: Clarendon Press, 1913.

————. *Greek Astronomy*. New York: E. P. Dutton and Company, Inc., 1932. Translations of selected texts.

————. *History of Greek Mathematics*. 2 vols. Oxford: Clarendon Press, 1921; New York: Oxford University Press.

Inge, William Ralph. *The Philosophy of Plotinus*. The Gifford Lectures at St. Andrews, 1917–18. (3rd ed.). 2 vols. New York: Longmans, Green & Co., Inc., 1929.
A standard work on the most important early Neoplatonist.

Klemm, Friedrich. *A History of Western Technology*. Trans. by Dorothea W. Singer. New York: Charles Scribner's Sons, 1959.

Concentrates on the relations between technology and intellectual climate.

Nahm, Milton C. (ed.). *Selections from Early Greek Philosophy*. (3rd ed.). New York: F. S. Crofts & Co., 1947.
Inexpensive collection with introduction reprinted from Theodore Gomperz, *Greek Thinkers: A History of Ancient Philosophy*. 4 vols. New York: Humanities Press, Inc.

Neugebauer, Otto. *The Exact Sciences in Antiquity*. (2nd ed.). Providence: Brown University Press, 1957.
On Babylonian, Egyptian, and Greek mathematics and astronomy.

Plutarch. *Moralia*. Trans. by Frank C. Babbitt et al., in Loeb Classical Library. 14 vols. Cambridge: Harvard University Press, 1927–1939.

*Ross, W. D. *Aristotle*. (5th ed.). London: Methuen & Co., Ltd., 1949; New York: Barnes & Noble, Inc., 1953; Meridian Books, Inc. (M65).
Standard analysis of Aristotle's works.

Rostovtsev, Mikhail Ivanovitch. *The Social and Economic History of the Hellenistic World*. 3 vols. Oxford: Clarendon Press, 1941; New York: Oxford University Press.
Agriculture, mining (in an appendix by R. B. Blake), trade, and industries in Ptolemaic Egypt.

Sambursky, Samuel. *The Physical World of the Greeks*. Trans. by Merton Dagut. New York: The Macmillan Company, 1956 (1954).
On the Greek (especially Stoic) conceptions of nature, by a distinguished Israeli physicist.

————. *Physics of the Stoics*. London: Routledge & Kegan Paul, Ltd., 1959; New York: The Macmillan Company.

Sarton, George. *A History of Science*. 2 vols. Cambridge: Harvard University Press, 1952–1959.
Detailed survey of the whole range of ancient science and its cultural connections.

Singer, Charles. *Greek Biology and Greek Medicine*. Oxford: Clarendon Press, 1922.

Singer, Charles, E. J. Holmyard, and A. R. Hall (eds.). *A History of Technology. Vol. 2. The Mediterranean Civilizations and the Middle Ages, c. 700 B.C. to A.D. 1500.*

Oxford: Clarendon Press, 1956; New York: Oxford University Press.

*Taylor, A. E. *Plato: the Man and His Work.* (6th ed.). New York: Meridian Books, Inc. (MG7).
Standard work-by-work analysis.

Thomson, James Oliver. *History of Ancient Geography.* London: Cambridge University Press, 1948.

van der Waerden, B. L. *Science Awakening.* Trans. by A. Dresden. Groningen: Erven P. Noordhoff, 1954.
Concerned with a reconstruction of the methods of Babylonian, Egyptian, and Greek mathematics, largely on the basis of Neugebauer's work.

*Zeller, Eduard. *Outlines of the History of Greek Philosophy.* Ed. by Wilhelm Nestle. Trans. by L. R. Palmer. (13th ed.). New York: Meridian Books, Inc. (M9), 1955.
Standard systematic survey, first published 1883.

INDEX